S0-BOA-469

Lewis and Lewis

JOHN JUXON

Ticknor & Fields
NEW YORK
1984

First American edition 1984

Printed in the United States of America

Library of Congress Cataloging in Publication Data

Juxon, John.
Lewis and Lewis.

Bibliography: p.
Includes index.
1. Lewis, George, Sir, 1833-1911. 2. Lawyers—Great Britain—Biography. I. Title.
KD631.L48J89 1984 349.41'092'4 [B] 83-24198
ISBN 0-89919-277-7 344.100924 [B]

V 10 9 8 7 6 5 4 3 2 1

Contents

Illustrations

Following p. 160

The Chief. Parnell around the time he first met Lewis.

'The Bayard of the Bar': Sir Edward Clarke QC. (*Mansell Collection*)

Sir Charles Russell QC (later Lord Russell of Killowen, Lord Chief Justice). (*Mansell Collection*)

Lewis in caricature. Drawings by 'Spy' of *Vanity Fair* (*Mansell Collection*) and Max Beerbohm. (*Garrick Club*)

'He knows all about us', Lewis at work, portrayed by Sir Philip Burne-Jones, Bart. (*Mrs Elizabeth Wansbrough*)

George Lewis by John Singer Sargent. (*Mrs Elizabeth Wansbrough*)

Sources and Acknowledgements

This is the first life of Sir George Lewis to be written. If he had not burned his papers, a solid 'authorized' biography would probably have appeared within a few years of his death. But the fact that Lewis's own documentation of his cases had been destroyed must have deterred possible biographers.

In the present book Lewis's professional life has been largely re-created from printed sources – the memoirs and biographies of his contemporaries; newspapers and periodicals of the time – in the manner of a palaeontologist recalling once-vivid life from surviving bones. In the absence of radio or television or any method of disseminating information to a mass-audience, the Victorian papers reported scandals and tragedies with a wealth of detail unimaginable today. Of many books consulted, I should mention Vincent Brome's *Reverse Your Verdict*, which illuminates the case of Serafino Pelizzioni and the role played in it by Henry Negretti. Kellow Chesney's *The Victorian Underworld* re-creates the criminal milieu that existed when George Lewis first began in practice. Ronald Pearsall's *The Worm in the Bud: The World of Victorian Sexuality* is mandatory reading for anyone who seeks to understand public and private attitudes as they developed through Victoria's long reign.

With regard to Lewis's private life, some family papers do exist. They are in the possession of Lewis's granddaughters, Mrs Elizabeth Wansbrough and Susan, Lady Karminski. Those held by Lady Karminski relate to the brilliant social life the Lewises enjoyed: their friendships with Burne-Jones, Whistler, Wilde, and many others – indeed, with anyone of any consequence in the arts at the time. The papers belonging to Mrs Wansbrough comprise letters, including Oscar Wilde's correspondence with the Lewises; family and social memorabilia; and newspaper cuttings illuminating different stages of George Lewis's career. I am most grateful to Lady Karminski and Mrs Wansbrough for letting me study these papers. Indeed, it would be true to say that, without Mrs Wansbrough's assistance, this biography could not have been written. I am particularly indebted to her for sharing with me her memories of her grandparents and for giving me the benefit of her insights into George Lewis's relationships with his children, and with Elizabeth, his second wife. I need hardly add that this expression of gratitude does not imply that Lady Karminski or Mrs Wansbrough necessarily endorse the contents of this book. They helped me; what I have written is my own.

I am also grateful to other members of the Lewis family: Sir Anthony Burney O.B.E., Lewis's grandson, and Mr Robin Jessel, his great-grandson, for their warm interest and co-operation.

In the early days of my research I was helped and encouraged by the late Judge Harry Leon, who gave pleasure to so many readers by the books he wrote as 'Henry Cecil'. Others who helped me greatly in different ways were: Mr Bruce Arnold, Mr C. C. Aronsfeld, Mr John Back (of the Archives Office, New Scotland Yard), Mr Henry Blyth, Mr Stephen Durbridge, Mr Joe Gaute, Mr George Macdonald Fraser, Mr H. Montgomery Hyde, Mr C. G. Mabey C.B.E. (of Penningtons, Solicitors), Mr Roy Russell and Mrs Barbara Russell, Mr Peyton Skipworth, and Mr Peter Strankland.

For permission to reproduce paintings and drawings in their possession, I have to thank: Mrs Elizabeth Wansbrough for a portrait of Sir George Lewis by John Singer Sargent and a painting of him at his desk by Philip Burne-Jones; Sir Anthony Burney O.B.E. and Lady Burney for Sargent's portrait of Lady Lewis; Mr Robin Jessel for Sir Edward Burne-Jones's drawing of Katie Lewis; Sir Anthony Burney (as a Trustee of the Garrick Club) and the Committee of the Garrick Club for the Max Beerbohm caricature. For permission to quote from the *Letters of Oscar Wilde* I am indebted to Sir Rupert Hart-Davis; and, for permission to quote from his *Sir Charles Dilke*, to the Rt Hon Roy Jenkins MP.

I am also grateful to Ms Anne Marie Erlich (art researcher), to my editor Ms Hilary Davies for her sympathetic guidance, and – as always – to Mr Richard Simon and Ms Vivien Green for their unfailing support.

Foreword by John Mortimer

> He comes towards them with his usual methodical pace which is never quickened, never slackened. He wears his usual expressionless mask—and carries family secrets in every limb of his body, and every crease of his dress. Whether his whole soul is devoted to the great, or whether he yields them nothing beyond the service he sells, is his personal secret. He keeps it, as he keeps the secrets of his clients. . . .

So padded Mr. Tulkinghorn, the all-powerful family solicitor, through the pages of Charles Dickens' *Bleak House,* quietly saving a reputation here or settling a damaging action there—but here it becomes necessary to explain what, in the English legal system, a "solicitor" is. The word has nothing to do, of course, with "soliciting." Solicitors do not stand on street corners seducing clients with a smile, a flash of stocking, and a wink. Solicitors are highly respectable ladies and gentlemen, but they occupy, often to their chagrin, what is regarded as the lower drawer of the legal profession.

Let me explain. In England, if you commit a murder, or wish to sell your house, or get involved in a notorious divorce case, you go to your solicitor. He or she is a member of a firm and will be your confidant, your family doctor, and if possible, your friend. It is only if your case has to come to a public trial that the solicitor will instruct a "barrister," a free-lance legal performer, to represent you. For solicitors, although often eloquent and usually verbose, are, by English legal traditions, inaudible in the Higher Courts. Only a barrister can be heard, and then only if he is wearing a long black gown and a horsehair wig. If he is not in this fancy dress he is, of course, inaudible. But, to put it shortly, solicitors are the producers, the agents, the backers of our theatrical legal profession. Barristers are the stars; they face the footlights, the bouquets, or as often as not, the rotten tomatoes of a trial. Unlike the barrister—who turns up for a hasty conference before breezing into court armed only with such facts as the client chooses to tell him, and is off again in the twitch of a gown, with a congratulatory handshake or a word of commiseration—the solicitor lives for months, perhaps years, with the client and his anxieties. He sees the witnesses, he sends out the detectives to gather information, perhaps on occasion he protects the simple-minded barrister from the dangerous effects of too much information. If a young man in England goes into the law to enjoy the thrills and spills of show business, he will be a barrister. But if he wants to learn the secrets of the human heart, he'd better become a solicitor.

If Mr. Tulkinghorn served the Victorian upper classes, the pillar and prop of the flamboyant but somewhat gimcrack edifice of Edwardian society was Sir George Lewis, of Lewis and Lewis, solicitors of Ely Place. Did a deceived wife find a compromising letter from the Countess of Warwick while opening her husband's letters? Did the Prince of Wales, later Edward VII, learn that his darling Daisy had written such a letter? He called round to Ely Place and tried to get his hands on it. If a *cause célèbre* was brewing, both sides rushed to Lewis, and it was Oscar Wilde's terrible misfortune that the Marquis of Queensbury got there first, for Sir George, who was a man of infinite wisdom, would have advised him to throw the mad Marquis's insulting card (in which he accused the great playwright of "posing as a sodomite") into the fire, and the grisly tragedy of the Wilde trials would have been avoided.

But it was not only the great and famous who called at Ely Place; Lewis was engaged in most of the great murder trials of his period, and his first and most creditable success was a tireless fight to save the life of an Italian workman unjustly condemned to death for stabbing an Englishman in the Golden Anchor pub at Clerkenwell.

In this respect, Lewis's legal life was wider and perhaps more interesting than that of Mr. Tulkinghorn. To the respectable family solicitor, deft at settling disputes in high places, crime may seem a bit down market. Murder is to defamation, in the English legal world, rather as pushing a trolley round a supermarket is to a leisurely stroll round the food halls in Harrods. But in Mr. Juxon's life of Lewis, those accused of murder emerge as more sympathetic characters than the Prince of Wales and his cronies. The office in Ely Place was delighted to receive them all.

George Lewis sat in that office, frock-coated and monocled, with a long, intelligent Jewish face and Dundreary whiskers, his wastepaper basket overflowing. When he finished writing, he put on his fur coat and glossy silk hat to go down to Bow Street Magistrates Court or the Old Bailey. Lewis would succeed brilliantly in the lower courts, where he had a right of audience, and then hand over the main trial to some barrister, who occasionally made a mess of it. As time went on he found the perfect counsel in Edward Clarke, so perhaps his frustrations were less. He may have enjoyed being the great advocate's puppet master, and his team of dubious detectives, some curious ex-policemen among them, were sent out to gather the grubby facts that Clarke, known as the "Bayard of the Bar" for his perfect chivalry, would then lay reverently before the jury as though they were fragments of the Holy Grail.

George Lewis, who was painted by Sir Philip Burne-Jones, Bart., and his wife Elizabeth, who was painted by Sargent, were patrons of the arts. Henry James and Oscar Wilde, Ellen Terry and Max Beerbohm came to his house; but I'm sure he enjoyed the clients most. He was taken behind the scenes of polite society, and learnt about "Beautiful for Ever," a shop in New Bond Street where respectable married ladies met their lovers and were spied on through holes in the wall by elderly peers. He learnt of the corrupt practices of great city firms and probably knew more than anyone about the way that mysterious young barrister, Charles Bravo met his death. He also found time to promote the right of prisoners to give evidence, and the institution of the English Court of Criminal Appeal.

John Juxon's book makes marvelously entertaining reading. Who would not envy George Lewis with his monocle and his fur coat, with his all-knowing life as a high-society confidant and a backroom advocate? What a tremendous lot of fun the old boy must have had.

Prologue

In the early hours of Thursday, 7 December 1911, an old man lay dying in his house in Portland Place. He had been ill for some months but no one had expected the end to come as soon as this.

The old man was Sir George Lewis and he was the most famous lawyer in England. Not only in England: throughout America and the whole English-speaking world his name was known, embodying the fascination and danger of the law. For years the press had created a public stereotype for George Lewis. 'His eyeglass and fur coat were as famous as Mr Gladstone's collar or Mr Chamberlain's orchid.' 'He seemed to go through life with a footfall almost as soft as his voice or his manners.' 'He looked like a Jewish Voltaire.' 'Over a quarter of a century he has had a monopoly of those cases where the seamy side of society is unveiled and where the sins and follies of the wealthy classes threaten exposure and disaster.' As his friend King Edward VII said, 'George Lewis is the one man in England who should write his memoirs – and of course he never can.' Lewis had endorsed that when he burned all his papers on his retirement in 1909.

All this would be repeated – and enlarged and added to – when the evening papers announced his death this afternoon. Tomorrow *The Times* (which Lewis had bested when he successfully defended Parnell in the affair of the Pigott letters), the *Morning Post*, the *Daily Telegraph* (which he had represented in several libel actions), and the other dailies would add their voices to the chorus: unanimous in praise but perhaps a little facile in their assessments of a man's life.

But meanwhile he lay here, not moving, so that it was hard to tell whether he was conscious or not: a man of seventy-eight who had looked for many years anything from fifty to seventy-five. His dark, bright eyes, which journalists had frequently called 'penetrating', were closed. His head was covered with an aureole of white hair, abundant even now; his face was narrow, framed in long whiskers.

As noises outside the house began to build up a picture of a London that started its business earlier than the present city – the rattle of milk-churns, the cries of newspaper boys, the sound of hooves on metalled roads – the woman who sat beside him moved uneasily, even angrily, cruelly aware of anything that might disturb her dying husband.

Elizabeth Lewis, born Elizabeth Eberstadt of Mannheim, Germany, was sixty-six in 1911; and she still retained much of the beauty that lit up Burne-Jones's portrait of her, painted when she was already in her forties. But, as her friend Elizabeth Robins wrote, 'her long-lasting beauty was the least of her'. The personality of Elizabeth Lewis – lively, astringent, a few might even say aggressive (for she didn't suffer fools gladly), transcended mere physical attraction. She had created a salon, here at Portland Place. The walls of this house were covered with pictures by friends of the Lewises: Whistler, Burne-Jones, Alma-Tadema, John Sargent (who said Elizabeth was the best sitter he had ever had). Thomas Hardy, George Meredith, and Henry James had all come here. The Lewises had befriended the young Oscar Wilde when he was still looking for a job as an inspector of schools. Paderewski had played in the drawing-room on the floor below. The Lewis children had taken part in a special performance to establish copyright for J. M. Barrie's play *The Little Minister*. Ellen Terry, Henry Irving, and the Bancrofts had enacted charades on the wide main staircase of the house. But, allowing for all this, perhaps Elizabeth's greatest achievement was that she had avoided the jealousies and enmities that beset later fashionable hostesses like Sybil Colefax and Ottoline Morell. Even Virginia Woolf had a kind word for 'old Lady Lewis' in her diary.

But at this moment Elizabeth could think only of her husband. He had lived for seventy-eight years, and now his life was coming to an end. Like all long lives, his had encompassed many changes, witnessed dramatic events – but, unlike most of the nameless, dumbly enduring majority, George Lewis had played his part in some of those events, had helped bring about some of the changes.

Born in the reign of William IV, he had lived right through the Victorian age – a blanket description which represents at least three distinct epochs. The brutal early days, with their echoes of the Regency – prize-fights and gutter journals like *The Town* mocking the young Queen and her Albert with lewd jokes about their honeymoon. Then the years leading on to the Crimean War, the Indian Mutiny, and the rise of Gladstone: stuffy, mid-century years when Dundreary whiskers were fashionable and people put frilly skirts on piano legs. Onwards, through the eighties and nineties, the high Victorian heyday, with the Widow withdrawn and reclusive at Windsor, and the Prince of Wales maintaining his own livelier court at Marlborough House. The eighties and nineties had been Lewis's heyday too: years that had seen him leave his beginnings far behind him – to become, not only the most successful solicitor in London, but the friend and confidant of the King.

He had begun as a clever young Jewish lawyer at a time when Jews in England still suffered various civil disabilities, and anti-semitism was an accepted attitude at every level of English life. From practising in the police courts, he had gone on to fight for defrauded shareholders in the great bank frauds of the 1860s; and then onwards to an ever-growing fame through one *cause célèbre* after another: the Bravo case, the Stauntons, W. T. Stead's 'abduction' of Elizabeth Armstrong, the Dilke divorce, the Baccarat Scandal. This last set the seal on his friendship with the Prince of Wales. Edward admitted that on this and other occasions Lewis's advice had enabled him to ride out a scandal and retain – sometimes even increase – his popularity with his subjects. Edward had been grateful: Lewis had been knighted in 1892, made a baronet at Edward's Coronation in 1902. He and Elizabeth were frequent guests at Sandringham, and Lewis was often with Edward at Homburg and, later, at Marienbad, the German spas he made fashionable.

Of course all this had to be paid for. Lewis had his enemies. The bland words of the obituaries would revive old grudges in their minds. Reminded that Lewis believed in 'my client, right or wrong', they would recall that he had been described as not so much a lawyer as a shrewd private enquiry agent, 'often playing the game in defiance of the rules'. Indeed many people, not least his fellow lawyers, resented his use of a network of spies and informers – ex-convicts, some of them, like Meiklejohn, a former detective inspector at Scotland Yard. Resented even more was the vigour with which Lewis fought the most doubtful cause.

The truth was that Lewis treated the law as a game and played to win. All successful lawyers do. This does not mean that they do not have a regard for justice and fairness, but the legal system – and human nature itself – compel them to work within a gameplayer's rationale. Consider the practice of the law in these terms and some cruelties and anomalies become more understandable, if not more tolerable.

This concept of the law is not acceptable to those who see the question in purely human terms, as Charles Dickens did. The legal system Dickens attacked and satirized was the one Lewis confronted when he was admitted a solicitor in 1856. If many of the laws on the statute book were less harsh and unfair in 1911, when he died, than they had been in 1856, then even Lewis's enemies would have to admit that he had played his part in changing them. The right of a married woman to keep her own property (without needing lawyers to draw up elaborate marriage settlements to protect her); the right of a prisoner to give evidence on his own behalf; the establishment of the Court of Criminal Appeal: Lewis fought for all these causes, just as he fought for George Edjali and Adolf Beck, victims of other lawyers who had been determined to win *their* game at any cost.

But which of these was the 'real' Lewis? The man who cared for justice, who wanted to reform the law – not always to the advantage of lawyers – or the man who fought to win, never mind the merits of his case or of his client?

The answer is: both. George Lewis would play the game of the law with all the skill he could command, even though he might be fighting for someone whose conduct he deplored. But to let his personal opinion of a client colour his judgement would have struck Lewis as mere self-indulgence. He would be guided by other considerations, with the one proviso that he must be told the truth, whatever his client wanted to say in court.

Thus he often appeared to be 'on the wrong side', championing a perjurer like Mrs Crawford or a swindler like Whitaker Wright. But Lewis was not just a grand master of the legal game. He was a sensitive and compassionate man – and this was why he fought for victims like Edjali or Beck, or went against the establishment of the day in representing Parnell, smeared by forged letters *The Times* had published without checking their origin.

Royal confidant and champion of the underdog, law reformer and ruthless fighter for his client, George Lewis was a complex man. The easy judgements of the obituaries cannot wholly contain him, this Jewish Voltaire with the monocle and the big fur coat, trustee of a thousand secrets he will carry to the grave.

He died at seven o'clock that morning. Her sad vigil ended, Elizabeth may have remembered that the best epitaph on her husband had already been written, by Oscar Wilde:

'George Lewis? Brilliant. Formidable. Concerned in every great case in England. Oh – he knows all about us, and he forgives us all.'

1

Beginnings

GEORGE HENRY LEWIS belonged to a family of Sephardic Jews from the Netherlands who settled in England in the eighteenth century, afterwards changing their name from Loew to Lewis. George Lewis's father, James Graham Lewis, was born at St Pancras, London, in 1804. He was admitted a solicitor in January 1829 and married Harriet Davis, also of London, on 11 March of the same year. He set up in practice at 10 Ely Place, Holborn (where the firm of Lewis and Lewis was to remain for over a century). As was the custom at the time, James Lewis and his bride made their home in an upper part of the house, the public office being on the ground floor.

All the Lewis children were to be born at Ely Place. George Henry Lewis, born on 21 April 1833, was the second of four boys; he had one elder and three younger sisters. His elder brother was Edward John Lewis, born 24 May 1831; his elder sister, Esther Lewis, born 6 February 1830. His younger brothers were Frederick Hyman Lewis, born 23 June 1834, and Louis Lewis, born 5 December 1837. His younger sisters were Fanny Lewis, born 7 January 1836, Harriet Lewis, born 30 June 1839, and Emmeline, born 19 March 1841.

It was not an unusually large family by Victorian standards. Lewis was a happy child; indeed he displayed all his life the self-confidence that is said to be the gift of an unthreatened childhood. Fifty years later he recalled for an interviewer what life had been like at Ely Place. His father's work was usually done by four o'clock in the afternoon: the briefs and papers were removed from the long table in the dining-room and a linen cloth laid in their place. James Lewis knew all the theatrical celebrities of the day – among them Charles Matthews, Madame Vestris, the Keans. Charles Kean was very fond of children and he would take young George on his knee and then move his fingers on the tablecloth in imitation of a dancer, to the small boy's delight.

Being a Jew, the young Lewis could not at that time go to Oxford or Cambridge. Equally, he was effectively barred from attending a public school (it is hard to imagine him at Thring's Uppingham or Arnold's Rugby). In the event the Lewises had a governess, a Miss Parry. She taught the older children, Esther, Edward, and George, to read and write. (Miss Parry later became headmistress of Queen's College, Harley Street. Lewis always kept in touch with her.) When George was a little older, he was sent to a private Jewish school in Edmonton, where he soon displayed the tact and shrewdness that later enabled him to settle hundreds of cases before they ever came to court. As he put it himself many years later, 'I always managed to get out of any scrape I got into.' He was good at cricket and appears, in the main, to have enjoyed his time at Edmonton, although he later suggested that anti-semitic prejudice cast a shadow over his school-days: 'Remember I am referring to the time when it was forbidden for a Jew to go to college. This then existing prejudice was so strong that the boys felt it as severely as their fathers and mothers.'

How severe were the disabilities endured by English Jews at this period? Since the reign of Charles II the Test and Corporation Acts had maintained a form of discrimination against those who were not members of the Church of England. This legislation worked against Roman Catholics, Protestant dissenters (like Congregationalists and Methodists), and, of course, Jews. Anyone outside the Church of England was barred from holding any civil or military office under the Crown and from attending a university. Naturally such laws bred intense resentment among the minorities concerned. In 1828 and 1829 these laws were mitigated to a considerable extent for dissenters and Catholics. But the declaration required of all office-holders and Members of Parliament 'on the faith of a Christian' meant that Jews were still excluded. (Disraeli became a Christian in 1817 and could therefore pursue a political career.)

In 1847 Lewis went to University College, London, a pioneer in its freedom from sectarian prejudices (earning it the description 'that godless institution in Gower Street'). He remained there for three years and then, in late 1850, at the age of seventeen and a half, he was articled to his father.

By this time the firm was known as 'Lewis and Lewis'. In 1834, five years after he started in practice, James Lewis had taken his brother, George Hamilton Coleman Lewis, into partnership.

As we have seen, at first the business was conducted from James

Lewis's house at 10 Ely Place. Later, numbers 11 and 12 would also be acquired and the three houses knocked into one, giving a total of twenty-two rooms in all. At that time – and for many years afterwards – Ely Place remained a unique backwater in the heart of London. Governed by a separate Act of Parliament, it was the only place in London where a porter called out the hour, upon the hour, throughout the night.

Years later, when George Lewis had made the firm famous, more than one journalist would describe the offices in Ely Place: the wide doors with LEWIS AND LEWIS blazoned across them in great brass letters; the spacious rooms with their thick Turkish carpets and heavy mahogany furniture; the portraits of judges and other dignitaries that lined the walls.

Things were different in 1850, when Lewis was first articled to his father. Montagu Williams, later a leading counsel who was often briefed by Lewis, spoke of going to Ely Place as a young barrister. He described it as a 'very dirty, dull, and depressing place'. Around the same time, a wealthy client, Lionel Lawson, one of the owners of the *Daily Telegraph*, called there. He was shown into a back room and kept waiting for half an hour. It was, he said, 'for all the world like a prison cell and when I had been there ten minutes I felt convinced that I was a felon of some kind, and before I left I was perfectly certain that I had committed every crime known to the criminal law'.

Lewis and Lewis were specialists in the criminal law. All through the 1830s and 1840s they had gained more and more criminal business in London. At that time, indeed, such business was the virtual monopoly of three firms: Humphreys and Morgan; Wontner and Son; and Lewis and Lewis.

Lewis and Lewis had other interests as well. George Hamilton Lewis ('Uncle George' to everyone in the firm) dealt with the civil side of the practice, being particularly concerned with bankruptcy. He was expert in 'arranging' the insolvencies of gentlemen of the 'leisured and professional classes'. When their yapping creditors had been dealt with by Uncle George, after a decent interval these gentlemen could again saunter down Pall Mall with head held high, to enjoy a drink at the club untroubled by any memory of the sordid business recently enacted by the Registrar in Bankruptcy in Carey Street.

And then there were the firm's strong theatrical connections. The half-forgotten stars Lewis remembered from his childhood had all been clients of his father; and his uncle George was solicitor to the Dramatic Authors' Society, which brought him into contact with writers like Tom Taylor, Dion Boucicault, and T. W. Robertson. (All this foreshadowed Lewis's later friendship with theatre people like Henry Irving, Ellen Terry, and the Bancrofts, who years later were to throng Elizabeth Lewis's soirées at Portland Place.)

The portraits of James Lewis show a genial, relaxed-looking man, his face fringed with beard, who looks more like a sea captain than a lawyer. He was famous for his generosity. He would often act for a client who could not possibly pay him and this won him the title of 'the Poor Man's Lawyer'. He is said to have inspired the character of Mr Jaggers in Dickens's *Great Expectations*. Benevolent but dictatorial, Mr Jaggers has a unique standing among the criminal classes. He announces that he never locks the front door of his house at night, extending an open invitation to all the burglars of his acquaintance: 'Why don't you try me?' Naturally, no one responds to his sardonic appeal. Jaggers flaunts his valuable watch and chain under the nose of hardened thieves – and of course no one dares steal them. No one can afford to make an enemy of Mr Jaggers. He is held in such respect that his house and person are sacrosanct.

The scene in the novel where Jaggers is besieged by eager clients, all begging him to act for them, undoubtedly reflects James Lewis's huge practice among the struggling, half-submerged masses. But while Dickens keeps an aura of mystery around Mr Jaggers, there was nothing in the least mysterious about James Lewis. Something much more than a clever 'mouthpiece', he was respected not just as a brilliant lawyer but as a humane and compassionate man – and therefore a unique and inspiring figure to most of his clients.

As late as the 1850s there were huge areas of London that were simply enclaves of crime. The capital at mid-century was a strange mixture of squalor and elegance. The windows of the rich often overlooked terrible alleys and courts that were rife with crime and disease. Pockets of intense poverty and suffering could extend for yards, or for miles. Some of the worst rookeries had gone by the time the young Lewis began in practice, but many remained, usually because they were so densely populated that they were very profitable to landlords, though recurrent cholera epidemics – there was a particularly bad one in London in 1855 – did direct public attention with more and more urgency towards the slums.

Many of these slums were 'no go' areas as far as the police were concerned. Probably the most famous of them was the 'Holy Land', the St Giles rookery, which took in an area extending from Great Russell Street to St Giles High Street. The Holy Land was a valuable sanctuary for villains operating on the relatively well-lit streets of the West End. Once inside that labyrinth of tortuous alleys and foul, interconnected cellars, it was almost impossible for the police to catch up with a fugitive criminal. Some of James Lewis's clients came from the Holy Land. Others came from further afield: from Jacob's Island, in Bermondsey, or the dreadful dens of the Ratcliffe Highway. Some of the most successful street thieves often did not come from the rookeries at all, but from respectable suburbs like Hackney or Camden Town.

The classification 'street thief' takes in everything from wretched children to members of the 'swell mob' – that is, superior pickpockets who dressed well and confined themselves to victims who were also well dressed and well off. There were women who specialized in stealing from shops; the feminine styles of the time, with ankle-length skirts and petticoats, facilitated concealment. There were 'dragsmen', who worked with one or two accomplices and whose aim was stealing luggage. A coach would leave one of the big London railway stations and the dragsmen would follow in a light cart or trap. Then, when an opportunity offered, one of the dragsmen would jump out and, clinging for a moment to the back of the cab, would dislodge several items of the luggage piled on the roof, causing them to fall out on to the road – without, it was hoped, the occupants of the cab noticing, although the cab driver was often an accomplice of the dragsmen.

These were only a few of the street crimes that were rife when George Lewis was first admitted a solicitor. More sinister – and more suggestive of our own day – were the crimes against the person. It was dangerous to walk the London Streets in the 1850s and 1860s. There were 'rampsmen', who used an attractive woman as a decoy to lure a man away from his companions so that they could then attack and rob him. Around 1861 there was an epidemic of garrotting in London and other big cities. Like modern muggers, garrotters often worked in teams. Two of them might carry out the attack while a third kept watch. The usual procedure was to mark down the victim in a quiet street; then attack him from behind, pinioning his arms and throwing an arm around his neck – starting to choke him – and dragging him back. Usually shock and fear rendered the victim helpless while the garrotters went through his pockets.

Garrotting reached such proportions in 1862 – an MP was garrotted off Pall Mall; a jeweller was killed while being robbed – that parties of vigilantes with swordsticks began to patrol the streets. In 1863 what was known as the Garrotting Act was passed. This provided for the flogging of anyone convicted of garrotting. This measure appeared to work, for cases of garrotting grew less frequent and eventually the crime disappeared altogether.

Street crime, however, represented a small and relatively unprofitable part of the Lewis business. Street robbers were regarded as small fry by the high-class professionals who crowded James Lewis's waiting-room at Ely Place. The real aristocrats were the skilled cracksmen, who robbed banks and business houses and the mansions of the rich; but these experts were facing something of a professional crisis. A safe-making firm in Sheffield had perfected a steel that defied the cracksmen's old-style drills. Safe-blowing was not possible with gunpowder, which was all that was then available. The cracksmen's art was thus in abeyance. Their only hope was to bribe a clerk or servant into lending a key to the safe, which could then be copied.

Lacking the social status of the cracksmen but just as important were the fences, the receivers of stolen property. Often disliked or distrusted, they were still essential to the criminal fraternity. Without their co-operation, the most ingenious robbery was pointless. Someone had to dispose of the goods.

Most fences were involved in a 'legitimate' business that served them both as a front and as a channel through which stolen goods could be funnelled – first to be 'laundered' (for instance, stolen jewels might be reset or recut) and then sold to an innocent member of the public. Jewellery was the most obvious target for the high-class operator, but there were fences who would handle anything. In Petticoat Lane there was a market where anything could be disposed of – from fancy buttons to coffins.

Street thieves, cracksmen, fences, macers (sharpers), shofulmen (coiners), prostitutes – they all came to Ely Place, and James Lewis did his best for all of them. When young George finished his articles and became a solicitor in 1856, this was the world that faced him, and – not forgetting Uncle George's gentlemanly bankrupts – the kind of practice he would eventually inherit from his father. Presumably young Lewis accepted this but, by the time he did take over Lewis and Lewis, he had realized that the role of Mr Jaggers was not for him.

2

Police Court Advocate

WHILE JAMES LEWIS continued to 'attend to the criminal classes indoors' – evocative phrase! – and Uncle George dealt with his bankrupts in a room at the top of the house, young George began to display a rather unexpected gift for advocacy. He started to appear on behalf of the firm's clients in the London police courts (as a solicitor he was not, of course, allowed to plead in the superior courts). He was soon recognized as a brilliant cross-examiner, displaying an instant grasp of any set of facts, however complex; and thus began the process that was to transform Lewis and Lewis's practice and bring George Lewis to the top of his profession within ten years.

The bulk of the firm's business was done at the Bow Street and Marlborough Street courts. At that time Bow Street court was held in two private houses knocked into one (on the other side of the road from where the present court stands). Nearby was a public-house called the Garrick's Head where, with the notorious 'Baron' Renton Nicholson as judge and the customers as jury, lewd mock-trials for rape and 'crim-con' (adultery) were acted out.

George Lewis's first appearance as an advocate was at the Westminster magistrate's court in 1856. His father was away that morning. A big, matronly-looking woman rushed into Ely Place, demanding to see 'Mr Lewis'.

'I'm Mr Lewis.'

The big woman shook her head. 'No – no – you can't be.'

Lewis explained that he certainly was Mr Lewis, adding that his father happened to be away that morning. At that, the woman appeared distraught. Lewis was aware of the extraordinary faith his father's clients had in him and tried to reassure the lady as best he could. He assumed an air of assurance he hardly felt and told her that she had nothing to worry about: he would handle her case in his father's absence.

But the woman did not appear reassured. Was his father coming back within the next hour? No, Lewis told her, his father might not return that day.

At last she calmed down enough to tell him that her son had been taken into custody. He was now at Westminster court, charged with robbing the till at a pub called the Black Lion. Lewis knew the place. It was notable for entertainments by a negro boxer called Sambo Sutton, whose accomplishments included dancing a hornpipe upside down. The woman said that her son, a lad of eighteen employed as a kitchen porter, had been in the public bar having a drink. Suddenly a row had started between two dollymops – girls of easy virtue but not full-time prostitutes – and this caught everyone's attention. The boy had been watching the girls as they shouted abuse and eventually started to hit each other. Finally the barman had vaulted over the counter and chased the girls out into the street. The girls made off but, when the barman got back, he found that £7.15s had been taken from the till. The woman's son had been standing closer to the open till than had anyone else; therefore – according to the barman and the landlord – he must have stolen the money. The police had been called and the lad arrested.

Although Lewis was to say forty years later that he had been so nervous that he didn't know whether he was standing on his head or his heels, he grasped the essentials of the case at once. In the first place it seemed likely that the woman's son was a victim of the hysteria that shouts 'Stop thief!' at what may well be an innocent bystander. And the case – what there was of it – was based on purely circumstantial evidence. Intuitively aware that in advocacy attack is often the best line of defence, Lewis interviewed the other people who had been in the bar and elicited the fact that a 'furtive-looking youth' in flashy clothes had been standing even closer to the till than the accused. What was more, Lewis was able to establish that this youth had disappeared from the bar at around the time the dollymops had been thrown out. He had been there when they had been fighting; when they had gone, so had he. In court Lewis argued that this youth was the real thief. No one had seen the money taken. What was most likely was that the furtive youth was an accomplice of the dollymops, poised to snatch the money during the diversion they created. It need have taken no more than a minute – then he had slipped out of the bar.

Lewis's theory had to remain unproven, but he managed to arouse sufficient doubt in the magistrate's mind for the charge to be dismissed.

The accused lad's mother was waiting for Lewis outside the court. As Lewis described it many years later, 'The mother was a big, muscular woman. I was made very happy by the words which accompanied her too-enthusiastic smack on the back: "Well done, young 'un!" But her enthusiasm hurt.'

During the next few years minor cases like this were to occupy most of George Lewis's time. In fact he soon found himself handling all this side of the firm's business. At the higher courts, like the Old Bailey, the Middlesex Sessions, and the Surrey Sessions, counsel had to be briefed. Lewis and Lewis had a shortlist of barristers who got most of their work: Serjeants Ballantine, Sleigh, and Parry as leaders; often Montagu Williams and Douglas Straight as juniors.

It was a surprise to George when his brother Frederick – who was a little more than a year younger than himself – decided to go to the bar. James Lewis had been disappointed that only George had elected to go into the family firm; but, he was to say later, he had not realized that George would do the work of four ordinary men. Frederick had resolutely declined to join Lewis and Lewis. Only the bar would satisfy him and he became a member of the Inner Temple. He had a moderately successful career – briefed by his brother on many occasions – and died in 1889.

His younger brother's determination to be a barrister held a certain irony for George. As he discovered his own great gifts as an advocate, he began to wonder if he had taken the right course himself. Should he, like Freddy, have gone to the bar? He could still do so; he could still change course, but what would his father say – and do? James Lewis relied on George to take over the firm; it would be mere self-indulgence to turn his back on that obligation because he enjoyed his work in court so much. Here duty seemed to clash with ambition. In terms of fame and personal achievement, the bar appeared to offer so much. Then – much more than now – leading counsel were star performers with all the world watching the play. The links between the stage and the bar were evident in the florid, histrionic style of advocacy in vogue at that time. Young barristers regarded the leaders of their profession with a mixture of envy and awe. Anecdotes were whispered about the great men; if one of them wanted to honour a diligent assistant – 'devil' in the argot of the Temple – he would give him a red bag to keep his briefs in, so that his fellow-strugglers would know the high esteem in which his master held him. The absolute beginners, wearing new snow-white wigs, would sit at the back of the court, listening to Henry Hawkins or John Duke Coleridge (or, a few years later, Charles Russell or Edward Clarke) rather as a novice actor, standing in the wings, might have watched Irving.

And yet Lewis, already assured of his gifts, knowing the wealth and honours a career at the bar could bring him, decided to remain a solicitor. By the time he accepted his father's offer of a partnership in the firm (in 1858), there was no doubt left in his mind. Apart from loyalty to his father, he believed that his achievement could be greater if he remained with Lewis and Lewis.

Indeed, he was to come to believe that, paradoxically, a solicitor often has more power than a barrister to influence the progress of a case. Of course the spotlight is always focused on counsel, but the solicitor behind him can to a great extent determine the way things go. Or at least should do – if he understands the rules of the game well enough and is playing to win. After all, the solicitor is responsible for the case from the beginning.

Assuming a case had to go to court, a great deal depended on the brief sent to counsel. Lewis treated each case as a puzzle: a puzzle that, unlike a jigsaw, could fall into more than one pattern. Spotting the right pattern demanded a blend of calculation and intuition (with Lewis, the intuitive element developed over the years), and counsel's response to the facts the brief enshrined might not accord with yours.

So everything had to be gone into. Discussed. Argued over. Prepared. There must be no possibility of any misunderstanding between solicitor and counsel.

And then there were the witnesses. A lot depended on how you handled them. Some lawyers never met their witnesses before they saw them in court – or they had a hurried consultation with them just before before the court sat. But Lewis insisted that every detail of a witness's testimony had to be checked and re-checked. Clarity and consistency were all-important. Indeed, Lewis was to become famous for the way he handled his witnesses. Enemies would allege he dragooned them: coaching, rehearsing them till they were like circus dogs, ready to jump through hoops of Lewis's devising – to the great advantage of his case.

One of the first murder cases Lewis had to deal with had all the pathos of one of the drawing-room ballads so popular at the time. It was the first time Lewis worked with a young barrister he was later to brief on many occasions. Montagu Williams had been to Eton and, after a spell as an actor, had been called to the bar. His apprenticeship in the theatre hardly seems a coincidence. He was a master of the histrionic style favoured in the 1860s (which was soon to be succeeded by the quieter, less impassioned manner that Lewis himself preferred).

Williams had a personal link with the case. He was a member of a dining club which met once a week at the Café de l'Europe. The café had been run by a man named Hicks, who had been declared bankrupt some time earlier. When the crash came, his nineteen-year-old daughter Floretta had decided to go on the stage (whether or not to mend the family fortunes is not recorded). Floretta had talent enough to get a job in a fourth-rate *opéra bouffe* company. Touring the provinces, staying in grisly theatrical lodgings, Floretta had fallen in love with the manager of the company, a glib Lothario with long waxed moustaches. Their romance proceeded along sadly conventional lines: soon Floretta found herself pregnant, whereupon the manager abandoned her (he was, inevitably, already married).

The girl returned to London. Rejected by her parents, she took a garret in Soho. There, in due course, her child was born. Some days later, a little girl's body was found wrapped in sacking at the bottom of some cellar stairs.

Medical opinion was divided as to whether or not the baby had died of natural causes, due in some measure to the mother's appalling situation, or whether this was a case of infanticide. The police considered that this was a question for a jury to decide. Floretta Hicks was arrested and charged with murder.

The members of the dining club were shocked. They had all known Floretta. She had waited on them at table many times. They started a subscription list to get her the best legal assistance. The chairman of the club, a Mr Watkins, who knew Lewis and Lewis by reputation, went to James Lewis and told him that the club would meet all the costs of the defence. Because Williams was a member of the club, Watkins suggested that he should defend Floretta – although he was a mere beginner at the bar. Tactfully, James Lewis suggested that a charge as serious as murder demanded a man of some experience. He proposed that Serjeant Ballantine should lead young Williams, and Wakins agreed.

The trial duly opened at the Old Bailey. Lewis had taken over the case from his father, who was attending the Middlesex Sessions. After senior treasury counsel had opened for the Crown, seeking to persuade the jury that Floretta had found her baby 'an intolerable burden' and had murdered her in a mood of anger and despair, Serjeant Ballantine was called away to appear in another case in the Court of Common Pleas. Lewis and Williams were on their own.

Williams was full of doubts. There was no point of law to argue. And there was no doubt about the facts. The body of the little girl had been found at the foot of the stairs and Floretta was the only person who could have placed her there.

There was only one thing to do, Lewis said. Make an emotional appeal to the jury. Aim at their hearts, not their heads. Williams had been an actor, hadn't he?

Williams took Lewis's advice. He addressed the jury in emotional terms. Here – he pointed to Floretta as she sat weeping in the dock – was a true unfortunate, barely twenty years of age. Who could imagine the agony, physical and mental, that this poor girl had endured? Who was to blame for her hideous predicament? Not herself, not society. Only one person was to blame: the cruel seducer whose victim she was.

Williams went on to describe the character of the theatrical manager in vivid terms. Quoting from *Othello*:

> 'O Heavens! That such companions thou'dst unfold,
> And put in every honest hand a whip
> To lash the rascals through the world.'

he denounced the baby's father as the real murderer. From whatever cause this unfortunate infant had died, he, the faithless progenitor, was responsible.

The jury withdrew for a short time and then brought in a verdict of not guilty – important not only to the unfortunate Floretta but to Montagu Williams too, for, as he put it himself, 'from that moment my fortune was safe' and he began to get briefs.

As for Lewis, his strategy had proved itself. Granted that poor Floretta had to stand in the dock at all, Williams's well-chosen fustian had been necessary to save her from the gallows.

3

Marriage and a Murder

By 1862 Lewis had been a partner in his father's firm for four years. Things at Ely Place seemed little changed. James Lewis continued to wear the persona of Mr Jaggers. 'Uncle George' went on arranging his bankruptcies. 'Young Mr Lewis' was consolidating his reputation in the courts, particularly as a cross-examiner of terrier-like tenacity.

But things *were* changing. James Lewis was gradually yielding control to his son. More and more often, he would confer with George about important cases. And the lines dividing the responsibilities of the three partners were becoming less well defined. This was a deliberate policy on James's part and Uncle George did not resent it. The future of the firm must lie with young George.

Lewis was twenty-nine that year. With his smooth brow and slim build, women often thought he looked younger (this, of course, was a period when a man of thirty-five was often considered to be well on into middle age). But the essentials of his appearance that would later make him an easy mark for caricaturists like Max Beerbohm and 'Spy' were already there: the slight figure; the long face framed in long whiskers; the look of imposed calm that masked a hair-trigger alertness. He already wore an eyeglass; he had not yet acquired the fur coat.

For several years now he had been taking his holidays in Germany. No need for an Englishman to apologize for that: not for another fifty years. Quite apart from the royal connection – and Victoria's beloved Albert Edward had died only the year before – the Germany of the 1860s was still for most people the pleasant land of *Gemütlichkeit* that conjured up fantasies of gentle blue-eyed young giants drinking beer out of long steins and smoking clay pipes, while at their side sat blonde *Gretchens* with their hair tied in pigtails. A Germany of storybook castles perched high among pine forests; the sentimental land that had wept over the sorrows of Werther. A very different Germany from the menacing creation of blood and iron that was to emerge under Kaiser Wilhelm II.

But a darker truth overshadowed these pleasant fantasies and, as a Jew, Lewis was aware of it. Whatever anti-semitic feeling there might be in England, it was a mild, desultory thing compared with the savage German anti-semitism that went back to medieval times. And so, in the nineteenth century, many German Jews tended to look towards England as an almost ideal haven of tolerance. The man who was to become Edward VII's physician, Sir Felix Semon, left Germany in 1875 because of 'religious intolerance'. Ludwig Mond, the great chemist, left because his mother 'had always suffered from the persecution put upon her race by the German people'.

While the German Jews looked towards England as offering tolerance and greater opportunity, English Jews regarded with admiration the artistic and cultural traditions of Germany Jewry. Certainly, at this time stronger links extended between English and German Jews than ever existed before or since. The Lewises had many friends among the German Jewish community.

None of this is to suggest that Lewis was necessarily preoccupied with such heavy matters when he went on holiday to Germany. He loved the Rhine. He knew every mile of it, particularly the Rhine-Highland between Bingen and Bonn. He was fond, too, of Mannheim, the ancient river city and former capital of the Rhonish Palatinate, later the capital of the Grand Dukes of Baden. He had friends there, the Eberstadts. Helena Eberstadt had married an Englishman called Henry Cannen, who was on the wool exchange in Coleman Street. The Cannens lived in Addison Road, Kensington, where Lewis sometimes went to dine with them. Helena was the eldest of the four daughters of Ferdinand Eberstadt. They were known collectively as 'The Four Beautiful Sisters of Mannheim', and Lewis had met another of them, Helena's younger sister Elizabeth, who was considered to be the most beautiful of the four. She was certainly the most energetic and high-spirited.

It was not to Mannheim, however, that Lewis went on holiday in the summer of 1862. He went to Frankfurt-am-Main, a larger city than Mannheim, with a history going back to Charlemagne, and famous for its trade fair, which dated back to 1240. Lewis had friends in Frankfurt too, the Kanns, and they came from the same Jewish banking and merchant caste as the Eberstadts. That summer he was going to visit Victorine, the twenty-two-year-old daughter of Philip Kann, the girl he had already asked to be his wife.

Because she died so young, Victorine Kann remains a shadowy figure. She is known to have been small and fair; she is said to have been gentle, almost timid. This said, it would be fanciful to cast her as Dora to Lewis's Copperfield; merely imaginative to endow her with Dora's childish dependence.

George Lewis and Victorine Kann were married on 29 March 1863 and spent their honeymoon travelling in France and Germany. Lewis's parents had moved to a house in Euston Square so that the young couple could begin their life together at Ely Place.

The first twelve months of their marriage was a time of happiness – and no doubt, as for any young couple, a time also of extraordinary adjustments. Victorine became pregnant almost immediately: the child was expected in the spring of the following year. 'Living above the shop', as they did in Ely Place, Lewis was able to go upstairs to see Victorine from time to time during the day. When he knew he would be absent for a long period – in court all day or out of London – he would arrange for his mother or his sister Esther (who lived in Brunswick Square) to sit with Victorine. Sometimes Helena Cannen would come, and occasionally Victorine would summon up enough energy to return the call and got to tea at Addison Road.

Lewis's marriage had coincided with mounting pressures at the firm. He was becoming better known, and that meant more work, with only him to do it, for he certainly could not ask his father or Uncle George for help. This was an added tension for Lewis, already anxious about Victorine's pregnancy. Bearing a child was still a dangerous adventure in 1864.

He consoled himself with the thought that her health appeared to be good. The doctor called almost every day. He sought to reassure Lewis by telling him that small, apparently delicate women often made the best mothers – in the biological sense. A small lady like Victorine was often better able to survive the strain of childbirth than some buxom, Junoesque creature.

Grateful for the doctor's assurances, Lewis still felt tense, sensing that the physician was perhaps voicing his own anxiety for his patient as well as consoling her husband.

For her part Victorine was in good spirits. She professed herself astonished at Lewis's anxieties; laughed gently at his wish that their first child should be born in the same first-floor room at Ely Place where Lewis himself had been born, thirty-two years earlier.

As December waned, Lewis got busier and busier. Everyone was preparing for Christmas and the weather co-operated: snow melted into steam as it dropped off the gas-lamps that lit the streets. Then, on Boxing Night, 26 December 1864, a young Italian knocked at the door of 10 Ely Place.

He was in a state of great excitement. 'Come with me! Come with me!' he kept begging Lewis. 'Where?' Lewis demanded, and 'Why?' and eventually the Italian – whose knowledge of English was limited – explained that he meant the police-station, the station-house in Clerkenwell. A thirty-two-year-old glass-silverer called Serafino Pelizzioni was being held there on a charge of stabbing an Englishman, Michael Harrington, during a fracas between English and Italians at a public house known as the Golden Anchor.

With a little reluctance – it was getting late, it was very cold, and he didn't want to leave Victorine – Lewis agreed to go with the messenger. The station house wasn't far from Ely Place. On the way, the young Italian told him more about the case.

As the Italian gave the facts to Lewis, in a clumsy and disjointed way, speaking in heavily accented English, Lewis never guessed that the stabbing of Michael Harrington was not only to be his biggest case to date, but was to remain unique in British criminal annals right up to the present day.

On the surface it all sounded commonplace enough. An Italian had stabbed an Englishman in a bar-room brawl. The kind of crime that – then, as now – springs from a lethal combination of alcohol and ethnic prejudice.

Serafino Pelizzioni lived in what was then London's Little Italy, the district known as Saffron Hill. There was and is a thoroughfare called Saffron Hill. It begins at Clerkenwell Road and ends at Charterhouse Street (very close to Ely Place). This whole area was at that time an Italian enclave, housing hundreds of immigrants and their families, most of whom earned a living through traditional skills like glass-silvering (in the making of mirrors) or terrazzo work (as in the laying of mosaic pavements in churches). Others worked in restaurants and some – no doubt to English eyes the most traditional of all – sold ice-cream or took out a barrel-organ to play in the streets. (Up to the 1920s or later, there were firms in Clerkenwell where a barrel-organ could be hired by the hour or day, complete with monkey.)

Although the Golden Anchor was patronized to a great extent by Italians, the landlord was an Englishman called Frederick Shaw. Lewis and his father both knew the pub and knew, too, that, with his mixed clientele of English and Italians, Shaw had a difficult time maintaining the peace. There had been fights at the Golden Anchor before, and there was always the danger that knives would be drawn. On Boxing Night they *had* been.

Lewis was told that the wounded man, Harrington, had been taken to St Bartholomew's Hospital, and that the police had brought Pelizzioni there too, for some kind of identification parade.

By the time Lewis arrived at the station house, Pelizzioni had been returned there and was lodged in a cell. Before seeing him, however, Lewis talked to an Inspector Potter, whom he already knew well through his police-court practice. Potter told Lewis that Pelizzioni had been arrested by a constable called Fawel, who had been called to the pub after reports of a brawl between English and Italians. Fawel had brought Pelizzioni back to the station house, where he had been charged with the stabbing of both Harrington and the potman at the Golden Anchor, a man called Rebbeck. While Rebbeck was not severely injured, the doctors at St Bartholomew's did not believe Harrington could live through the night.

The police version of events was largely based on the statement of Shaw, the landlord, and Rebbeck, the potman. According to them, there had been several Italians in the bar-parlour that evening. Among them was a man they knew as Gregorio, a regular at the pub. Then Pelizzioni, another regular, entered. An argument developed and Pelizzioni got excited and said to Shaw, 'I could kill you or any six Englishmen like you.' (Later there was to be an argument as to whether Pelizzioni had used the word 'kill' or 'settle'.) In any case, Shaw ignored the remark.

After a few minutes Pelizzioni left the bar-parlour. A little later a much more serious row developed in the tap-room. (It was typical of the confusion of testimony that bedevilled this whole case that there was disagreement about whether it was the 'tap-room' or the 'bagatelle-room'.) Shaw tried to get into the tap-room in the hope of quelling the row, but some of the customers pushed him back – perhaps to save him from injury. A few minutes later he saw Michael Harrington being carried into the bar-parlour, bleeding from a stab-wound. Rebbeck, the potman, said he had seen Pelizzioni and another Italian going into the tap-room. He had said to Pelizzioni, 'We don't want any row here.' The Italian did not answer but a moment later pulled out a knife and stabbed Rebbeck in his right side. Rebbeck turned to run, but Pelizzioni jumped forward and stabbed him a second time. A moment after this Rebbeck turned and saw Pelizzioni 'on top of Harrington'. He moved to pull him off the wounded man but fainted before he could do so.

Inspector Potter told Lewis that there were other witnesses who would say that they saw Pelizzioni stab Harrington; and that, while there had been a number of Italians present earlier, only Pelizzioni had been there when the double stabbing took place. After Constable Fawel had arrested Pelizzioni, he had brought him to the station at Clerkenwell where he had been interviewed by Inspector Potter. Harrington had already been taken to Bart's Hospital, and Potter decided to take Pelizzioni by cab to the hospital, there to take part in what must surely have been the most bizarre identification parade in British legal history.

The inspector led Pelizzioni into the long ward where Harrington lay, screened off from the other patients. The hospital staff had momentarily withdrawn, but a number of men stood around Harrington's bed. They had been brought in at random, off the streets, as is usual with an identification parade.

The other men waited in silence. Potter approached the wounded man's bedside. Harrington had been stabbed six times in his abdomen, leaving a gaping wound from which his intestines actually protruded. He was in great pain, but – according to Potter – fully conscious and quite lucid.

In the flickering gaslight, Potter took Harrington's hand. He asked, 'Do you understand what I am saying to you?'

'Yes,' Harrington said.

Potter said, 'In consequence of what the doctor tells me, I must inform you that you have but a short time to live.'

'If I am to die,' Harrington said, 'may the Lord have mercy upon me.'

Then he appeared to doze, but Potter sought his attention again. He pointed to the men grouped around the bed. 'Look,' he said, 'there are twelve men there. Do you know any of them?'

Harrington indicated Pelizzioni. 'That is the man who did it. God bless him.' (Later, in court, Potter would say he was not sure whether

Harrington's words were 'God bless him' or 'God forgive him'.)

Harrington was now so weak that, throughout this scene, Inspector Potter had to hold up his head. A Sergeant Baldock stood close by, writing down all that was said. When he had finished, Harrington's words were shown to Pelizzioni, who said, 'I do not understand English writing.'

Potter replied, 'What Harrington has said is that you did it.'

'Oh,' Pelizzioni said, and that was all he did say, either then or later when he was cautioned and charged at Clerkenwell.

Having heard the case against Pelizzioni, Lewis went down to the cells to see him.

Serafino Pelizzioni was a tall, well-built young man, swarthy-complexioned, with a heavy moustache. He was wearing the smock-type overalls that made Italian workmen instantly recognizable in the London of that time. He appeared calm, even resigned. He merely nodded when Lewis told him that the charge against him must be one of murder, as the doctors thought Harrington would die that night. (In fact he died at three o'clock in the afternoon of the following day.)

Pelizzioni told Lewis he had been in England ten or eleven years. He spoke English 'a little bit', but hadn't understood much of what had been said to him that night. 'I know the constable read a paper to me; but I couldn't understand.' Pelizzioni said that Constable Fawel had examined his hands and found blood on them. Pelizzioni told Fawel he had been hit on the head and that was where the blood had come from.

The story Pelizzioni told Lewis differed widely from Shaw's and Rebbeck's – as conveyed to Lewis by Inspector Potter. Pelizzioni had not even been in the Golden Anchor when the row began, he told Lewis. So the 'kill any six Englishmen' conversation had never taken place. In fact, at the time Pelizzioni had been in another, Italian-owned public house called Bordessa's. He was standing in the bar there, talking to some Italians, when someone came in and said there was a row going on at the Golden Anchor. Pelizzioni's two cousins, Gregorio and Giovanni Mogni, were all down there.

Concerned for his cousins, Pelizzioni immediately started off for the Golden Anchor. He would try to stop them getting into any trouble. 'Directly I went into the tap-room I heard a woman scream,' he told Lewis. 'She was the landlady of the house. When she saw me, she called me by name. "Serafino," she said. "My God! Don't let them make no row." I said, "No, Eliza. Tell your husband to keep the

English people to one side. I shall try to take the Italians the other way."'

He left the landlady at the bar, and went into the bagatelle-room where he thought the row was. The moment he got into the room someone hit him on the head and he fell to the floor. Then he was grabbed and dragged into the bagatelle-room and kept on the floor till the policeman Fawel arrived.

Someone said to Fawel, 'I give you in charge of this man.'

'Who gives me in charge?' Pelizzioni demanded, and a woman said she would, claiming he had hit her in the mouth and then knocked her down. This was not true, Pelizzioni added. He did not even know the woman.

Lewis questioned the Italian but could not get him to contradict his original version of what had happened. As far as Lewis could judge, Pelizzioni was telling the truth, but it was going to be difficult to get him a fair trial. His halting, imperfect English set up a barrier even between him and Lewis – how much more would it damage Pelizzioni's chances in court? Lewis had no illusions about the amount of prejudice that would be generated against Pelizzioni. An Italian immigrant who had stabbed an Englishman in a bar-room brawl?

Lewis gave the man what reassurance he could and went back to Ely Place.

In the days that followed it became apparent to Lewis that this case endorsed a long-cherished theory of his: that, if three different persons witness the same event, whatever it may be – a child falling into a river; a thief picking a pocket; a burglar climbing into a window – each of the three will give a different account of it.

Lewis succeeded in getting several Italians to testify that there had been a general melée, a free-for-all, in which several Italians (including Pelizzioni's cousin Gregorio) had been seen to draw knives. Indeed, the impression was that total confusion had reigned in the Golden Anchor that night.

On 4 February 1865 Serafino Pelizzioni stood in the dock of the Old Bailey, charged with the murder of Michael Harrington. Baron Martin was the judge. Hardinge Giffard, later Lord Halsbury, Lord Chancellor, led for the prosecution. Mr Ribton led for the defence, with Lewis's brother Frederick as his junior. The presence of a large number of Italian immigrants in the public gallery imparted an extra tension to the proceedings: the Italians applauded defence counsel loudly when they entered the court.

The Crown case was based on the sequence of events Inspector Potter had outlined for Lewis the night Pelizzioni had been arrested. The first witness for the prosecution was the landlord, Shaw. He was cross-examined about 'kill any six Englishmen' and conceded that Pelizzioni might after all have said 'settle any six Englishmen . . .' More curiously, he now said that Pelizzioni's cousin, Gregorio Mogni, had not only quarrelled with him (Shaw) but had struck him in the face.

'But, Mr Shaw,' Ribton said, 'I have before me two depositions of yours, one before the magistrate and one before the coroner, in which there is no reference whatever to Gregorio having struck you.'

'But he did. He struck me on the mouth and then rushed into the tap-room. I saw no more of him.'

The potman, Rebbeck, was called next. He claimed to have seen Pelizzioni and 'many others' in the tap-room. He then said that he had seen one of the Italians knock down a woman who was in the doorway of the tap-room. (Could this be the woman who claimed Pelizzioni had struck her?) Rebbeck then described the stabbing again.

It was evident to Lewis that the prosecution intended, if possible, to focus all the attention on Pelizzioni – playing down the involvement of all the other Italians who had undoubtedly been present. Counsel for the Crown was as aware as Lewis was that, to the English habitués of the pub, all the Italians tended to look alike, which made identification – always difficult – more difficult than ever. But, if the prosecution could show that Pelizzioni was the only Italian in the bagatelle-room at the time of the murder, they would almost certainly get a conviction.

The defence, therefore, had to pursue a different line: stressing the confusion caused by the presence of so many Italians, all much alike in dress and appearance – mostly with heavy moustaches and wearing overalls.

Mr Ribton held to this line in cross-examining the police constable Fawel and another constable, Eliot, who had arrived a little later. Fawel denied that he had been making enquiries about Pelizzioni's cousin, Gregorio Mogni. (Which would imply that the police were not absolutely sure they had the right man.)

Inspector Potter was closely questioned about the identification parade by the dying man's bedside. Ribton elicited the fact that, while Sergeant Baldock had taken down Michael Harrington's statement identifying Pelizzioni as his assailant, Harrington had not signed it.

'How was that?' Ribton demanded.

'He did not seem ready to sign.'

'*Ready* to sign? Do you mean he was unwilling to sign?'

'I do not know exactly why he did not want to sign.'

'Do you think it was possible he did not sign because there was some doubt in his mind about the man he had identified as his murderer?'

'No, sir. He was quite firm on that.'

'Is it correct to say that you have been making enquiries about other Italians who might be involved in the case?'

'That is so.'

'And have any of them been identified as being concerned in this affray in any way?'

'No, sir. None.'

In all eight witnesses testified that Harrington had been stabbed by Pelizzioni. Lewis did not feel hopeful as Ribton opened the case for the defence.

His was an able speech enough. He stuck to the question of identity – this was clearly the best line the defence had. The defence contended (Ribton said) that Pelizzioni was, quite simply, the wrong man. He had not stabbed anyone that fateful Boxing Night: he had, in fact, been attempting to act as peacemaker.

The first witness for the defence was a woman called Anne Sams. She had been at the Golden Anchor at about five in the afternoon. She had been dancing with Pelizzioni. Later a violent row had developed between the English and the Italians. But, she said, Pelizzioni had left before the brawl began.

'Were other Italians present?' Ribton asked.

'Another Italian who was very like Pelizzioni was there with his brother and I saw one of them strike Mr Shaw.'

Cross-examining her, counsel for the Crown concentrated on her evidence that Pelizzioni had actually left the Golden Anchor before the row started.

'The prisoner had left the pub after he had danced with you?'

'That is so.'

'In fact you do not know what happened to him after that?'

'No.'

'He could have returned to the pub and entered the bagatelle-room later?'

'I suppose he could.'

'You were not, in fact, in the bagatelle-room when the stabbing occurred?'

'No, not the actual stabbing.'

While this last admission may appear to render all Anne Sam's evidence inconclusive, her words 'another Italian who was very like Pelizzioni' stood at the very heart of the defence. And indeed, Lewis had located two more witnesses, a terrazzo worker called Angelinetta and another called Mossi who deposed that Serafino Pelizzioni closely resembled his cousin Gregorio Mogni.

The defence now went into the question of the knife that had killed Harrington – a question that the prosecution had, significantly, said very little about.

What had happened to the knife that had inflicted the fatal wound? Ribton demanded. Why had the police not produced it in court? It was in their possession, was it not?

There were in fact apparently two knives in question. A witness called Cetti swore that after the fight Gregorio Mogni had approached him with a knife in his hand. Afterwards Mogni had thrown this knife away in the yard of the pub called Bordessa's (mentioned, it will be remembered, by Pelizzioni to Lewis). The potboy at Bordessa's found the knife and the next day handed it over to the police.

The defence recalled Inspector Potter to the witness box and asked why the knife had not been produced as an exhibit in the case. Potter prevaricated; he gave no satisfactory answer, but eventually produced a knife which he said was the one the potboy at Bordessa's had given him. Recalled, the potboy said that the knife now exhibited was not the one he had found.

A second knife was now produced, which, it was claimed, had been found near the Golden Anchor. It had blood on it, while the one taken from Bordessa's yard did not. It was hard for Lewis to gauge the effect of this confusing evidence on the jury: the true ownership of the knives could not be established and at that time forensic methods did not permit accurate matching of the blood on the second knife with that of the dead man, Michael Harrington.

Lewis felt the atmosphere of the court was heavy with prejudice. If Pelizzioni had been an Englishman, he could have been fairly certain of an acquittal. As it was, the judge summed up for a conviction. Baron Martin appeared to be merely impatient over the question of identification. He failed to remind the jury that more than one witness had remarked on the likeness between Pelizzioni and his cousin Mogni.

Lewis could sense the intolerance in the judge's attitude. Damned foreigners! Compounding the insolence of coming to England at all by drinking and brawling and then killing an Englishman!

It only took the jury ten minutes to arrive at their verdict of guilty. Before passing sentence, the judge chose to remark that the 'evidence in this case was about the clearest and most direct I have ever known'. He then passed sentence of death. Pelizzioni – who had sat silent and impassive throughout the trial – began to protest his innocence, clinging to the rail around the dock until he was dragged away by warders.

Lewis was disappointed but not surprised. Identification – direct identification by eye-witnesses – was often unsatisfactory, and dangerous to an accused person. And he doubted if the jury had made anything of the question of the murder-knives.

The verdict caused a sensation among the Italian community in London. The Italian ambassador and Count Maffei, the secretary to the legation, saw a junior minister at the Home Office to make representations to save Pelizzioni's life. There was correspondence in both *The Times* and the *Daily Telegraph*. In view of the likeness between Pelizzioni and Mogni, the lack of interest in Mogni on the part of the police was remarkable. No attempt had been made to call him at the trial and now he was said to have 'disappeared'. It was obvious to Lewis that the police, glad to have secured a conviction, and with Pelizzioni awaiting execution in Newgate, were satisfied enough to do nothing more.

Italians in London felt angry and dissatisfied. Their ambassador's representations had been ignored. The truth was, of course, that the British establishment did not need to listen to the Italians: they could not conceive of any circumstance in which the goodwill of the Italian government could possibly be of use to Britain.

But one prominent member of the Italian community would not accept no for an answer. This was Henry Negretti, one of the founders of the famous firm of Negretti and Zambra, the instrument-makers. He had attended every day of the trial: he had not missed one word of the evidence against his fellow countryman. Naturally he had been appalled at the way the verdict had been steamrollered through, despite all the doubts and contradictions in the prosecution's case. Pelizzioni was innocent, Negretti believed, and he was to be hanged for a crime he did not commit.

Not if Henry Negretti could prevent it! He went to see Lewis at Ely Place. There he poured out all the shock and anger he felt.

While recognizing that Negretti's reaction to Pelizzioni's conviction was an emotional one, Lewis agreed with every word he said. All the same, he pointed out to Negretti, the case now looked almost hopeless. (It will be remembered that there was no court of criminal appeal at that time.) Pelizzioni had been duly taken by the police, tried, convicted. It was hard to see any way in which the case could be reopened.

Calmer now, Negretti told Lewis that he understood all that. The difficulties were immense. But he was determined to fight for Pelizzioni's life, and he believed he was not alone. He had the backing of every Italian in England – ranging from wealthy businessmen like himself and his partner to newly arrived immigrants. Did he have Lewis's support too?

Lewis shook him by the hand and assured him he did. But what did he propose to do?

Mogni, Negretti said. Gregorio Mogni was the key to the case. This was a case of mistaken identity: there was little doubt of that. Locate Mogni and the case could be reopened.

How? Lewis asked.

Negretti said he had a friend, a Mr Negroni. Negroni had a vast acquaintanceship among the Italians in England. If Gregorio Mogni were still in England – and Negretti did not think it likely that he would have been able to return to Italy – then Negroni would find him.

Leaving the search to Negroni, Negretti went on, he, Negretti, would organize a public campaign to save the condemned man. His partner, Mr Zambra, would take over the running of the firm; he himself would concentrate on saving Pelizzioni. For what they were worth, official representations would be continued. More importantly, he would keep the controversy alive in the correspondence columns of the *Daily Telegraph* and *The Times*.

Both Lewis and Negretti were acutely aware of how little time they had. Less than three weeks. In less than twenty days' time, Pelizzioni would walk from the condemned cell at Newgate on to the gallows.

If Negretti or his friend Negroni could find Mogni in that time, Lewis said, he could probably find grounds to reopen the case. But, even if Mogni were found, they would still confront difficulties that were almost unique in the history of the criminal law. Once a man was convicted of murder, only the Crown could show clemency and commute the death sentence – and this rarely happened. Having obtained a conviction, the police and the Home Office behind them would be most reluctant to disturb it. Why should they? They would have everything to lose and nothing to gain. Even if Mogni were found – even if he admitted his guilt – the evidence against him would have to be overwhelming to disturb the position of the authorities.

But Negretti, his decision taken, and assured of Lewis's support, appeared full of confidence. His first action was to visit Pelizzioni in Newgate and pledge the support of the whole Italian community. Then he opened his campaign for a reappraisal of the case with a broadside in *The Times* in which he discussed the strange situation of the *two* knives being found, one covered with blood and the other not, and the indifference of the police to establishing which knife was actually the murder-weapon. He also stressed the confusion of identities: the amount of evidence pointing to Gregorio Mogni.

Naturally there were establishment voices raised in defence of the police. Continuing his campaign, Negretti raised the matter of the identification parade that had taken place beside the dying man's bedside. Pelizzioni was a typical Italian: swarthy-skinned, heavily moustached, wearing workman's garb that was almost a uniform. The six or more other men grouped around the bed had all been Englishmen – most of them fair-skinned and clean-shaven. Would not almost anyone – let alone a dying man, heavily sedated with laudanum – have picked out *any* Italian in that group? What could Harrington's identification really be worth?

The battle went on, with Negretti shooting his darts at the elephantine hide of the police, who ignored them all. Both Negretti and Lewis realized it was no good going on scoring debating points, however unanswerable. Time was running out. One morning, soon, the hangman was going to lead Pelizzioni out on to the gallows.

Just as time was running out for Serafino Pelizzioni, so Victorine's confinement drew nearer and nearer. A week or two more at the most. The doctor was still confident that all would go well, but Lewis suspected a growing anxiety behind the apparent optimism. All he could do was wait: aware of the irony that seemed to link the birth of his child with the fate of a condemned man.

Then, suddenly, Mogni surfaced. Negretti received a note from him. He was in Birmingham. He had made his confession to an Italian priest there and the priest had persuaded him to write to Negretti.

Negretti left immediately for Birmingham, catching an express at twenty minutes' notice. Arriving, he went to the address on Mogni's note. It turned out to be a carpenter's workshop.

'You rascal!' Negretti cried the moment he saw Mogni. 'Is it possible you can't get into a fight without using a knife?'

Mogni appeared stunned by this. He said, 'Mr Negretti, you would have done the same in my place.'

Negretti said, 'Do you know your cousin Serafino Pelizzioni is going to be hanged?'

'No,' Mogni said. 'I did not know it.' He shook his head. 'It is not possible. It cannot be true.'

'It is true. He is going to be hanged.'

Negretti told Lewis afterwards that Mogni appeared to be dazed and confused. Slowly and patiently, Negretti went over the circumstances of the trial. He reiterated that Pelizzioni lay in Newgate under sentence of death. Only Mogni could save him.

After a few minutes, Mogni took down his coat from a nail on the wall and said, 'Mr Negretti, I am ready to come with you. My cousin shan't be hanged for me.'

They took the train to London. During the journey, Mogni talked freely about the crime: 'On the night of the murder I had been drinking a good deal of rum. We Italians were all treating each other, till I was the worse for liquor. Then there was a fight between the English and the Italians. I went to my brother Giovanni's aid. The fight took place in the bagatelle-room and at the time my cousin Pelizzioni was not there.'

When they arrived in London – having sent a message to Lewis – Negretti immediately took Mogni to King's Cross police station. He explained the circumstances – rather naively, it must be said, expecting the police to respond with some kind of positive action.

In fact their reaction to Gregorio Mogni was wholly negative. Mogni? Who was he? And why should they be interested in him? He wasn't on their files. Again rather naively, Negretti was appalled to realize that they had no intention of arresting Mogni for a murder they had already solved. A man was going to be hanged for the Saffron Hill murder in a week or so's time: that was an end of it.

When they met, Lewis reminded Negretti that he had expected this. It would be hard to shift the elephant, but perhaps not impossible.

Next day, Lewis wrote to the Home Office, enclosing a deposition from Mogni himself, and demanding a full enquiry. The reply was as he had expected: Her Majesty's Government saw no reason to question the correctness of the verdict arrived at in the case of *Regina* v. *Pelizzioni.*

Lewis's next move was to test the strength of official confidence in the verdict. He sent Mogni's deposition to the Treasury (along with other evidence garnered since the trial and relating to the confusion of identities between Mogni and Pelizzioni). In fact he was inviting the Treasury to back their expressed belief in the rightness of Pelizzioni's conviction by undertaking to defend Gregorio Mogni – which would have been something without precedent in the history of the law.

Meanwhile, however, Lewis had achieved the most important objective of all: Serafino Pelizzioni's execution was postponed.

As to defending Mogni, the Treasury did not rise to the bait. With Pelizzioni granted at least a temporary reprieve, Lewis was not too concerned at this. He expected strategic delays, obfuscation, prevarication. These were the natural weapons of officialdom, and naturally the Treasury would use them. He began a complex series of exchanges with the Treasury Solicitor: proposal and counter-proposal.

Lewis and Negretti had good reason to feel satisfied so far. But they were a long way from getting the Crown to release Pelizzioni and indict Mogni for the murder in his place.

For a second time, Negretti stepped in and offered to solve the problem in his own unorthodox fashion. What about a private prosecution? What if he guaranteed the costs of the prosecution against Gregorio Mogni?

Again, Lewis agreed. Mogni went on trial at the Old Bailey on 2 March 1865. The indictment said 'manslaughter', but in effect he was being tried for the murder of Michael Harrington. Serjeant Ballantine and Frederick Lewis conducted the prosecution. Mogni was not represented but Montagu Williams accepted a 'dock brief' on his behalf.

A new witness had come forward: Mrs Shaw, wife of the landlord of the Golden Anchor. Inexplicably, she had not been called at the first trial. Now she deposed that, as Harrington was entering the tap-room, she had seen him grabbed by Gregorio Mogni; and that she saw Mogni raise his hand as if to strike Harrington, although she did not actually see the fatal stabbing.

A witness of even greater importance was Giovanni Mogni, brother of the accused. He said he had been at the Golden Anchor on the night of 26 December. During the row in the bagatelle-room he was badly beaten. His face was covered with blood. He was terrified and cried out to Gregorio, 'Brother, they kill me!' Gregorio put his hand into his pocket and pulled out a knife. He started to strike out wildly with it, although, again, Giovanni did not actually see him stab Harrington with it.

A knife was handed up to Giovanni and he was asked if he knew its owner. He identified it as his brother's. He was then asked if his cousin Serafino Pelizzioni had been in the bagatelle-room when the fight was in progress. Giovanni said he had not.

Lastly, like Mrs Shaw, he confirmed that he had not been called at the earlier trial.

A glass-silverer called Maraggi testified to seeing Gregorio Mogni with a knife in his hand. Maraggi had said, 'Gregorio, for God's sake put away that knife!'

Finally – and this was when legal history was made – Pelizzioni himself entered the witness box. His testimony embodied everything he had told Lewis the night they first met at the Clerkenwell station house. But he dealt also with the question of the two knives. When arrested, he had no weapon in his possession. But he did have a small penknife, which was taken by the police. This bore no resemblance to either of the two knives which had been found. With regard to the deathbed identification he said, 'I didn't make any statements by the bedside of the dead man, as the police say I did. I didn't understand what the dead man said.'

A Giovanni Schiena, who lived in Birmingham, gave evidence that he had met Mogni there. Mogni told him he had left London because he was in trouble, as he was the man who had killed 'the Englishman'.

Doing his best with his dock brief, Montagu Williams tried to turn the clock back to the first trial by calling some of the original witnesses who had identified Pelizzioni as Harrington's assailant, but his client Mogni had already given himself away.

Mr Justice Byles summoned up. The jury retired. They were out for an hour. Then they returned to announce that they found Gregorio Mogni guilty of manslaughter. However, they recommended him to mercy on account of the provocation received and the injury done to his brother, Giovanni Mogni. The judge then sentenced him to five years penal servitude.

The situation that now existed was utterly without precedent. Pelizzioni still sat in the condemned cell at Newgate, still under sentence of death for Harrington's murder. Gregorio Mogni was in prison at Millbank, a couple of miles away, about to begin a sentence of penal servitude for the manslaughter of the same man.

Lewis continued to make representations to the Home Secretary for Pelizzioni's release, but the Home Office refused to budge. Serafino Pelizzioni had been duly convicted of murder: there was no more to be said.

The next day Lewis thought of a possible way out of the impasse. An indictment against Pelizzioni for the attempted murder of Rebbeck, the potman, remained on the file. This could offer the authorities what would today be called a 'face-saving formula', and, after some wrangling between Lewis and the Treasury Solicitor, the trial was set for the second week in April. The Crown considered the case of such importance that two judges were named to preside, instead of the usual one.

This time, the charge was one of 'feloniously wounding, with intent to murder, one Alfred Rebbeck'. Hardinge Giffard led for the Crown, with Mr Besley as his junior. Sergeant Ballantine, Mr Ribton, and Frederick Lewis represented Pelizzioni.

Again, Rebbeck was called for the prosecution. Again, he swore that Pelizzioni had stabbed him. The Crown also called the police constable, Fawel, who gave some inconclusive evidence about the two knives. It was obvious, however, that these were last-ditch efforts. The steam had gone out of the prosecution. How could it not have when Mogni had admitted stabbing Harrington?

At last, after what was still an exhaustive sifting of the evidence, the judge summed up in Pelizzioni's favour. The jury returned a verdict of not guilty. A few days later, Serafino Pelizzioni was granted a royal pardon and was released.

Lewis was naturally intensely gratified, although he gave most of the credit for Pelizzioni's deliverance to Henry Negretti. If it had not been for Negretti's faith and determination, Pelizzioni would have died on the gibbet, a victim of mistaken identification who had not been helped by the 'all coons look alike to me' attitude of some witnesses, nor by prejudice against the Italians of Saffron Hill as a noisy, quarrelsome minority.

Most importantly, this case confirmed for Lewis the need to right an injustice that bore heavily on anyone accused of a crime. No accused person could go into the witness box and give evidence on their own behalf. In 1848 it had been laid down by statute that a prisoner need not make a statement unless he so wished. It was argued that the inability to give evidence on his own behalf was no disadvantage to a prisoner able to afford an adequate defence – but proponents of reform maintained that the intention in 1848 had been merely to remove all question of *compelling* a prisoner to give evidence; the absolute bar defeated the administration of justice. Lewis himself had always believed that the accused should be able to go into the box, but not until 1898 did the Prisoners Evidence Act make this possible. All too often, the outcome of a case was determined by the fact that an accused person had to stand mute in the dock, listening to prosecuting counsel build up a case against him when the evidence he could have given on his own behalf might have saved him.

Lewis's existing convictions were strengthened by the Pelizzioni case. If the Italian had been able to give evidence on his own behalf at his first trial, he might well have been acquitted; he would not have needed the superhuman energies of a Henry Negretti to save him.

4

Tragedy

ON 15 MARCH 1865 Victorine gave birth to a daughter, a small but beautiful baby whom her parents called Alice Victorine. As Lewis had wished, she had been born at 10 Ely Place.

Of course the birth of his daughter brought Lewis such joy as to transcend even his obsessive concern for Pelizzioni – the case was then at its most crucial stage – but, within days, that joy was clouded by his concern for Victorine's health. Reassuring as ever, the doctor said that the actual birth had gone smoothly enough, but it was soon evident that she was in a state of physical collapse. The days passed and, as she lay on in bed, hardly moving, showing no signs of recovery, Lewis was gripped by a kind of terror. Victorine had never been robust, but she had always been healthy: there was a distinction, the doctor told him. Certainly Victorine had never been the pale, languishing lady that was part of the mythology of the day, but now a malign fate appeared to have cast her for the role. Almost palpably, it seemed, life and energy were draining away from her.

The wet-nurse was actually living at Ely Place. She would bring the infant Alice in to see her mother and these visits were a source of great joy to Victorine: she would lie there, eyes closed, exuding an air of rapture.

Victorine had few visitors. She had never possessed a gift for making friends – she had been too shy for that, Lewis thought with a kind of loving exasperation. Helena Cannen came over from Addison Road, of course; and Lewis's sister Esther and his mother came when they could.

Lewis tried to visit her as often as he could during the day, but sometimes it was difficult, particularly if he were detained at court. And the daily, bread-and-butter work of the firm had to go on. Not only was Lewis carrying on the traditional practice of Lewis and

Lewis – defending the criminal fraternity: the cracksmen, street thieves, fences, and dragsmen from the Holy Land and other rookeries – but he was extending the practice into other areas.

Over several weeks Victorine's condition remained unchanged. Then, one afternoon, Lewis came back to Ely Place to find her worse. All the doctor's vague talk – of 'debility', of 'a natural weakness after childbed' – suddenly seemed full of menace. Victorine was sinking fast, a victim, almost certainly, of purpureal fever, a common hazard for Victorian mothers after childbirth and one that, lacking modern antibiotics, was often fatal.

Lewis was at Victorine's side when, on 21 April 1865, she died.

His response to the tragedy was conventional enough: he buried himself in work. In those first weeks after Victorine's death some self-regulating gyroscope in his brain must have taken over. He functioned, it seemed, in a dream and yet he made no blunders; never let the mask of professional assurance slip for a moment.

His family and friends wondered about him. They did not doubt his anguish but they did not know how to penetrate his reserve. The tragic young widower whose wife has died in childbirth is an archetype of Victorian fiction, and now Lewis found himself shouldering the unlikely role. While he stood at the farthest remove from the gloomy widowers in the novels who reject the child that has unwittingly robbed them of its mother, he still faced the problem of who was to take care of his baby daughter. He did not want to put Alice in the hands of strangers, but his own mother was old and in poor health; and, with the exception of Esther, his sisters were widely dispersed, mostly with young children of their own.

There could be no question of his mother or Esther taking Alice to live with them. He hoped, however, that they could exercise a motherly surveillance over whoever he employed to look after the child. In fact it was decided that, once the wet-nurse left, a reliable person, middle-aged and 'settled' would be sought to take charge of Alice. She would have a young girl to assist her.

Lewis was now thirty-three. Slowly but surely over the last few years he had taken command of Lewis and Lewis. The firm was forging ahead. The case of Serafino Pelizzioni had been widely reported. Never before or since has a man under sentence of death come into the witness box and testified against another man accused of the same crime. (Pelizzioni had been able to do so as a prosecution witness against Mogni; he was, of course, barred from giving evidence for himself when he was the accused.) A good deal of professional credit accrued to Lewis, even though he believed Henry Negretti had done more than anyone else to save Pelizzioni.

This was a time of great change and development in the English legal system. Reform was in the air. Anyone who has read *Bleak House*, with its gallery of rogues and grotesques – a daunting vision of a system ossified into lunatic futility – may find this hard to believe, but such is the distorting power of Dickens's genius that we have come to accept his vision of the law in Victorian times. In fact the whole system was in the process of transformation and Lewis welcomed the changes.

It was generally agreed that drastic reforms were needed, particularly in the Chancery court, the target of Dickens's most biting satire. But the courts of common law were a scene of appalling confusion, with three courts – Queen's Bench, Exchequer, and Common Pleas – all claiming jurisdiction over many classes of cases and actually in competition with each other over who should try them.

The opposition to reform came, as usual, from those with vested interests at stake. The existing system had created many well-paid sinecures – and no one ever gave up a sinecure without protest. The question of patronage was also involved. Both the government and the judges had a large number of these appointments in their gift. Of course the wretched litigant ultimately paid for all this, yet he could expect neither courtesy nor efficiency from the gorged drones the system had called into being.

The process of reforming the courts went on right through the nineteenth century but the process was, of necessity, a piecemeal one. Then, in 1873, a clean sweep was made. The Judicature Act abolished the old courts of Queen's Bench, Common Pleas, and Exchequer in favour of the High Court, which at first sat in five divisions: Chancery, Queen's Bench, Exchequer, Common Pleas and (a new creation) Probate, Divorce, and Admiralty. Then, in 1881, all the common law divisions were amalgamated into the Queen's Bench Division.

Naturally these changes did not affect Lewis directly or all at once, but it should be remembered that he practised during a period when an archaic system was giving way to a more modern one. There was professional success, then; an abundance of work; more money. But, as Lewis went to and from the courts or worked in his first-floor office in Ely Place, he did not find his sense of grief and loneliness growing less. Every day he saw little Alice – not once but several times: morning, midday (if he wasn't in court), and in the evening. These, he told himself, were landmarks in his day. But the blackness and blankness remained. Work was not the anodyne it was claimed to be.

But the work went on and he was grateful for it. One afternoon a middle-aged man came to Ely Place and asked to see Lewis. He gave his name as 'Captain Leyland', but he didn't look like a seaman and still less like a soldier.

A seaman he was, however, although he struck Lewis as too uncertain of himself to be someone used to command. He was clearly very worried about something. He started by asking Lewis for an assurance that all he said would be regarded as 'confidential'. Lewis told him that anything a client said to his lawyer was always in confidence.

Captain Hugh Leyland was in fact a master mariner of great experience. Now, through the sinking of his most recent ship, the *Severn*, he faced ruin. Unless he could clear his name, he might never get another command – indeed, might never get the chance to go to sea again. Worst of all, he could soon find himself in jail.

He went on to tell Lewis that the *Severn* had been lost as the result of a criminal conspiracy. He, Leyland, had taken no part in it, but he was afraid he would be accused of giving tacit approval to the conspirators and thus be regarded as their accomplice.

Lewis told Leyland that in his experience it was always best to tell the truth. The fact that Leyland was here at Ely Place meant that he had already accepted the necessity for this in his own mind.

The whole case, Leyland said, began with his meeting an insurance agent and shipbroker named Lionel Holdsworth. (Lewis had had some dealings with Holdsworth through his representing Lloyds Salvage Association.) Holdsworth had negotiated an earlier command for Leyland, and the ship involved, the *Thames*, had been lost in a gale off the west coast of Scotland. Then a year before Leyland's meeting with Lewis, Holdsworth had told Leyland to hold himself in readiness for a new command: the *Severn*. Naturally Leyland was delighted. Ships were hard to come by. Later, however, as Holdsworth told him more, he became a little uneasy.

After he had first mentioned the *Severn* to Leyland, Holdsworth suggested Leyland come to see him at his office in Fenchurch Street.

(Holdsworth's clerk, Joseph Dean, was also present on that occasion.)

Holdsworth told Leyland that a consortium of his friends had bought the *Severn* and she would soon be leaving London for Newport. From there she would be chartered to Shanghai. At this meeting Leyland was offered a definite contract to take command of the *Severn*, which he accepted. It was arranged that he should go home and await instructions.

He did so and soon received a telegram telling him to go to Newport. There he found Holdsworth and a man called Berwick awaiting him. Berwick was one of the owners of the *Severn*, Holdsworth told him, a member of the consortium. The three of them dined together. During the meal Berwick said that, during a recent visit to London, he had engaged a young man named Charles Webb who would serve as mate. He added that he had known young Webb for many years; Leyland could rely on him.

Holdsworth said it would cost £7000 to render the *Severn* seaworthy and fit her out for the voyage; thus it would be necessary to insure her for a large sum.

So far, Leyland thought, everything had gone splendidly. He congratulated himself on getting a command in such difficult times. He relaxed and drank some more wine. He was enjoying himself.

'Of course,' Holdsworth said, 'we don't expect the *Severn* will ever reach China.' He paused. 'Do we, Tom?'

This last was addressed to Berwick, who grinned and said, 'No, we don't. And I think we can promise you, Captain, that if she don't arrive you will receive seven hundred pounds.'

Leyland was clearly embarrassed when, telling his story to Lewis, he reached this point. He did not say – claimed he 'didn't remember' – what his reply to that had been. Whatever it was, his hosts must have felt encouraged to go on talking.

What they wanted, they said, was a man they could rely on. And an important condition to their deal with Leyland was his promise not to interfere with his first mate, Charles Webb. Webb must be allowed to act as he thought fit. Not that Captain Leyland wasn't in command; he would be totally responsible for the navigation of the ship. But, apart from that, Webb must be given his head.

Again, Leyland must have given the impression of agreeing to what they said, for his two new employers rose from the table apparently well pleased. On a personal note, they said, they would advise him to insure his own belongings for two hundred pounds.

Before the *Severn* sailed, many large cases were taken on board as part of the cargo. The consignors were William Allsopp and Co and the bill of lading specified that the cases contained rifles, carbines, sabres, and swords. Holdsworth made himself responsible for ordering all stores and provisions for the voyage; and in due course the *Severn* sailed, with Leyland in command and Charles Webb as mate.

When they had been some days at sea, Webb emerged one day from the hold and approached the captain. He was grinning.

'What is it you find so amusing?' Leyland asked.

'Those cases,' Webb said. 'They're full of salt.'

'You had no right to touch them,' Leyland said.

Webb said he had been anxious to know exactly what was in the cases. (It was later revealed that Webb was right. The cases contained only salt, to the total value of three pounds.)

They had good weather until they arrived off Cape St Vincent. Then a gale struck them, but a gale far short of a storm – nothing, as Captain Leyland emphasized, that could threaten the safety of the ship. And yet soon afterwards it was reported to the captain that the *Severn* had sprung a leak and was taking in water.

The leak got worse. For the next two weeks the pumps were going all the time. The gale only lasted for one day. They now had fine weather – the trade winds set in – but they had to keep at the pumps harder than ever.

On 14 June it was reported to the captain that the *Severn* was shipping a greatly increased quantity of water. Webb came to Leyland and told him to have the boats manned in readiness to abandon ship. The pumps were no longer able to cope with the amount of water pouring in through the leak. The *Severn* was sinking.

Leyland accused Webb of tampering with the ship.

Webb replied, 'It is done now and cannot be undone.'

'What do you mean?' Leyland demanded.

'I bored a hole,' Webb said. 'Later I tried to stop it by driving a plug in, but it's no good. The plug broke as I was doing it and now the water is pouring in. I can't stop it.'

'Then you'd better go below and try again,' Leyland told him. 'You must be mad to do such a thing when we're so far from land.'

He added that it would be plain to everyone that the ship had been scuttled.

Webb did go below but returned ten minutes later. It was impossible to stop the leak now, he said, as the pressure of water had made the hole bigger. Leyland retorted that they would all drown as the result of Webb's folly.

'Then you'd better get out the boats,' Webb said.

The *Severn* was now in mid-Atlantic some 180 miles west of the Cape Verde Islands. The crew were divided into three watches, and the pumps were worked continuously.

On 15 June the situation looked so bad that Leyland ordered the boats to be held in readiness to be lowered. They were already provisioned for twenty days. The longboat was manned and then lowered and moored astern.

A few moments later Webb told the captain that the men in the longboat were crying out that they could see two holes bored in the stern of the ship. Webb added that he himself was going on board the longboat, which would then be cast off from the *Severn*. Webb climbed into the longboat, and its crew rowed away some distance from the ship but still in sight of her.

About six that evening the longboat came up alongside the *Severn* again and Webb came aboard.

'A child could see what has happened here,' Leyland said.

'Don't worry,' Webb said. 'I can square any of this lot [the crew]. I don't believe any of them can actually have *seen* those holes.' He paused. 'Why don't you abandon ship? She hasn't much longer to go.'

'I'd rather go down with her than face the disgrace that is going to come upon me,' Leyland retorted.

'Do as you please,' Webb said and climbed into the longboat, which rowed away again.

The carpenter, the boatswain, and three others – the crew of the gig – remained on board with the captain. The boatswain and the others kept urging Leyland to abandon ship and at eight o'clock he did so. The six of them boarded the gig and rowed clear of the ship.

Less than an hour later, the *Severn* heeled over. For what seemed to the men in the gig a long time – in fact, it could only have been a few moments – she appeared to remain stationary, although half submerged, then she sank.

The captain and the crew of the gig rowed around till next morning, when they sighted the longboat carrying Webb and the rest of the crew. The following day they were sighted by the *Arequipa*.

They were taken aboard and later landed at Recife (Pernambuco) in Brazil, where Webb and the captain, forced together in uneasy companionship, had plenty of time to reflect on their situation.

Webb had kept the *Severn*'s logbook and, when Leyland looked through it, he pronounced it 'exaggerated'. Webb decided to cut out some of the pages and rewrite certain key portions.

The steamship *Oneida* eventually brought them back to Southampton. Leyland and Webb shared a cabin on the voyage home. According to Leyland, Webb talked freely about his crimes. He admitted he had bored three separate holes in the bottom of the *Severn*. He even admitted to doing the same thing on board another ship he had served on, the *Jane Brown*. 'I'm an expert,' he boasted. 'I know all the tricks. I can put the plugs in and take them out again at pleasure.'

Arrived at Southampton, Captain Leyland telegraphed Holdsworth and then immediately travelled up to London, where he confronted Holdsworth in his office.

'This thing is going to be found out,' he told him. 'The crew know the ship was scuttled. They saw those holes. Do you think they're not going to tell what they know?'

Holdsworth was evasive. The whole thing was most unfortunate. He would be seeing Webb in the morning and would hear what he had to say.

As he was leaving, Leyland added, 'On top of everything else, that ship was lost in a dead calm. Do you think that won't be noticed?'

He went to see Holdsworth again next day. This time Webb was there. He greeted Leyland in jaunty fashion and said there was nothing for any of them to worry about. He had met some of the *Severn*'s crew on the train up from Southampton and they had appeared friendly enough.

'It's all right, I tell you,' Webb went on. 'Only Kelly [a seaman] and the boatswain saw the holes, and I've talked to them and I can promise you we shall hear no more about it.'

The logbook remained a problem. It had obviously been tampered with. Holdsworth and Webb decided that the only hope was to concoct a new, false logbook, and this they started to do, with the help of Holdsworth's clerk, Joseph Dean.

'You're living in a fool's paradise,' Leyland said. 'None of this is any good. That logbook won't deceive anyone. It's brand new.'

While Dean was throwing the faked logbook on the floor, rubbing it in the dust to give it a suitably battered appearance, Holdsworth tried to reassure Leyland.

'It's all right,' he said. 'Webb can square those fellows with a few sovereigns apiece. And look here,' he added, 'I'll give you ten pounds a month to keep you going till the insurance on the *Severn* is paid.'

But after more argument, ending in angry words, Leyland left and, after a day spent in agonized consideration of the situation, came to see Lewis.

It was obvious that Leyland was to some extent compromised. Lewis thought his professional reputation was probably ruined; no one was going to give him a command again when they heard what happened to the *Severn*. But it was not for Lewis to say this and further discourage a badly shaken man.

So he told Leyland that he believed he could save himself from prosecution by telling the whole story to the authorities and thus ensuring the conviction of Holdsworth and the other conspirators. And in any case, Lewis said, Lloyds Salvage Association, which he himself represented, would be most anxious to have the kind of information about the loss of the *Severn* that only Captain Leyland could supply.

Lewis was right on both points. Leyland was not prosecuted. He was the chief witness at the trial of Lionel Holdsworth, Charles Webb, Thomas Berwick, and Joseph Dean, indicted for 'the scuttling and casting away of the ship *Severn*' at the Old Bailey (which had at that time Admiralty jurisdiction that enabled its judges to try people accused of committing offences on British vessels sailing on the high seas). Hardinge Giffard, Montagu Williams, and Frederick Lewis prosecuted. Webb was defended by Warner Sleigh; Berwick by Serjeant Ballantine; Holdsworth, organizer and evil genius of the whole plot, by Serjeant Tindall Atkinson.

Defence counsel did their best, but Leyland's evidence was damning. Further testimony was given about the dummy cargo and the insurance effected on the ship before she sailed. Then the judge summed up and the jury retired. They came back almost immediately, finding all the defendants guilty. Holdsworth and Berwick were sentenced to twenty years penal servitude; Webb to ten years; Dean to five.

Lewis felt sorry for Captain Leyland. He was clearly an honest man who had not fully resisted temptation on a single, damning occasion. If only he had stood up and walked out when the conversation took such a strange turn at Holdsworth's dinner party!

In 1866 Lewis had more cases in the police courts than ever, and late in that year there was an arson attempt at the offices of the *Daily Telegraph*. An employee called Poole started a fire on the paper's premises at Peterborough Court, off Fleet Street. There had been a smaller fire there three days earlier. Poole had been alone in the office at the time and he had greatly exaggerated its extent, presumably anxious that his prowess as a fire-fighter should be appreciated. Fortunately the manager of the paper had returned to the office and at once noticed smoke bellowing up from a lower floor. Poole was arrested and tried at the Old Bailey. Lewis represented the *Daily Telegraph*, briefing the ubiquitous Montagu Williams. The wretched Poole really had no defence. Today, he might have been sent for a psychiatrist's report; then, he got five years' penal servitude.

Despite being so busy, Lewis found that the classic remedy for grief, hard work, was still not working for him, although everyone – parents, brothers and sisters, friends, and fellow lawyers – all assured him that it was only a matter of time before it did. They were all aware of his sadness. George had always been quiet and self-contained; now they sensed the strain under the controlled mask.

Even so, everyone except his parents and his sister Esther were very surprised when, on 10 February 1867, Lewis married Elizabeth Eberstadt, daughter of Ferdinand Eberstadt of Mannheim, Germany: the youngest and most beautiful of the Four Beautiful Sisters of Mannheim.

The first summer after Victorine's death Lewis had gone to Germany on holiday, as he always did. Certainly no one had been surprised that he had stayed only briefly with his in-laws, the Kanns, in Frankfurt – the associations there must have been intolerably sad – and had then gone on to Mannheim to visit the Eberstadts. After all, Mannheim was a lovely city too. Not as old as Frankfurt, but the former seat of the Electors Palatine, with a splendid castle and some fine eighteenth-century churches.

The Eberstadts were, of course, old friends of Lewis. If he had been close enough to anyone to discuss such a thing – which he was not – he could have pointed out that he had known Elizabeth Eberstadt before he met Victorine Kann. Elizabeth had been in her teens then, with the immature, still-to-be-unfolded beauty of a young girl.

Perhaps some unconscious censor in the quiet, restrained Lewis prevented him from falling in love with the sixteen-year-old Elizabeth when he first met her? Instead, he turned away from her dark challenge to marry Victorine – gentle and fair and even quieter in manner than himself.

But meeting Elizabeth again now, when he was thirty-three and she twenty-one, everything was changed. Now the promise of her youthful beauty *had* unfolded; now she was a woman and she dazzled him, set his senses spinning with her gaiety and attack. And, beautiful as she was, her intelligence transcended her beauty, giving her a confidence that was more than mere boldness, a courage that would confront anything life might offer. While Lewis might hesitate, carefully analysing a situation, Elizabeth would act – always decisively, not always wisely – and these contrasting patterns of behaviour were established from the very beginning of their marriage. Elizabeth could be courageous to the point of being aggressive. Razor-sharp, her tongue could wound, but she never sulked or held a grudge – though the slower-witted victims of her disapproval rarely forgave her.

If Lewis had had a 'soft' marriage with his first wife Victorine, then his relationship with Elizabeth was tonic and challenging. Certainly there was often an undertow of conflict between them. Not that they quarrelled often. In fact they usually agreed. Lewis was temperamentally incapable of quarrelling. Quarrels were a ludicrous expense of spirit, he maintained. From the start they established separate spheres of influence. Lewis had his professional life. Elizabeth had the house and all matters domestic; soon she was to have children, and a social life that was to burgeon in an extraordinary fashion over the next ten years.

One wonders whether this undertow of conflict between the quiet but forcible Lewis and the more ebullient Elizabeth generated a power between them that otherwise might not have existed. Did their marriage act as a catalyst, evoke powers in them that neither could have developed alone?

Certainly, if Lewis had not married Elizabeth, his career might have developed along different lines. Lewis alone, or even Lewis with Victorine, might simply have become a more powerful and sophisticated version of his father. His drive towards professional success would have been as great as ever – but he would have been a different man. The Lewis we shall come to know – 'Sir George'; the friend of the King; the connoisseur of 'the follies of the famous'; the caricaturist's stand-by; the victor of a hundred *causes célèbres* – *this* man was in some part Elizabeth's creation. When they married, Lewis was a lawyer with a successful criminal practice; when he died, he was *the* lawyer in London, the only solicitor whose name ever became a household word.

From the earliest days of their marriage, Elizabeth's ambitions were boundless. To fulfil them she needed the continuous thrust of George's professional success: a drive upwards so steady and relentless that it carried the Lewises with it like a tide.

But all this was still in the future. Now Elizabeth decided to begin as she meant to go on. She and Lewis were not going to 'live over the shop' at Ely Place. On their marriage they moved to 19 Taviton Street in Bloomsbury.

5

By Swift Dromedaries

By the time of Lewis's second marriage in 1867, he had already begun to establish that network of agents and information-gatherers that was to become an important part of his legend. (A less-than-friendly source once described it as a 'spider's web of narks and informers'.) Some of his agents were professional criminals who had been defended by Lewis and Lewis and felt they owed Lewis or his father a debt of gratitude; others belonged to the large class of louche persons like prostitutes and the keepers of 'assignation houses' (often masked as cheap hotels), who operated on the farther side of the law.

But the newly married Lewis would not have needed any spy or informer to tell him about Sarah Rachel Leverson. A contemporary journalist described her as 'a coarse-looking middle-aged woman with a persuasive manner'. Coarse-looking she may have been, but her powers of persuasion deserved to be celebrated more eloquently than that. They had made her rich and, by 1867, famous. She was known professionally as 'Madame Rachel' and with that name was linked the compelling slogan 'Beautiful for Ever'.

'Beautiful for Ever' was painted above Madame Rachel's elegant shopfront at 47A New Bond Street. Inside, Sarah Leverson presided over a temple devoted to the beautification of women. Whatever her age, race, or creed (Madame Sarah's promotional material proclaimed), no woman could pass through these portals and emerge again without being revivified, transmogrified, born anew. Not only would she have a choice of innumerable powders, oils, washes, soaps, and perfumes, but she could also have one of Madame's celebrated Arabian Baths (bran infused in hot water) or wash her face in Precious Jordan Water (without bran). Or she might like to have a Royal Bridal Toilet Cabinet, as used by the Sultaness of Turkey, at a thousand guineas.

There were plenty of women eager to try anything Madame had to offer. Some of them were young, but most were older women fighting a rearguard action against middle age. It should be remembered that, at that time, the mere act of making up one's face held a hint of impropriety. Cosmetics were permitted, if at all, only to the 'mature' woman; and this meant that most of Madame Rachel's clients were old and well off.

Sarah Leverson had built up her business in a few years through a promotional campaign of great intensity, which had included the issue of a brochure called (inevitably) *Beautiful For Ever.* Who could resist

the Magnetic Rock Dew Water from the interior
of the Sahara or the Great Desert where
a Magnetic Rock distils water
in the form of dew which is possessed
of an extraordinary property. Whether a latent electricity
is imparted by magnetism or an additional quantity
of oxygen enters into its composition
it is not easy to say. But it restores
the colour to grey hair, apparently
by renewing the circulation in the capillary tubes,
the cessation of which causes greyness
and it gives the appearance of increasing youth *to* persons of considerable antiquity.
This water is brought to Morocco by swift dromedaries
for the use of the Court
and its virtues are much extolled
by their physicians. . .

The inspired copywriter is thought to have been Madame Rachel's solicitor (and possibly her financial backer), James Haynes, who had his office in St James's Street.

Successful as all this was, Madame Rachel was rumoured to offer other, more interesting, services. For instance, despite its overwhelmingly feminine atmosphere, men were often to be seen at Madame Rachel's. Raffish older men of the stage-door-johnny type, and also much younger men: grooms, ostlers, ex-soldiers. It was whispered that there were cunningly placed peep-holes through which gentlemen could watch the ladies taking their Arabian Baths.

Whatever the truth of such rumours, Madame Rachel prospered. She had a house in Blackheath and another in Maddox Street, off

Bond Street. She ran a coach and pair and thought nothing of taking a box at the opera at £400 for the season. In 1868, when she first crossed Lewis's path, she was at the peak of her success.

Little was known of her origins. She was said to have been born in the north of England around 1806 and to have married a man called Jacob Moses who had been drowned at sea. A few years later she had married again a man called Philip Leverson, who remains a shadowy figure. She became an old-clothes dealer and somehow, by the early 1860s, had saved enough money to buy the Bond Street premises. Within months, thanks to her brilliant advertising, she was on the way to becoming a rich woman.

Lewis had heard a number of damaging reports about Madame Rachel. It was clear that it was only a matter of time before someone moved against her. One story concerned the admiral (not one of Lewis's clients) whose wife had gone to Rachel's to buy some ordinary perfume but had been persuaded to buy some of the more exotic and expensive brands. Later, the admiral got a bill for £1000. He was furious and disputed the bill. He soon received another letter saying the sum demanded was really for curing the admiral's wife of the unpleasant skin condition known as scabies. More furious than ever, the admiral still refused to pay. A third letter from Madame Rachel hinted that his wife had caught scabies as a result of some sexual encounter which had taken place at the Beautiful For Ever shop in Bond Street. Fortunately for his wife, the admiral refused to believe this and simply ignored any further threatening letters.

From this and other stories, Lewis concluded that blackmail was probably an important part of Madame Rachel's business. Lewis didn't know exactly what went on at the Bond Street premises, but there seemed little doubt that some of the ladies would pay up rather than have Madame Rachel write to their husbands – some of whom might not be as trusting as the admiral.

Lewis wondered if he would ever be professionally involved with Sarah Leverson. It seemed possible and, one morning in March 1868, a Mr Arthur Esdaile, a city stockbroker, called at Ely Place by appointment. Esdaile was middle-aged, his wife some twenty years younger.

Esdaile made small-talk at first; he seemed reluctant to come to the point. Mrs Esdaile was attractive and fashionably dressed but she, too, appeared ill at ease. Gradually, by avoiding any hint of pressure, Lewis got them to tell their story.

Mrs Esdaile was a client of Madame Rachel's. Like other customers, she had gone there first to buy perfume; then, captured by Rachel's dynamic salesmanship, she had agreed to take a course of Arabian Baths. This had lasted six months and she was coming to the end of it.

Three weeks ago she had left her diamond rings and earrings in a changing-room before she went to take her bath (she had done this many times before). Returning, she had found both ring and earrings missing. She called one of the attendants, a girl in quasi-Arab dress, and asked to see Madame Rachel. When she told Rachel about the missing jewellery, the older woman amazed her by telling her bluntly, 'You must be mistaken!' Before Mrs Esdaile could reply, Rachel added, 'If you had left your jewellery there when you undressed, it would still be there. You must have left it at home.'

When Mrs Esdaile persisted that she was absolutely certain, Madame Rachel got aggressive and ordered her to leave, 'before I have you thrown out'. Then she told Mrs Esdaile to wait a moment. Madame Rachel called the girl attendant in and asked her if she had noticed whether Mrs Esdaile was wearing her rings and earrings that morning. The attendant swore she was not. 'There – you see?' Madame Rachel demanded.

Arriving home, Mrs Esdaile had found it impossible to conceal her distress from her husband, who said they must consult Lewis and Lewis at once.

Lewis's professional antennae warned him that, while Mrs Esdaile might not be lying, she was not telling the whole truth either. He felt sure she would not have consulted him if her husband had not insisted.

With this impression in his mind, Lewis had so far been noncommittal in his remarks. Then, out of the corner of his eye, he happened to see Mrs Esdaile put her gloves down on the table. He had a notion he knew why she did this, so he told Mr Esdaile that he must give the question of possible action against Madame Rachel further thought. He would write to Mr Esdaile in a few days' time. When they rose to go, Lewis did not call Mrs Esdaile's attention to the gloves she had left on the table; nor did she pick them up.

As he expected, Mrs Esdaile returned to Ely Place later that day – without appointment – and asked to see Lewis. Apparently relieved to be able to unburden herself, she poured out her whole story. What she said confirmed the rumours Lewis had heard about Madame Rachel's.

Mrs Esdaile had been meeting a lover at Beautiful for Ever. Under the cover of her course of Arabian Baths, Mrs Esdaile had enjoyed twice-weekly assignations with a young man named Raikes, an out-of-work music hall artiste. After bathing, she would go into a cubicle with her lover – other cubicles, she told Lewis, had been similarly occupied. Madame Rachel demanded extra fees for thus facilitating her and, as the six months wore on, asked for more and more to cover 'extra expenses'. Mrs Esdaile tried to keep up with this extortion, but the theft of her jewellery had been the last straw. Madame Rachel, she said, had been even more menacing than she had described this morning, threatening to tell her husband 'what you really come here for! Something young Raikes has got which your husband hasn't!'

Lewis asked Mrs Esdaile to tell him more about the Bond Street establishment. She said a number of women went there because they genuinely believed in the powers of Circassian Bloom or the Magnetic Rock Dew Water from the Sahara. Others went because it was the most discreet assignation house in London and Madame Rachel one of the most efficient procurers. She could always offer handsome young men – footmen out of a situation; stable boys; occasionally deserters from the army. In theory, what the lady paid Madame Rachel covered payment to the young stud; in fact, most of the ladies gave their young men handsome presents as well. Mrs Esdaile assured Lewis that she was an exception: Madame Rachel had not procured Mr Raikes for her; they had met at a concert. Lewis doubted that.

He asked Mrs Esdaile about the older, stage-door-johnny types seen hanging around the Bond Street shop. She professed to have hardly noticed them – Mr Raikes had taken up most of her attention – but thought they were mostly voyeurs who had come to see the ladies bathing. Yes, it was true about the peep-holes. 'Did you know men were watching you when you were bathing?' Lewis asked. 'Oh, yes,' Mrs Esdaile said without embarrassment. 'I knew.'

Lewis had heard enough. A day or so later, he wrote to Mr Esdaile regretting that, in his opinion, no effective action could be taken about his wife's jewellery.

One morning, late in April 1868, Lewis was told that a Mr Cope, a city merchant, was awaiting his convenience in the outer office.

Introducing himself, Cope apologized for not making an appointment. However, this was a matter of urgency. His wife's sister, a Mrs Mary Tucker Borradaile, had been arrested for debt. They – the family, her relatives – had been appalled. Mrs Borradaile was a most respectable person – in fact she was the widow of a colonel in the Indian Army. She was about fifty; not rich but comfortably situated. She had some property and a pension of £300 a year.

Now she appeared to be destitute, and totally in the power of the woman who called herself Madame Rachel.

Her story according to what Cope told Lewis, ran along familiar lines. She had first gone to Madame Rachel's shop because she was impressed by Rachel's claim to be 'purveyor of cosmetics to the Queen'. Through 1864 and 1865 she went on buying there, spending more and more money, fully believing Madame Rachel's claim that she would make Mrs Borradaile 'beautiful for ever'.

One day in 1866 she came to Bond Street to undergo further beauty treatments. Madame Rachel called her into a private office. She had something very confidential to tell her. A gentleman was in love with her.

Mrs Borradaile was naturally overwhelmed at the thought. Flattered, intrigued – but not, apparently, in the least disbelieving.

'Who is he?' she demanded. 'You must tell me his name!'

Madame Rachel was coy. 'A good man. And very rich.'

'His name?'

'Can't you guess?' Madame Rachel paused. 'Lord Ranelagh.'

Lord Ranelagh was one of the oldest of the elderly bucks who hung around the shop. Mrs Borradaile had seen him there, although she had never spoken to him. Her excitement can be imagined. Lord Ranelagh in love with *her*?

A few days later Mrs Borradaile was sitting in the shop when she heard Madame Rachel talking to an elderly man whom she addressed as 'Lord Ranelagh'. Mrs Borradaile asked him if he were Lord Ranelagh. 'Yes,' he said, 'and this is my card.'

That was the only time Mrs Borradaile spoke to the man she believed to be Lord Ranelagh. She saw him in the shop on one other occasion, when he bowed to her without speaking.

From such tiny beginnings Madame Rachel wove an extraordinary web of fantasy, to which Mrs Borradaile abandoned herself totally. She kept assuring Mrs Borradaile that Lord Ranelagh had fallen madly in love with her. He had told her (Madame Rachel) that, many times. And – it was quite naughty but love conquers all! – she would tell Mrs Borradaile a secret. He had confessed to watching Mrs Borradaile having her Arabian Bath. He had been glued to a peep-hole, feasting his eyes on her nakedness! This had happened not once but several times. No wonder his lordship's passions were inflamed beyond restraint.

At this point it is worth quoting Montagu Williams, whom Lewis later briefed to represent Mrs Borradaile. He described her as 'a spare, thin, scraggy-looking woman, wholly devoid of figure; her hair was dyed a bright yellow; her face was raddled with paint. She had a silly, giggling, half-hysterical way of talking. . .'

Madame Rachel went on building up Mrs Borradaile's hopes. Lord Ranelagh was nothing if not a gentleman: he was offering Mrs Borradaile marriage. Unfortunately, his family was likely to put obstacles in the way. And before Mary Borradaile became Lady Ranelagh she would have to undergo further treatments that would make her even more beautiful than she was now. This would cost £1000. And then the wife of a peer would need jewellery. A diamond tiara was essential. This would cost around £1400. Then there was lace for the wedding dress – another expensive item, for a large quantity would have to be bought. And a carriage. Lady Ranelagh would have to have a carriage of her own.

To lend her depredations extra credibility, Madame Rachel introduced Mrs Borradaile to her solicitor, James Haynes. With his support, the wretched Borradaile was soon stripped of most of her property. One day she went to the City with Madame Rachel to 'sell out money in the Funds' (government stocks) amounting to £963, and that was only the beginning. Madame Rachel and Haynes took Mrs Borradaile to a livery stable in the West End to select a suitable carriage. And then there was the matter of a trousseau. Clothes, quantities of expensive lace, and jewellery – including a diamond tiara – had to be bought. To meet these expenses, Mrs Borradaile sold out more and more money in the Funds until there was nothing left to sell. Presumably these purchases of a carriage, clothes and so on were all bogus – executed with the connivance of the traders involved – because not one of these items, on which, in total, thousands of pounds had been spent, was ever given to her. And when Madame Rachel had exhausted all possible wedding preparations, as a final twist of the screw, she told Mrs Borradaile that her affianced, Lord Ranelagh, was temporarily embarrassed financially and needed a loan! The volunteer corps he commanded had to go to Belgium on manoeuvres. Mrs Borradaile was delighted to help – and this finally cleaned her out: she sold a property in Streatham for £1600, and the cheque for this was taken by Madame Rachel for Lord Ranelagh.

The Ranelagh–Borradaile marriage fantasy had been intensified while the fleecing had been going on. Madame Rachel showed Mrs Borradaile an old-fashioned coronet, said to have belonged to Lord Ranelagh's mother, which would have to be altered to fit Mrs Borradaile. Madame Rachel began to give her letters which she said came from Lord Ranelagh. She also told Mrs Borradaile that she was to be 'married by proxy'. This was perfectly legal: it was done by letter-writing. She had married two couples in this way. Mrs Borradaile would be the third.

Madame Rachel explained an odd feature of the letters she had passed on to Mrs Borradaile. Although Lord Ranelagh's christian name was 'Thomas', the letters were signed 'William'. This was a ruse to put Lord Ranelagh's family off the scent.

Rachel also gave Mrs Borradaile a vinaigrette and a pencil case, accompanied by a letter bearing Lord Ranelagh's crest and monogram. It was addressed to 'My own dearly loved Mary' and had some muddled talk about 'Granny' [Madame Rachel] smoothing things out for the lovers. The perfume box and pencil case enclosed had belonged to Lord Ranelagh's mother, he said, and he signed off as 'your ugly old donkey'.

Around this time Madame Rachel brought Mrs Borradaile a lighted cigar and told her that Lord Ranelagh's love for her was as hot as its burning tip.

With the house in Streatham sold, Mrs Borradaile was penniless. But there was still her pension as a colonel's widow. Rachel Leverson wanted that too. Haynes advised her she was entitled to it by virtue of one of the bonds Mrs Borradaile had signed. But Madame Rachel had finally gone too far. Mrs Borradaile refused to make the pension over to her. Furious, Madame Rachel had her arrested for debt.

Now, at last, Mrs Borradaile's relations – long aware that she was in the clutches of the abominable Rachel – were able to take action. That was why Mr Cope had come to Ely Place.

The first objective was to get Mrs Borradaile released from Newgate. This achieved, Lewis suggested that Mrs Borradaile and Cope go together to New Bond Street and confront Mrs Leverson.

Predictably, Rachel denied ever having had any money from Mrs Borradaile and would give no information about Lord Ranelagh.

The swindle had been so well orchestrated that Lewis doubted if a civil action for damages could succeed. And what about Lord Ranelagh? What was the truth of his role in the affair? Of course, no one credited the story of his wishing to marry the pathetic Borradaile – but there were several questions to be asked. It was not denied that he had been introduced to Mrs Borradaile and had given her his card. Why? And, while no one believed that the letter signed 'William' had actually been written by him, the writing-paper embossed with his crest and monogram was genuine enough. Had he agreed to lend his name to the swindle, for an appropriate fee?

The best course seemed to be a criminal prosecution. In August 1868 Sarah Rachel Leverson appeared before Russell Gurney, the Recorder of London, at the Old Bailey. For the prosecution, Serjeant Ballantine, Montagu Williams, and Douglas Straight; for the defence – which drew the comment that Madame could afford the most expensive legal talent – the fashionable Digby Seymour, QC, Serjeant Parry, and Serjeant Sleigh.

Madame Rachel was charged with obtaining £600 by false pretences; and of conspiring to defraud Mary Tucker Borradaile of various other sums totalling £3000.

Even before the trial, Lewis had realized that they could expect no easy verdict in their favour. Mrs Borradaile was not a witness who would evoke sympathy from judge or jury. She affected a coy, self-satisfied air everyone found irritating.

When Serjeant Ballantine had outlined the story of the fraud, Mrs Borradaile went into the witness box. Giving evidence about the letters signed 'William', she said that they were in more than one handwriting. Madame Rachel told her that Lord Ranelagh had hurt his arm and therefore his servant had written some of the letters. Mrs Borradaile gave a poor impression even when she was being examined by her own counsel, Ballantine; in cross-examination by Digby Seymour she did even worse. She refused to give her age, and pompously announced, 'I have been in India and have always associated with people of the highest principles and rank. I am acquainted with the styles and usages of polite society; but I know nothing about business.'

Realizing that she was their greatest asset, the defence attacked her savagely. How dare she invoke the name of Lord Ranelagh? Allege that a man of his rank and position would even deign to speak to her?

Sleigh counter-attacked with the suggestion that Mrs Borradaile had never believed the letters were from Lord Ranelagh. 'William' was a real lover. Attributing the letters to Lord Ranelagh was an afterthought – as was her attempt to blame Madame Rachel for the fact that she had beggared herself pouring out money on gifts for this young lover.

Madame Rachel then went into the box and swore that 'William' did in truth exist. She had warned Mary Borradaile against wasting her small fortune on this man. All the large sums that had been spent – alleged by the prosecution to have been obtained by Rachel as bogus wedding preparations – had in fact gone to this mysterious lover of Mrs Borradaile. When he disappeared with her cash, she had turned in fury on the unfortunate Madame Rachel.

Against this, of course, Ballantine asked, 'Where is this man? Why has the defence not produced him? I will tell you why: he does not exist.'

Lord Ranelagh certainly existed but, if Lewis had cherished any hopes that his role in the affair would be clarified, they vanished when he entered the court. The noble lord was literally fawned on, invited to sit on the bench beside the judge; treated with a servility remarkable even for the period. Lounging beside the Recorder, he smirked in a self-satisfied way every time his name was mentioned. When the letters from 'William' were being read aloud by counsel, he was observed (in the words of one report) 'to be joining in the general merriment'.

When the time came for him to be called, he left his place on the bench and strolled down to the witness box. Treated with great deference by counsel on both sides, he admitted he had frequently been in Madame Rachel's shop.

Sleigh asked, 'My lord – may I ask what was the attraction that took you to Madame Rachel's?'

Lord Ranelagh answered, 'Curiosity led me to the shop. You don't suppose I went there to be enamelled? I used to go in for a chat with Madame Rachel. I think I saw Mrs Borradaile there once.'

Certainly he did not want to be 'enamelled'; and Lewis wondered if he found Mrs Leverson's conversation so very engaging. Presumably he was there to enjoy the peep-holes.

No one asked him about the occasion when Mrs Borradaile was

introduced to a man said to be Lord Ranelagh who gave her a visiting card. And what of the writing paper with his crest on it? Lewis thought the mentality of this man was such that he might well have regarded the deception played on this ugly, middle-aged, middle-class woman as a huge joke.

The jury disagreed. A new trial was ordered. Lewis knew that nothing could be done to make Mrs Borradaile more appealing; but a court-room takes its orientation from the judge and the Recorder had not even bothered to conceal his bias for Madame Rachel.

The second trial of Rachel Leverson began some two weeks later, on Friday, 25 September, before Mr Commissioner Kerr. The same evidence was given for the prosecution. The defence called Mrs Leverson's two daughters to say, simply, that their mother had not robbed Mrs Borradaile; but this achieved little. In contrast to the Recorder, Commissioner Kerr was clearly not impressed by Madame Rachel. He brushed aside her counter-accusations against Mrs Borradaile. He was noncommittal about Lord Ranelagh, but the court could sense that the tide had turned against Madame Rachel. After a much briefer withdrawal than at the first trial, the jury found her guilty. She was sentenced to five years penal servitude.

Lewis was never vindictive, but he was pleased with the verdict in this case. He did not like Mrs Borradaile personally – who did? – but he had been sickened by the almost gladiatorial atmosphere at the first trial. The implication had been that because Mrs Borradaile was ageing and stupid she somehow *deserved* to be swindled. This was one of the first of many cases in which Lewis was shocked by the hostility and derision unleashed on any woman – especially a woman with prentensions to 'gentility' – who was considered to have compromised herself: to have, through her own behaviour, lost caste. The press had savaged 'the boot-faced Borradaile', calling her a 'Senescent Sappho' and making her a laughing-stock. Particularly unpleasant had been the way the court-room had rocked with merriment at the idea of this middle-aged widow daring to link her name with that of the dashing nobleman, Lord Ranelagh – who was far from young himself and appears to have sought fulfilment through watching naked women through peep-holes.

It is hard not to feel some sympathy for Mrs Borradaile, however tiresome she was. Like most Victorian ladies who lost their reputations, she was the victim of the hypocritical romantic gloss that was applied to 'ladies' in general. The men who put them on a pedestal were usually only too pleased to see them topple off again.

6

Gaining Speed

WITH HIS MARRIAGE to Elizabeth Eberstadt, Lewis found his true centre: the axis upon which his life could appropriately turn. During the months that he was crossing swords with Madame Rachel Elizabeth was carrying their first child. Lewis could not but contrast poor Victorine's attitude to her pregnancy – a gentle calm, with an air of resignation about it – with Elizabeth's solid confidence. Elizabeth gave him the impression that she would not *allow* anything to go wrong.

Nothing did. Lewis's only son, George James Graham Lewis, was born on 12 September 1868 at Taviton Place, Bloomsbury, thus breaking the tradition that all the Lewises had to be born at Ely Place.

The birth of a son confirmed his happiness. Inevitably, Elizabeth referred to the baby boy as 'George the Second' (although, if one counted 'Uncle George', he was really the Third), but with the self-mockery that redeemed the touch of grandeur always implicit in her utterances – for behind the twenty-one-year-old bride could be discerned the shade of the great lady she would one day become.

From now on, Elizabeth determined the outward pattern of their lives. Professionally, Lewis was very successful, but his recent triumphs were nothing to what was to come. And she – she would help him. She was young; she had enormous self-confidence; she was very beautiful in her dark, challenging way. Everyone thought, What a contrast to poor Victorine! – but of course they did not say it in Lewis's hearing, still less in Elizabeth's.

No one was more aware of the contrast than Elizabeth herself. Poor Victorine. It had been a tragedy – and yet she, Elizabeth, knew she could make Lewis happier than Victorine would have done, had she lived. Elizabeth never doubted that for a second.

Towards the end of the 1860s she began to entertain at Taviton

Street. It was not as large or as grand a house as she would have wished, but it would do for the time being.

It was at Taviton Street that George and Elizabeth began to coalesce into 'The Lewises' – a formidable social entity, two-headed but indivisible – and it was appropriate that the first friend to become a regular visitor at Taviton Street should be an artist, a painter. For it was her feeling for art – in the widest sense – and her understanding of artists that was to distinguish Elizabeth Lewis as a hostess. All her life she could spot originality or potential excellence. Far from being 'a typical Jewish flair for the market' that a rival hostess would bitchily attribute to her thirty years on, Elizabeth's gift lay in the sympathy and understanding she offered. She was the best friend a young artist could have, precisely because her appreciation was informed and critical, never merely well-meaning. Her patronage – hard to win but, once given, never withdrawn – was so subtle in essence as to be acceptable to the prickliest talent.

But this was in the future. The first friend to come to Taviton Street – a friend who would also become closer to the Lewises than almost anyone else they ever knew – was Edward Burne-Jones.

Burne-Jones was born in 1833, the same year as Lewis; he was thus his exact contemporary, although very different in background and temperament. Lewis had known the painter slightly when Burne-Jones was living in Great Russell Street; then, in 1867, Burne-Jones and his wife had moved to the Grange, North End Road, West Kensington. Little known when he began to live there, Burne-Jones stayed at the Grange for the rest of his life, working hard, and meeting increasing fame with the modesty that endeared him to the Lewises and indeed to all his friends. His character never changed: he was gentle and shy, almost diffident, and he aroused a protective loyalty in both Lewis and Elizabeth.

In those first years, when the Lewises were at Taviton Street and the Burne-Joneses had not been long at the Grange, both families stood at a similar point: poised and waiting to enter a wider world of fame and success. Both the Lewises and the Burne-Joneses would attain these over the next ten years; and the lives of both couples would be enhanced by the friendship they shared.

While Lewis had been preparing for Madame Rachel's second trial, Edward Lawson, one of the proprietors of the *Daily Telegraph*, had consulted him about a libel action that was being brought against the paper by an Egyptian called Risk Allah. He had been tried for murder in Brussels and after a hearing lasting nine days had been acquitted. The *Telegraph*'s special correspondent in Brussels had reported the case – and now Risk Allah was suing the paper for libel. It was unusual for a libel to straddle the Channel, so to speak; still more unusual was the fact that a commission had been established in Brussels for the purpose of taking depositions that would later be used at the hearing of the libel action in Britain. This meant that the witnesses who had testified at the original trial would not have to come to London to give evidence again.

Soon afterwards, Lewis heard that he and Montagu Williams (who would represent the *Daily Telegraph* when the case came to court) had to go to Brussels to attend the hearings of the commission. Montagu Williams always retained a certain schoolboyish zest; he was delighted to get to Brussels, all expenses paid. Lewis was not so pleased. He was not anxious to leave Elizabeth at this time. But the overall strategy of the case lay in his hands; he admitted that Lawson, his client, was right in asking him to attend.

As he had expected, Lewis did not enjoy their stay in Brussels as much as Williams did. They put up at the Hotel de Flandre, where the commission was sitting in a large room on the ground floor.

Lewis had a letter of introduction to the Procureur Général in Brussels. One day, he invited Lewis and Montagu Williams to attend the trial of two men accused of fraud. Lewis was amused at the casual air of these proceedings, heard before three judges. The two prisoners sat in a dock that was luxury itself by Old Bailey standards and, at a crucial moment of the Procureur Général's speech for the prosecution, one of the prisoners produced a snuff box and took a huge pinch of snuff. After he had done so, the Procureur Général (who stood only a few feet from the dock) smiled at the prisoner and helped himself to the open snuff box. Then he continued his speech. All very different, Lewis thought, from the solemn pageantry of the Old Bailey.

The commission sat for three weeks, and then Lewis and Williams returned to London, taking with them the depositions that would be used at the forthcoming trial in the court of Queen's Bench.

Risk Allah was an Assyrian who had been educated for the priesthood of the Greek Orthodox Church. Abandoning theology, he had come to London and studied medicine at King's College Hospital. He had later served as a medical officer with the Turkish army during the Crimean War; at the end of the campaign he was awarded the Crimean Medal of England and Turkey. Returning to England, he married a rich widow, a Mrs Lewis. At the same time he became friendly with her nephew, a young man named Readley.

Through the complexity of a marriage settlement, Risk Allah stood to inherit some £5000 in the event of Readley's death. Thus, when Readley was found shot dead in a hotel room at Spa in Belgium, Risk Allah – who was staying at the same hotel – fell under suspicion. The circumstances of the young man's death were certainly curious: he was found lying naked on a bed with a gun beside him and a note that said, 'I've done it.' But this, it was later alleged, was a forgery.

Although the weight of the expert evidence concerning the gun and its position, and the wound it had produced, appeared to indicate suicide, Risk Allah was put on trial for murder in Brussels and acquitted. The libel action against the *Daily Telegraph* related to the manner in which that trial had been reported. At the London trial Risk Allah's counsel pointed out that this was a matter of insinuation and innuendo rather than direct comment. Even so – as Lewis was well aware – the fact that Risk Allah had been found not guilty in Brussels made it very hard for the *Daily Telegraph* to win the case. And, after a short retirement, the jury did in fact find for him, awarding him £960 damages.

This was the first well-publicized libel case in which Lewis acted. There were to be many more. By 1868 (when this case was heard), the press was getting better-mannered – at least compared with its style earlier in the century – but by modern standards it was still capable of a slashing brutality, and it reported divorce cases with a wealth of salacious detail unthinkable today.

In the Risk Allah case, the *Telegraph* graciously accepted the verdict in a leading article, quoting the emollient words of the judge: 'The higher the character of the paper and the more extensive its influence, the more serious are the consequences to the individual whom it wrongs.'

Lewis was to act for the *Daily Telegraph* in a number of libel cases in the future. In fact, Lewis and Lewis were to gain a reputation as specialists in libel, largely owing to Lewis's friendship with a man whose career, if not exactly built on libel, certainly took innumerable libel actions in its stride. His name was Henry Labouchere.

Labouchere was one of those paradoxical figures that the Victorian age threw up in such abundance: quintessentially English in his John Bullish individuality and yet French in name, ancestry, and appearance. His extraordinary career as the scourge and flail of the nineteenth-century establishment pivoted on the weekly magazine *Truth* – which he owned and, at times, largely wrote. *Truth* has been described as the Victorian equivalent of *Private Eye*, with which it had some features in common.

But *Truth* was not founded till 1877. When Lewis and Labouchere first met, shortly before Lewis's second marriage, Labouchere was thirty-six. His grandfather had been a Frenchman who came to England and made a fortune as a banker. His son (Henry Labouchere's father) concerned himself with the evangelical pieties of Exeter Hall – difficult to be more stodgily English than that! – and in his lifetime deplored almost everything his son Henry did.

Henry Labouchere had all the advantages Lewis's Jewish blood had denied him: Eton and Trinity College, Cambridge (sent down in 1852). By the time he was twenty-five he had travelled in America and Mexico; taken part in the Californian gold-rush of 1853; lived with Red Indians. At last, through parental influence, he was appointed to the British diplomatic service, in Washington, and later in Munich and St Petersburg. Tiring of the Diplomatic – his career had not been helped by his obsessive gambling – he went into politics and at the time he first met Lewis had just been elected to Parliament as member for Middlesex.

Lewis shared with Labouchere an interest in the theatre, although Labouchere, unlike Lewis, had no childhood memories of an earlier generation of performers. Labouchere, in fact, had only lately become involved with theatrical matters – for the good reason that he was living with an actress. This was a lady Lewis already knew slightly: Henrietta Hodson. Lewis had met her through his friends the Bancrofts, with whom she had been acting.

Labouchere's entry into theatrical management may well have sprung from a desire to further Henrietta Hodson's career; late in 1867 he opened the Queen's Theatre in Long Acre. On Boxing Night 1867 Lewis and Elizabeth attended the first night of David Garrick's version of *The Taming of the Shrew*. Henry Irving and Ellen Terry appeared in this (the first time they acted together). Both, of course, were to become friends of the Lewises, and in later years enliven gatherings at Portland Place with their contribution to the Lewises' 'charades' – which were often not charades at all but sophisticated parodies of current plays.

Lewis's friendship with Henry Labouchere lasted forty years – for the rest of his life in fact. In some respects it was the most important friendship Lewis ever enjoyed, both personally and professionally.

It is not recorded what Elizabeth thought of the smart quasi-Bohemianism of Labouchere and Henrietta Hodson (who was still, at this time, married to a solicitor called Pigeon, whom Lewis also knew slightly). Perhaps their raffishness jarred a little on her German sobriety. If it did, she was already too subtle and instinctive a hostess to show it.

7

Overend Gurney

ALTHOUGH LEWIS AND LEWIS continued to 'attend to the criminal classes indoors' – and outdoors too – the late 1860s and the beginning of the 1870s brought a change in the general nature of the cases the firm undertook. Like most truly significant changes, this took place slowly but was unmistakable in its effects. The old savage, noisy underworld – that had its roots in the eighteenth-century London of Jack Sheppard and the thief-taker Jonathan Wild – was gradually being replaced by a more sophisticated criminal milieu.

Lewis noticed this change working in the great increase in what would today be called 'white-collar crime'. There had always been a good deal of petty swindling and cheating: hucksters who sold worthless goods by convincing the mugs that they were getting a bargain – like 'mock auctioneers' today; magsmen who ran crooked gambling games; but these were small fry, even by underworld standards. What Lewis began to confront now was crime on a financial scale and of a social import beyond the capacity of James Lewis's old lags to even comprehend. Crime executed not by underworld figures but by rich men who were themselves of the establishment and thus able to dazzle the authority-conscious middle-class who were their natural victims.

There had been swindles on a grand scale before, of course. The biggest financial débâcle in British history had occurred as early as 1711, when Robert Harley persuaded a company of merchants to buy up the floating national debt of £10 million on a government guarantee of 6 per cent interest. A frenzy of speculation ensured that all the shares were taken up and ten years later the entire national debt of £30 million had been taken over. Then the South Sea Bubble burst (the chairman and several directors of the company had sold out just before) and thousands of people throughout the country were ruined.

Fortunately no disaster of that magnitude ever happened again. However, the extraordinary speed of industrial development during the first half of the nineteenth century brought new legislation relating to joint stock companies that opened the door to widespread exploitation. The Limited Liability Act of 1855 (essentially an amendment of an earlier act of 1844) enabled joint stock companies to limit the liability of their members. This was to prove somewhat two-edged in its effects. It could be claimed to have inaugurated the golden age of the company promoter: the silver-tongued rogue with impressive connections in the City of London who had the power to hypnotize the small investor into parting with millions. The purpose of the act was to protect investors; but it was no coincidence that the 1860s saw a vast proliferation of fraud. Particularly vulnerable, it appeared, were private banks, and a number of these failed through fraud and mismanagement – the latter was often alleged as a cover for the former. In late 1868 came the case that was to gain Lewis national attention and to give his practice a new dimension: fighting for the victims of these new and predatory 'entrepreneurs'.

The disaster that had overtaken the great financial house of Overend Gurney went back more than two years. On a Thursday afternoon, 10 May 1866, the company was forced to suspend payment. The news sped around the City with the speed of the recently developed electric telegraph. A huge crowd gathered outside the firm's impressive headquarters at the corner of Lombard Street. The massive doors – closed since three o'clock the previous afternoon – were besieged by a solid mass of people. For most of them their savings were at stake: they had money deposited with Overend Gurney. They were still dazed; incredulous. It wasn't possible. Overend Gurney? The biggest house in the City?

The crash was not entirely unexpected. There had been rumours circulating for several days that Overend were in trouble, but experienced City hands discounted them.

The firm had been established by John Overend and Thomas Richardson in 1810. A few years later they were joined by Samuel Gurney of Norwich; and the three original partners all continued in business for the next fifty years. Then in the early 1860s all three died within months of each other. They were replaced by another Samuel Gurney, Edward Gurney (kinsmen of the original Gurney), and Robert Birkbeck. A few years after taking control of the company the new partners decided to sell the firm – till now a private partnership –

to a limited company that would be formed (with the same name). The public would then be invited to subscribe for shares in the new company. It was, in fact, a classic exercise in 'going public': the long-established reputation of the private firm appeared to investors to guarantee the new public company. The issue was a great success. Two of the partners in the private firm – Edward Gurney and Robert Birkbeck – joined the board of the new company, along with three new directors: John Henry Gurney, Henry Barclay, and Thomas Gibb.

On the day after Overend Gurney closed, Friday 11 May, panic gripped the City. A run started on the banks, a number of which opened an hour earlier that morning – 'to give confidence to investors' – but against that, some closed their doors early, presumably afraid that their reserves might be depleted too fast. A journalist wrote:

> Many ladies were seen to enter the different banks, their faces deadly pale, only to reappear – now with faint smiles on their faces – closely hugging leather bags. Where were they going to put their rescued wealth? One lady happened to know a Governor of the Bank of England, so she hastened to him and demanded, 'Where shall I put my money now?' The banker countered, 'Where have you taken it from?' 'From the London and Westminster Bank.' 'Then put it back there,' he told her.

But to some extent the panic was justified. Now the English Joint Stock Bank followed Overend Gurney into liquidation. Apart from being hit by Overend's failure, the English Joint Stock Bank had overextended itself when it recently took on the business of Olding and Co. (the banking business in which Samuel Rogers, the poet, had been a partner).

The panic intensified. At first Overend's liabilities were thought to be between £10 million and £12 million. The issued capital of the company was £5 million, divided into 100,000 £50 shares (only £15 had been paid up on each share).

As with a great ship sinking and dragging a number of smaller craft down with it, the effects of Overend Gurney's failure were felt in the City for months. If Overend was responsible for ruining the English Joint Stock Bank (as its directors alleged), then there were many smaller victims too: notably the Merchant's Bank.

Lewis and Lewis had already been involved in the many bankruptcies stemming from Overend's failure when, at a stormy shareholders' meeting, it was decided to institute criminal proceedings against the directors of Overend Gurney Ltd. Prominent among the shareholders was a Dr Thorn, a member of the Canadian bar, and allied with him was an accountant called William Howell. Thorn only held a few shares, but he was very determined and served as a focus for the accumulated anger and frustration of his fellow shareholders. Howell, the only man who could unravel the tangled finances of Overend Gurney, was described to Lewis as 'a demon with books'; and he spent long days investigating the huge pile of ledgers that were brought to the Mansion House every morning in two or three horse-drawn wagons, and every evening collected and taken back to official custody. Lewis had been retained by the shareholders to conduct their prosecution against the Overend directors and he knew that Howell's researches would be very important to their case.

The committal proceedings were held at the Mansion House, which had the standing of a magistrate's court, so Lewis was entitled to plead in it. He opened for the prosecution on New Year's Day 1869; and he was ranged against experienced counsel – Serjeant Ballantine for John Gurney and Robert Birkbeck; Serjeant Parry for Henry Barclay; Hardinge Giffard for Thomas Gibb. The charge was that the defendants had conspired by false pretences to induce Adam Thorn and other persons to become shareholders in Overend Gurney 'with intent to cheat and defraud'.

Lewis rose to present the case for the prosecution – a lone solicitor ranging himself against the acknowledged leaders of the bar.

The essence of the case, as Lewis saw it, was the question of intention. He knew that casual opinion in the City tended to excuse the Overend Gurney directors on the grounds of carelessness – 'They just didn't realize what was happening; men of that calibre don't perpetrate fraud' – but Lewis had seen the results of Howell's researches. These men *had* perpetrated fraud. Despite their background and impeccable connections, these solid City burghers had cold-bloodedly gulled the public into subscribing millions of pounds for shares in a concern they knew was hopelessly insolvent.

Thanks to Hovell, Lewis was able to go back at least a decade in Overend Gurney's finances. For the first fifty years of its life the old private partnership had conducted its affairs with caution – and had been very successful. Over the years millions had been made.

Then, around 1859, the partners had changed their policy altogether. Whether they doubted if the firm could continue to prosper along the traditional lines or whether they had become possessed by some madness of greed, Lewis did not know. What was certain was that the partners had plunged into speculation on a huge scale. Railways, shipping, mining, commodities – they had entered every speculative field, always with disastrous results. By 1865 the firm was insolvent, owing more than £15 million, while assets hardly totalled £3 million.

'And this' – so far Lewis's delivery had been relentlessly quiet but now his voice struck steel-sharp across the court – 'this was the moment they chose to offer this concern to an unsuspecting public in the shape of one hundred thousand £50 shares.' The prospectus, Lewis continued, was a monstrous attempt to persuade the public to put their hard-earned savings into an already bankrupt concern. 'In fact,' Lewis said, 'Overend Gurney was already a sinking ship. Not only were the original partners abandoning it, but they were inviting the unfortunate shareholders to board it as passengers!' This was not a question of negligence – it was cold-blooded fraud. The biggest fraud since the South Sea Bubble. Lewis would ask the Lord Mayor and his colleagues on the bench to remember that the men behind the South Sea Bubble had been highly placed in the government of their day. Then – as now with Overend Gurney – ordinary hard-working citizens had been ruined by specious promises made by those they thought they had every reason to trust. Any plea of negligence on the part of the Overend Gurney directors was an empty excuse. The prospectus issued to the public offering shares in the new public company was a thoroughly dishonest document, putting forward claims its authors knew to be false.

As Lewis had expected, Serjeants Ballantine and Parry opened the defence with mind-bludgeoning bursts of rhetoric. The prosecution had dared accuse these men of being swindlers! Did Mr Lewis have any inkling of the standing they enjoyed in the City of London? These were men of wealth and integrity. It might be that these gentlemen had been negligent – although that was by no means admitted. Guilty of fraud – never! Perhaps the prospectus inviting the public to buy shares had been sanguine in tone: nothing criminal in that. Mr Lewis had talked of 'false statements': would it not be fairer to call them 'mis-statements'? That would not, perhaps, altogether preclude the possibility of some degree of negligence being admitted. But, as to the use of the word 'dishonest', well really, it was necessary to protest at that. These were men from families respected in the world of commerce and trade; for Mr Lewis to cast a slur on their good names. . .

And so the word-spinning went on, always seeking to obscure the fact that the direction had invited the public to subscribe to an enterprise they already knew to be insolvent.

But the eloquence of defence counsel did not prevail with the Lord Mayor and his colleagues. They had evidently listened to Lewis, for the Overend Gurney directors were committed for trial at the Old Bailey. (Later, through the exercise of private influence, the venue was changed to the court of Queen's Bench.)

The trial of John Gurney and his fellow directors did not take place until December 1869. (In the interim they were allowed to remain at liberty, on heavy bail). Meanwhile Lewis, reversing roles, had defended one of the directors of the Merchant's Bank, which Overend Gurney had dragged down with it. The proceedings again took place at the Mansion House and Lewis appeared for Richard Stuart Lane.

This time, the prosecution was conducted by Douglas Straight and the Crown case appeared to mirror that against the Overend Gurney directors, if on a smaller scale. A circular had been sent out to prospective investors, making statements which the directors 'well knew to be false', and inviting the public to buy shares in a concern which they, the directors, knew to be insolvent.

Lewis argued that the evidence against Lane and his co-directors was far from conclusive. At the time of the flotation they had no reason to suppose that Lane, Hanbury and Co. (the private partnership that 'went public' as the Merchant's Bank) was not perfectly solvent.

Perhaps the Crown lacked a Howell to marshal the facts. In the event, after a hearing lasting several days, Douglas Straight asked if the Lord Mayor would agree for the case to be withdrawn as the authorities had reason to believe that there was no hope of obtaining a conviction.

Later that year, on 13 December 1869, the trial of the Overend Gurney directors began in the court of Queen's Bench. As a solicitor, Lewis could not, of course, appear here; but his overall responsibility for the case remained, acting as he was for the hundreds of shareholders who were personified by Dr Thorn.

The case was heard before the Lord Chief Justice. Dr Kenealy QC replaced Lewis for the prosecution. The then Solicitor General, Sir John Duke Coleridge, led an expensive team of counsel for the defence.

From the first, it was obvious that Lewis's success in the lower court was not going to be repeated. How far this was due to the legal personalities involved is not clear, but Kenealy (notorious for professional misconduct during the famous Tichborne Claimant case) hardly inspired confidence – especially when opposed by the 'silver-tongued' John Duke Coleridge.

The arguments on both sides were those already heard before the Lord Mayor. But before the Lord Chief Justice the defence grew bold, even arrogant. How dare these shareholders, men of straw as they were, bring a prosecution against gentlemen of wealth and position? Sensing his lordship's mood, Coleridge blatantly toadied to the judge's establishment prejudices. Working himself into a rhetorical frenzy, Coleridge denied that his clients could, under any circumstances, be guilty of fraud: 'If the partners are men of large fortunes and ample private means, what evidence of fraud is there?'

His speech was an extraordinary exercise in forensic incantation, apparently hypnotic in its effect. Again and again he used key-words like 'power' and 'money' and 'position' to deaden judge and jury to the plain facts of fraud and deceit. Plain facts got short shrift with Coleridge, later characterized by Sir Edward Clarke as a cross-examiner of 'studious unfairness'. He was certainly a master of relentless double-talk: 'As to the mention of a guarantee, did not that in itself make men of experience in business aware that there had been a loss, that there were liabilities which would require a guarantee.'

Coleridge achieved his aim of obscuring the truth with a web of words. The Lord Chief Justice took up the same refrain in his summing-up. Like Coleridge, he emphasized again and again the wealth and importance of the accused and huffed and puffed at the audacity of the shareholders in bringing this prosecution at all.

The jury retired for a quarter of an hour and then returned with a verdict of not guilty. 'Really,' the Lord Chief Justice said, 'I cannot for the life of me see why this prosecution was ever brought.'

The verdict cannot have surprised Lewis. The advocate in him must have wondered whether he would have done better than Dr Kenealy did. The player of the legal game perhaps reflected that he had got Lane of the Merchant's Bank off without his even being sent for trial. This would confirm Lewis's view that it was sometimes possible to win simply by playing well, according to the rules – and sometimes impossible, however good your case, because prejudice, or entrenched power, social or financial, prevented it. This had happened when the case of Overend Gurney had reached the higher court. Not only had justice not been done; it had been seen not to be done: and this was because the Lord Chief Justice had quite openly identified himself with the rich and powerful directors of Overend Gurney. What did he care for these wretched shopkeepers and clergymen's widows who complained of being cheated? He knew the defendants, attended the same City banquets as they did, drank the same wines.

The social reformer in Lewis must have felt bitter chagrin at the suffering and deprivation inflicted on hundreds of people as a result of the Overend Gurney swindle. None of the investors ever got any money back. More than thirty years later, Lewis heard of the suicide of a retired army officer who had been living in the Lambeth Workhouse. The report of the inquest recalled that the deceased 'had lost his savings in the collapse of Overend Gurney'.

8

By Royal Command

ON 5 MAY 1869 Lewis's mother died. This was sad but not unexpected: she had been failing for a long time. Her husband and all her eight children were present at her bedside. Lewis might have consoled himself with the thought that she had lived to see him achieve a considerable professional success. And, grieved as she had been by Victorine's tragic death, she had been glad that he had been able to find happiness in a second marriage so soon, though perhaps she had found Elizabeth a little overwhelming in her beauty and audacity. And it must have been a great joy to her to hold her first male grandchild in her arms: George James Graham Lewis, named both for his father and for his grandfather, her husband.

She loved her son's other child too, of course: Alice, poor Victorine's daughter. Sometimes Lewis wondered uneasily if the shadow of Victorine's death did not still hang over his firstborn child. There was no question of Elizabeth's not being fond of her, still less of her not treating her well, and yet for some reason Alice was never the centre of attention, as every child should be on occasion. She was now four years old, an age when (Lewis's sisters told him) even a small girl should have been getting a little noisier, making her presence felt rather more. Alice appeared all too happy to stay in the shadows.

Lewis could not do anything about this himself – he was busier than ever; the practice was getting bigger all the time – and Elizabeth was too brisk, moved too fast in everything somehow, to understand how he felt. When he had sought to voice these misgivings she had chosen to see them as an indication of some doubt or depression in himself. Alice? Why should he be worried over Alice? The child was in the best of health. If she did seem a little shy and hesitant – well, she would come out of her shell in her own good time.

Lewis would accept that, of course, and Elizabeth would bustle on, Alice forgotten, to start something else.

Active as he was professionally, Lewis was aware that, compared with Elizabeth, his natural forces ran slow and deep, an underground river to her dashing Niagara. Sometimes he wondered how he could ever keep up with her. She never stopped. Not only entertaining, but listening to music, looking at paintings, reading, studying. She spoke English perfectly (although to the end of her life she was to retain a slight German accent); she was scarcely less fluent in French and Italian.

Apart from Edward Burne-Jones and his wife, whom the Lewises saw constantly – both when visiting the Grange and when receiving the Burne-Joneses at Taviton Street – by 1869 Elizabeth was also entertaining George and Emma Du Maurier; Lawrence Alma-Tadema – a future Royal Academician and founder of the so-called 'Marble School'; and a man who was certainly Alma-Tadema's artistic antithesis, James McNeill Whistler. Elizabeth's career as a hostess had begun, although her drawing-room at Taviton Street was never a *salon* – as the great room on the first floor of 88 Portland Place was to be.

But these were artists – exactly the kind of people, the establishment voices would have said, you would expect a clever foreign Jewess to entertain. More important – and very annoying to that same establishment, which disapproved of both artists and Jews – was the fact that 1869 was the year in which Lewis first became friendly with the Prince of Wales.

Edward Albert, Prince of Wales, was then twenty-eight. He had married Princess Alexandra of Schleswig-Holstein in 1863. Despite her youth and beauty and the fact that she had already given him four children (including the future King George V), by 1869 the Prince had already adopted the rakish persona that was to be his for the next forty years. During those forty years his popularity with his subjects waxed and waned with feverish inconsistency, only settling into the acceptance his mother the Queen had always enjoyed when he himself became King, at nearly sixty years of age.

Most of Edward's biographers blame the Queen for the problems that beset the Prince throughout the half-century of waiting he endured. His father, the Prince Consort, had designed a monstrous system of education for him, which naturally met with Victoria's enthusiastic approval; in the words of the then Bishop of Oxford it was calculated to 'make him the most perfect man who ever lived'. Predictably the experiment failed.

After he reached manhood, the Queen's attitude towards her son was, if possible, even more insensitive. She was happy to let him lay an unlimited number of foundation stones: that appeared to be his main function in life, as someone sardonically observed. Certainly she ruthlessly – some thought almost maliciously – denied him any of the cultural functions his father, Prince Albert, had enjoyed. The Prince of Wales was not allowed to give his patronage to any of the charities or learned societies which owed so much to his father's encouragement. Excluded from power, in the truest sense unemployed, the Prince was left with only one accessible objective: the pursuit of pleasure – and he pursued it relentlessly.

He could have created a court of his own, in the manner of a Hanoverian Prince of Wales, but 'Bertie' (as his mother called him) was too loyal to do this, at least in the political sense. Certainly he created his own court in the social sense, and it soon acquired a name: the Marlborough House set. Its manners and morals were as far as possible removed from those of the Queen's court at Windsor, and she was soon bitterly hostile to anyone who belonged to it. She believed, with some justification, that the main pursuits of those in the Prince's entourage were charades, masked balls, whist, baccarat ('baccy' in the set), and adultery – which had to be conducted discreetly, with certain ground rules strictly observed by all the parties. It was these last two diversions that were to cause the Prince the greatest annoyance during the long years while he waited to be King.

Lewis met the Prince through Lord Marcus Beresford, son of the Marquis of Waterford and one of the Prince's oldest friends. Good-natured and boyish in manner (the memoir writers say), a superb horseman, Lord Marcus Beresford trained the Prince's horses and three times won the Derby for him. He was Edward's adviser on everything connected with racing – a passion with the Prince that would grow stronger as he got older.

Marcus Beresford had met Lewis through an incident that had occurred some years before. Always extravagant, Beresford had got himself into the clutches of a moneylender who had his office just off Piccadilly. He owed this man a large sum at an outrageous rate of interest. One day, Lord Marcus was walking in the Park with a friend, Lord Charles Kerr. Leaving Hyde Park, they suddenly encountered the moneylender. There was some talk – at first cool, then angry. Tempers mounted; blows were exchanged. Marcus Beresford was more than equal to the moneylender; in fact, he gave the man a beating.

Lewis knew it was impossible to escape a conviction. This case was so clear-cut that being a 'swell' could not help Beresford. He was charged with 'assault occasioning actual bodily harm and common assault'.

Lord Marcus pocketed his pride and offered an apology. This the moneylender would not accept. The case came to court at Marlborough Street, and Lewis briefed Montagu Williams to represent Beresford. He was committed for trial at the Middlesex Sessions.

The sessions happened to coincide with the Liverpool Races. To his surprise, while he was on his feet addressing the court on Beresford's behalf, Montagu Williams felt a tug at his gown. He looked down. A telegram was handed up to him. It gave a time and the name of a horse. Puzzled, Williams went on with his speech. Again and again, a hand tugged at his gown: each time a telegram was delivered to him. At last his clerk whispered an explanation. The telegrams were intended for Lord Marcus. They reported the fortunes of his various runners at the Liverpool meeting, but he had told his trainer to address them to Williams since he himself was in the dock.

Montagu Williams did his best for Beresford, stressing the extortionate rates of interest he was being charged; but nothing could alter the fact that he had assaulted the man. He was fined £100 and told by the chairman of the sessions that he was lucky to escape imprisonment. Unrepentant, but expressing deep gratitude to Lewis and Montagu Williams, Lord Marcus jumped on the evening train to Liverpool: to ride one of his own horses to second place in the Grand National a day later.

Despite his conviction, Lord Marcus had been impressed by his lawyer's performance. Thus it was that, when the Prince happened to mention that he was perturbed at his possible involvement in a divorce suit being brought by Sir Charles Mordaunt against his wife, Lord Marcus suggested that HRH should consult George Lewis.

9

And in Open Day

In 1866 Sir Charles Mordaunt, a baronet and a wealthy landowner, married Harriet Moncreiffe and brought her home to Walton Hall in Warwickshire. She was the daughter of Sir Thomas Moncreiffe, an even wealthier landowner in Perthshire. Only seventeen, she was one of eight sisters, known collectively as 'the beautiful Moncreiffes', all of whom had married well.

Despite her youth and beauty, Lady Mordaunt did not appear happy, and after a few years she became odd and unpredictable in her behaviour.

Soon after the birth of their first child, she called to her husband, 'Charles, I want to tell you something. I have been dreadfully wicked and I have done very wrong. I have been unfaithful to you. I have committed misconduct with Lord Cole, and with Sir Frederick Johnstone, the Prince of Wales, and others: often and in open day.' Then she added, 'It is Lord Cole who is the father of my baby.'

Sir Charles reacted in a predictable way to this confession. He at once set divorce proceedings in motion; and this fact was soon reported to the Prince of Wales.

The Mordaunts were members of the Marlborough House set and their divorce case was to cast a lurid glow on the social and sexual mores of the Prince's circle: particularly on his habit of calling on married ladies during the afternoon. (He might or might not know their husbands.) On such occasions, wrote Harry Tyrwhitt-Wilson, the Prince's equerry and unofficial procurer, in a directive to complaisant husbands, 'it is requested that the person called on shall receive no other visitors and that no other members of the family shall be present unless enquired for by the Prince'.

This meant, of course, that the lady and her royal caller had to be left uninterrupted for at least two or three hours. The husband was not to return home until at least tea time. Such was Edward's charm, and such was the prevailing attitude to royalty, that there is no doubt that most husbands in the Marlbough House set were genuinely delighted that their wives should be chosen for the Prince's enjoyment.

Not surprisingly, fashionable society took its cue from the Prince and his friends. What a relief, indeed, after the puritanism, the moral tight-lacing of Victoria and Albert! The Prince of Wales initiated the golden age of the *mari complaisant*. If you permitted the Prince – or indeed, any of your friends – to enjoy your wife's favours, then it was only fair for your friends to accord you similar privileges with their wives. In the Marlborough House set – in fact throughout smart society – it became acceptable for a young wife to provide the husband with some children (a son and heir and a few more to keep him company) and then to play the field in a discreet and tasteful way. Only occasionally, through stupidity or an excess of passion, did anyone rock the boat, and then the Prince – himself the trendsetter and a figure of symbolic importance – often got the blame.

The Queen was well aware of all this. She was always, in her letters, denouncing 'the frivolous, selfish and pleasure-seeking lives of the upper classes'. Characteristically, she feared it might nourish 'the spirit of democracy' among the lower classes. Meanwhile she abandoned herself wholly to the role of the Widow of Windsor: a dark icon symbolizing austerity, even repression – but with the might of an empire behind her.

It is not clear whether Sir Charles Mordaunt himself played by the Marlborough House rules, nor whether he would have overlooked his wife's confession if the Prince had been the only man she named.

Lady Mordaunt had known the Prince of Wales before she married Sir Charles, who was a good deal older than she and, after their marriage, kept up his lifelong habit of going off to Norway alone on fishing trips. The Prince, for his part, kept up his acquaintanceship with Lady Mordaunt. The Mordaunts had attended a ball at Abergeldie, the house the Prince owned near Balmoral; Lady Mordaunt was then pregnant. Her baby had been born in the spring of 1869 and, tragically, was found to be nearly blind. Naturaliy, Harriet Mordaunt was distraught; a week later she made her confession to her husband. It is significant that, having said that Lord Cole was the father of the baby, she then added, 'I am the cause of its [the baby's] blindness.' This implied that the baby's eye condition was due to inherited venereal infection, and (presumably) that it was Lord Cole who had given her, Lady Mordaunt, the disease.

After he had decided to sue for divorce, Sir Charles began to make intensive enquiries. He admitted afterwards that, despite the decision to divorce Harriet, he still hoped to find that it was 'all hysteria'.

He soon heard, however, that she had spoken to other people about her adulteries. They mentioned the Prince of Wales's visits to his wife – something which Sir Charles had tried to prevent: 'I told her that I had heard in various quarters certain circumstances connected with the Prince's character. I was not aware till after my wife's confinement that the Prince had been a constant visitor at my house and that any correspondence existed between them.' After his wife's confession, he had gone to an escritoire belonging to her. Forcing the lock, he found some letters from the Prince to Lady Mordaunt; some dried flowers; the verses of a valentine; a handkerchief belonging to the Prince.

The Prince's letters were certainly not incriminating – except of course that they provoked the obvious question: Why did he write them in the first place? Nothing could have been more harmless than their contents:

> I am so glad to hear that you have made so good a recovery [from measles] and will be able to go soon to Hastings, which is sure to do you a lot of good. I hope that perhaps on your return to London I may have the pleasure of seeing you.

Another letter tells her that his wife, Princess Alexandra, has given birth to their daughter Louise and hopes that Lady Mordaunt will come to the St James's Hall that week for a concert:

> There would, I am sure, be no harm in your remaining till Saturday in town. I should like to see you again.

In the escritoire Sir Charles also found letters from Lord Lucan – Crimean 'hero' and bungler of Homeric proportions – and hotel bills made out to Sir Frederick Johnstone.

None of this was conclusive in itself, but there was enough of it to convince Sir Charles that he had sufficient evidence to divorce his wife – a more difficult enterprise in 1870 than in 1983, although, as a man and a husband, all the cards were stacked in his favour.

Lewis had always been passionately concerned with the injustice to women inflicted by the divorce laws. All his life he was to fight, not only for a liberalization of English attitudes to divorce, but for equal treatment of men and women before the law.

Up to 1857 divorce was not available to the great mass of the population. (After obtaining a separation *a mensa et thoro* in the ecclesiastical courts, one had to get a private Act of Parliament passed granting a divorce.) The Matrimonial Causes Act of 1857 allowed divorce, but on conditions grossly unfair to women. The act allowed a man to divorce his wife for adultery alone, but before a woman could divorce her husband he had to be guilty, not only of adultery, but of some *additional* matrimonial offence – bigamy, rape, sodomy, bestiality, or cruelty. Most women seeking divorce had no option but to allege cruelty and this was notoriously hard to prove. A man could be flagrantly unfaithful – taunt his wife with the presence of a mistress, beget children by another woman – and yet the wife might never get any redress.

But, even in this one-sided situation, with all the odds weighing heavily in the husband's favour, a divorce suit in the nineteenth century could still prove a doubtful undertaking. Sir Charles Mordaunt worked hard at accumulating evidence. He had his wife examined by specialists in 'specific complaints' (a Victorian euphemism for venereal diseases); by an opthalmologist, who said that there was no proof that the condition of the child's eyes was due to gonorrhoea; by a gynaecologist – again, to determine whether she was suffering from a 'specific complaint'.

Sir Charles also busied himself below stairs. A housemaid said that Lady Mordaunt and a Captain Arthur Farquhar of the Guards had spent the night together in a London hotel, as well as at an address in Warwickshire. Various footmen told of the different men who had visited her ladyship at the Mordaunts' London house at Chesham Place: Lord Cole; Lord Newport; Sir Frederick Johnstone; and – again – Captain Farquhar. All these were prominent members of the Marlborough House set; and their visits had taken place while Sir Charles was away on his fishing trips on the Norwegian fiords.

While the trial was pending, Lady Mordaunt went to stay at her father's house in Perthshire. There she was examined by alienists (a nineteenth-century term for psychiatrists), who pronounced her insane.

But, even if she were, Sir Charles still wished to divorce her, and he evidently wanted to wash as much dirty linen as possible in the process. Indeed, the forthcoming trial offered the public almost everything: adultery, madness, and venereal disease.

And, as if all that were not enough, the Prince of Wales himself was involved! Lady Mordaunt's lawyers announced that they were going to subpoena the Prince as a witness for the defence, although it was not clear why, of the three alleged adulterers named by Lady Mordaunt – Sir Frederick Johnstone, Lord Cole, and the Prince – only the Prince was being called.

When the Prince got the subpoena, his first thought was of his mother, the Queen. She was naturally appalled, although not as angry as he had expected. But calling the Prince of Wales to give evidence in a filthy divorce court! It was practically *lèse majesté*. She was totally opposed to his going into the witness box. But could he refuse? She consulted the Lord Chancellor, Lord Hatherley. He shared her concern. This, he said, was 'as bad as a revolution in its effect on the Prince of Wales'. The Queen wrote back:

> The fact of the Prince of Wales's intimate acquaintanceship with a young married woman being publicly proclaimed will show an amount of imprudence which cannot but damage him in the eyes of the middle and lower classes, which is to be most deeply lamented.

Again, the Lord Chancellor agreed with her. But he was adamant that no question of privilege could keep the Prince out of the box. If the Prince were served with a subpoena, he had to appear – like everyone else.

It was at this juncture that the Prince consulted Lewis, who endorsed the Lord Chancellor's view. It would be most unwise to invoke any question of privilege. 'You must go into the witness box,' Lewis told the Prince. 'That is the only way to clear your name.'

This was sound advice, but Lewis might be considered a bold man to give it so bluntly. He was, after all, a stranger to the Prince. He was a Jew (he could not have known at that time that Edward was the least anti-semitic of men, and that Jews such as Sir Ernest Cassel and Lewis himself were to play an important part in his life). He was a lawyer and, although he recognized the need to consult them from time to time, the Prince did not like lawyers.

Whatever he may have thought, the Prince listened. He accepted the argument that it is never wise for a royal personage to stand on privilege alone – because doing this can only put a weapon in the hands of those who want to bring down the throne.

Perhaps the Prince was impressed because Republicanism was so much in the air at that time. In 1870 there were over fifty republican clubs in various parts of England and they were all dedicated to the overthrow of the monarchy.

He thanked Lewis for his advice and said he would take it. He would attend the Mordaunt trial and give evidence.

Lady Mordaunt's condition deteriorated rapidly and by the time the trial started, in February 1870, she had been certified as a lunatic and was under restraint in a hospital. Lord Penzance presided at the divorce hearing. Serjeant Ballantine appeared for Sir Charles Mordaunt; Dr Deane, QC, for her father, Sir Thomas Moncreiffe (her guardian while she remained certified insane).

The defence was a simple one: insanity. If the court agreed with the doctors Sir Thomas Moncreiffe called on his daughter's behalf, she must be found 'unfit to plead' and that would be the end of her husband's divorce action.

But this defence was strongly attacked by Ballantine. Lady Mordaunt's madness, he argued, was assumed – a wretched attempt to escape the consequences of her adulteries.

So all the evidence had to be gone through. Various chambermaids and footmen gave evidence about Lady Mordaunt's comings and goings. An entry in her diary was cited. Dated 5 April, it ran, '280 days from 27 June'. It referred, Sir Charles's counsel suggested, to the fact that she had conceived a child by Lord Cole on 27 June, while her husband was away in Norway on one of his fishing holidays.

After nearly a week of this kind of evidence, the moment that the Queen had been dreading came. HRH walked calmly across the court and up into the witness box.

Dr Deane examined the Prince, who answered the questions, it was reported, 'in a calm and undisturbed manner'.

In fact the questions were few enough, and simple enough. The Prince said he had known the Moncreiffe family some time before Lady Mordaunt's marriage. When she married, he wrote to her and sent her a wedding gift. He also confirmed that she had visited Marlborough House before her marriage.

'Did you see much of her in 1867?' Dr Deane asked.

'I did.'

'And in the year 1868?'

'I did also.'

Deane then sought to prove that Sir Charles Mordaunt knew the Prince a good deal better than he, Sir Charles, admitted; and that both had taken part in a pigeon-shooting match at Hurlingham.

Then at last Deane said, 'Only one more question with which to trouble your Royal Highness. Has there ever been any improper familiarity or criminal act between yourself and Lady Mordaunt?'

The Prince answered in a loud voice, 'There has not.'

And that was all. Serjeant Ballantine graciously waived the right to cross-examine. The Prince in the box had been the high-point: nothing else in the case could equal that. And nothing did. The rest was, in fact, anti-climactic.

Sir Frederick Johnstone asked if he might also deny the charge of adultery through counsel. This was allowed.

Sir Charles Mordaunt had told his wife that Sir Frederick Johnstone had never married because he had suffered from venereal disease. Not just once but repeatedly: he would get infected, be treated and apparently cured, only to get infected again. There came a flicker of black comedy when Johnstone said, 'A more unfounded statement was never made behind a man's back. It is perfectly untrue.'

But he was cross-examined. Ballantine asked, 'You do not mean to imply that you have never suffered?'

'Certainly not!' Sir Frederick replied. 'I have had youthful indiscretions.'

At last the judged summed up; and it can be assumed that the question of the Prince's involvement was on Lord Penzance's mind as he did so. It was later said that Gladstone, the then Prime Minister, had asked Lord Penzance to 'protect' the Prince if the examination or cross-examination of himself or anyone else appeared to threaten him.

After a retirement of only ten minutes the jury came back. They found that Lady Mordaunt was, by reason of insanity, unfit to plead. Sir Charles did not get his divorce (he was to get it five years later, citing only Lord Cole).

So it was all futile. As not uncommonly happened in Victorian divorce cases, nothing had been achieved by opening this can of worms.

For some weeks afterwards the Prince must have wondered if his mother had not been right in telling him to keep out of the witness box – and Lewis, therefore, wrong. There were a number of demonstrations of public feeling against the Prince. When he went to the theatre with Princess Alexandra, she was wildly cheered as they entered their box; *he* was even more loudly booed.

The Prince was too strong a character to be much disturbed by such an expression of public disapproval – but even so, it *was* disturbing, when he considered those fifty republican clubs. What worried the Queen more was the disapproval of a large class of censorious, puritanical people who could not boo the Prince in the theatre because they did not go there – they disapproved of that too – but were extremely vocal and influential, particularly in the press. Victoria was particularly sensitive to these groups because she shared their attitudes. This 'moral majority' in England would be sniping at the Prince and the Marlborough House set for the next thirty years. From now on – and right up to his accession to the throne – the Prince was to be lectured by clergymen and straight-from-the-shoulder journalists (often writing with their tongue in their cheek, giving the public what their editor thought it wanted); and, though Edward reacted with the kind of irritation with which one might respond to the persistent buzzing of a gnat, they were always there: a kind of perpetual opposition – carping and censorious – however hard he tried to ignore them.

In the main, though, he did ignore them and did what he wanted. And that, in the long run, did appeal to the majority of his subjects – especially his lower-middle- and working-class subjects, who liked their Prince (and later their King) to have a go, to have a bit of the devil in him. Thus he may be said to have 'created' his public, rather as a pop star creates his, living up to his 'image', behaving in the colourful way his fans expect.

Even as early as 1870, Lewis may have had some perception of this. And it soon became clear that he had been right in advising the Prince to give evidence in the Mordaunt case. Most people applauded his decision to come forward and speak up in open court. If he *had* been guilty of adultery, and had perjured himself denying it, what else could a gentleman have done? As a man of honour he could not blacken a lady's name. Even if he had lied in the witness box – and that was by no means certain – he had acted like a gentleman.

Lewis had been proved right. It could be argued that the Mordaunt episode marked the beginning of the Prince's popularity with the great mass of his people – which was consolidated when he nearly died of typhoid in 1871.

That popularity was not at all lessened by the occasionally scurrilous references to him in the press (which, in this, was harking back to an earlier, rougher tradition). There was a broadsheet that read:

> This lady's appetite
> It really is enormous,
> But whether right or wrong,
> The papers will inform us.
> She is fond of veal and ham,
> To feed she is a glutton.
> She got tired of Charley's lamb,
> And longed for royal mutton.

10

Mr Morris as Tenant

THE MORDAUNT DIVORCE CASE had evoked a great deal of publicity, and the fact that Lewis had been called on to offer advice to the Prince was more significant than either he or Elizabeth could have appreciated at the time.

Elizabeth would not have been surprised that the Prince of Wales wished to consult her husband professionally – to her, George was, quite obviously, the best lawyer alive – but, as a German Jewess by birth, keenly aware of anti-semitic feelings in her native land, this must have confirmed for her the fact that England was indeed the most liberal country in Europe: the best place to live. But even Elizabeth could not foresee Lewis's future relationship with Edward as Prince of Wales and, later, as King.

Nothing, in 1870, could have promised such a friendship. As Edward's sometime mistress Lady Warwick said of the Prince's entourage, 'As a class we did not like brains,' going on to add that, 'we acknowledged that pictures should be painted, books written, the law administered; we even acknowledged that there was a certain stratum whose job it might be to do these things.' She implies that the Prince and his circle did not want much contact with that 'stratum', but Lewis was to overcome the disabilities of both his brains and his profession.

Lewis was more than ever a family man now. His daughter Gertrude Rachel was born early in 1871. In years to come it would be said of her that she inherited her mother's beauty but not her temperament – quiet and gentle, she lacked Elizabeth's ebullient, positive attitude to life. Now of course she was simply a baby in a cradle, a source of great wonder and happiness to her sister Alice, who was now six years old.

Lewis's father took a particular delight in his grandchildren. A widower now, living alone in his house at Euston Square, he remained as cheerful as ever, his sardonic optimism unclouded by age, still playing his role of Mr Jaggers to the 'professionals', who now formed only a small section of Lewis and Lewis's clientele. Although effective command at the firm had already been transferred from father to son – a process gently accomplished over a number of years, with neither party to the transaction actually mentioning it – James Lewis continued to work his usual hours, coming to his office in Ely Place every morning at ten.

In late 1872 occurred what Lewis always described as the 'most ingenious' crime he had encountered in his long career, a crime that was totally successful in that its objectives were achieved and its perpetrators never caught. Lewis's role was necessarily that of a spectator; but to his own children and to interviewers who asked him about the case in later years he always expressed a grudging admiration – a connoisseur's appreciation of the cunning and resolution displayed by the thieves.

Lewis represented a number of insurance companies, acting for them in the litigation that frequently arose regarding the settlement of claims. Among these companies was the Alliance Marine; and it was from their woebegone manager, a Mr Charlton, that Lewis heard about the clever theft that had taken place in Hatton Garden, the next street to Ely Place.

Then as now, Hatton Garden was the centre of the diamond business; and the Alliance Marine Insurance Co., among its other interests, gave cover to many diamond merchants. This could be an undertaking attended with some doubt and difficulty, mainly because (in the words of the *Police Encyclopedia*), 'dealers in precious stones do not seem to exercise that vigilance in protecting their costly wares that one would expect under the circumstances'. Whoever planned the Hatton Garden robbery must have been at one with the *Encyclopedia* in noting this over-casual attitude – and acted accordingly.

One of the merchants insured with the Alliance Marine was a man called Ruben Spyzer, based in Amsterdam. He made fairly frequent visits to London, usually for the purpose of selling rough stones. When Lewis met Spyzer, after the robbery, he was able to establish that although Spyzer thought of his visits to London as casual and unplanned they in fact conformed to a consistent and indeed predictable pattern. Lewis discovered this by getting Spyzer's office staff to check back on the recorded dates of his London selling trips.

The gang who perpetrated the Hatton Garden robbery knew all about Spyzer; had observed his comings and goings; where he stayed; where he had his meals; with whom he did business. This was the aspect of the robbery that impressed Lewis most: the meticulous staff-work done months in advance. That – and the masterly simplicity of the whole plan.

Having worked out the date of Spyzer's next selling trip with the exactitude of an astronomer plotting the date of a forthcoming eclipse of the sun, the gang were ready to move into the second phase of the operation. About a week before Spyzer was due to arrive, a man giving his name as 'Frank Morris' rented an office on the first floor of 70 Hatton Garden, above a jeweller's shop. He was described as a 'gentlemanly man', well dressed and about forty-five years old. He gave his business as 'diamond merchant', not of course unusual in Hatton Garden which was then tenanted almost exclusively by diamond dealers and wholesale jewellers.

Mr Morris took possession the same day and about an hour later a van drove up to number 70. Some basic office furniture was unloaded – a table, an armchair, some smaller chairs, some deed boxes, a thick pile carpet, a roll-top desk, and (more unusual) a folding screen.

This furniture was taken out of the van and arranged in the office on the first floor. (With hindsight, it was easy for Lewis to see the purpose of the thick-pile carpet – perhaps unusually luxurious for the average office: footsteps could not be heard in the jeweller's shop below.) The deed boxes were arranged conspicuously against the wall; the roll-top desk in one corner; the folding screen up-ended by the fireplace, which it partly concealed. The armchair was placed with its back towards the screen.

The stage was set. Now Mr Morris had to 'establish' his character as a diamond merchant, rather as an actor establishes a character in a play. He had his name painted among the other names at the door of number 70, and also inside, on the panelling of the wall of the staircase. Letters arrived for him, which were seen to be addressed to 'Mr Frank Morris, Diamond Merchant, 70 Hatton Garden'. Messengers were seen coming and going: they carried small paper parcels in their hands, and Hatton Garden habitués knew that samples of rough stones were usually carried about in small paper parcels. In so far as anyone observed Mr Morris, he appeared to be a diamond dealer in a modest way of business; there was no reason to suppose he would not still be a tenant at 70 Hatton Garden ten years hence.

Now the third phase of the plan began. Spyzer duly arrived from Amsterdam exactly a week after Mr Morris moved into his office, as the gang had expected.

The morning after he arrived, Spyzer was sitting at a table in a café in Hatton Garden much frequented by diamond merchants – indeed, a good deal of business was transacted there. Spyzer had often done deals there in the past. He was drinking a cup of coffee and smoking a cigarette, turning over one or two prospective clients in his mind, when a gentlemanly man of about forty-five approached the table. The café was rather full; would there be any objection if he took the seat facing Spyzer? Of course not; he would be most welcome, Spyzer said.

The gentlemanly man clearly knew a good deal about diamonds. He was quite a connoisseur in fact, and Spyzer warmed to him. Like most dealers in precious stones, Spyzer had a genuine passion for the gems themselves. So he was soon lost in talk with the newcomer who informed him that he had recently purchased some really fine stones. This naturally caught Spyzer's attention: after all, he was here to sell some particularly good uncut diamonds. He mentioned this to his new friend, who expressed great interest.

'I have to tell you one thing, though,' the gentlemanly man said. 'Any stones I buy have to be of the finest quality.'

Spyzer's answer was to take a diamond from the leather bag beside him and hand it to his companion. The man studied it with an obviously professional eye. He did not say anything but produced a magnifying glass from his pocket and continued to examine the stone with that. Then, at last, he pronounced himself satisfied. 'That would be in my line of business all right,' he said.

After some further discussion, the man suggested that they meet again with a view to his making a large purchase of diamonds from Mr Spyzer. Why didn't Spyzer come to his office, bringing with him a parcel of his best stones?

Spyzer was delighted at the prospect of getting rid of his latest consignment in a single transaction. He agreed to call at his friend's office, bringing all the stones he had. Thursday, at 4 p.m.? Delighted.

Before they parted, the man handed Spyzer his card. It read: FRANK MORRIS, DIAMOND MERCHANT, 70 HATTON GARDEN.

The next Thursday, around four o'clock, Spyzer walked along

Hatton Garden and turned into number 70. He saw the name 'Frank Morris' on the stairwell and again on the glass door of the office on the first floor.

He knocked on the door and Mr Morris opened it and asked him to come in. Spyzer entered. Morris was smiling pleasantly; he asked Spyzer to sit down. (Spyzer was afterwards to say that this looked like any other office in Hatton Garden. He saw nothing to arouse his suspicions.)

A man sat at the table, writing letters. Morris's clerk, no doubt. Spyzer sat down opposite him, in the armchair which was placed with its back to the screen that blocked the fireplace. Then he began to unbuckle the leather wallet in which he had placed his diamonds.

He had unbuckled the wallet when he heard a rustling sound behind him. He half turned – to receive a blow on the head which sent him reeling back over the table. The screen in front of the fireplace had been pushed aside, and a man stood there. Dazed and terrified, Spyzer struggled to his feet, only to receive another, more violent, blow on the forehead. In great pain, blinded by the blood that was dripping down into his eyes, he felt a hand clapped tightly over his mouth and nose. This was – he learnt later – a chloroformed pad being applied.

Spyzer lost consciousness. When he came round, he found he was alone in the office. Going to the door, he discovered it locked, so he put his fist through the glass and managed to open it. His face was badly battered; his hair was matted with blood; his clothes, too, were torn and bloodied. The wallet of diamonds had been taken.

Stumbling down into the jeweller's shop, Spyzer told the jeweller's assistants what had happened. They sent for a doctor and the police.

A number of detectives arrived from Scotland Yard, headed by Inspector Leech, but by this time Mr Morris and his confrères had a good start. The police had little to go on, other than a description of 'Mr Morris' that would have fitted thousands of middle-aged men. The office at 70 Hatton Garden yielded no clues. The office furniture was there – the props in the play Morris and his gang had enacted – just as it had been delivered a week before.

The diamonds in Spyzer's wallet would have been readily identifiable had they been cut stones, but they were rough. A list of them was published in the police journal, *Hue and Cry*, but little was expected from this, and in fact the stones were never recovered. Nor was anything ever heard of Mr Morris and his gang. The usual watch was kept on the ports, because it was thought likely that they had gone to Amsterdam to dispose of the stones. If they did go there, they managed to slip out of the country unnoticed.

The unfortunate Spyzer's chagrin was matched by that of his insurers, the Alliance Marine. While they wanted to meet their commitment to Spyzer, the directors of the company cherished certain doubts. The whole robbery had an air of smoothly run clockwork about it: a lack of spontaneity. Had it really happened the way Spyzer told it? Everything fitted in so well – a bit too well, the directors thought. The diamonds he had brought to London were uncut and therefore untraceable. And the gang's knowledge of his movements had been so precise that Morris was able to intercept him while he sat drinking coffee at a certain time in a certain café. Was it possible that any group of criminals would devote such time and trouble, display such expertise, in setting up one diamond merchant on a visit from Amsterdam?

It was at this point that Alliance Marine's manager, Tom Charlton, invoked Lewis. He wanted him to meet Spyzer and tactfully question him about the circumstances of the robbery. There would be no question raised about payment on the claim – unless Lewis found some flaw in Spyzer's story.

The most obvious flaw would be some sign that the diamond merchant had himself been an accomplice in the plot. That is, that Spyzer had conspired with Morris and the others in letting himself be set up and robbed, with a view to claiming from his insurers a sum far in excess of the real worth of the 'stolen' diamonds. This excess would then, of course, be shared between Spyzer, Morris, and the rest.

Spyzer came to see Lewis at Ely Place. The insurance company had told him they wished him to call on their solicitor as a formality before they dealt with his claim.

Spyzer impressed Lewis as a truthful witness. He was clearly still suffering from the effects of the attack, but he told his story coherently, and the enquiries Lewis had already instituted in Amsterdam confirmed his reputation as an honest trader, a man of integrity. Certainly he appeared to have no links with the seamy, quasi-criminal side of the diamond business. As to the stones being uncut and therefore untraceable – well, he always sold uncut stones on his visits to London.

Lewis questioned Spyzer thoroughly, making sure that the merchant did not feel that his word was being doubted or that he was under suspicion. Lewis concluded that Spyzer had been selected by the gang as an ideal mark. He came to London at regular, predictable intervals; he was a man of clockwork regularity in his habits – always going to the same hotel, same cafés, coming to the 'Garden' at the same time each day; and he always carried a large quantity of uncut stones, worth many thousands of pounds, which made a single coup worth all the expensive waiting and planning.

So Lewis had no alternative but to advise Alliance Marine to pay up. When anyone disagreed with his description of the Hatton Garden robbery as the 'most ingenious crime' – what, after all, was so remarkable about just luring a man into an office and hitting him over the head? – he would reply, 'The logic! The planning! The patience displayed!'

If Edward and Georgiana Burne-Jones were the Lewises' closest friends, Henry Labouchere and Henrietta Hodson were the liveliest, the most unpredictable. And of course they provided a link with the theatre – and the theatre was in Lewis's blood. By this time, indeed, Lewis and Elizabeth were indefatigable first-nighters. They were to be indispensable figures at every important première for the next forty years. Pinero, Gilbert and Sullivan (after their famous quarrel they had to visit the Lewises on different nights), Wilde, Barrie – they all expected to see George and Elizabeth sitting in the stalls when the curtain went up for the first time.

Perhaps the most amusing first night the Lewises ever attended was that of *The Last Days of Pompeii*, which Labouchere put on for Henrietta Hodson at the Queen's Theatre in Long Acre. It opened in January 1872 and in the foyer Lewis introduced Elizabeth to a young barrister called Edward Clarke, who was soon to be briefed by Lewis and Lewis in several cases of great importance to both him and the firm.

As soon as the curtain went up, it was clear that Labouchere had spared no money on this production. The backdrops depicting ancient Rome were well designed, even impressive. There was a large cast, and the first part of the play went very well. But then things began to go wrong. The curtain rose on a scene set inside a Pompeiian villa. At the back of the stage was a lofty doorway; across it stretched a slackened cord. For some time the scene went on: a banquet was in progress and guests were lolling, Roman-fashion, as they ate. Then suddenly and inexplicably, a man appeared on a cord stretched across the back of the stage. Assuming the stance of a tightrope walker, he took a few steps along the cord, striving to maintain his balance, then caught his pole in the scenery and came crashing down.

The audience roared with laughter – and from behind the scenes could be heard a voice, presumably that of the stage manager, shouting abuse.

Almost immediately the man was out on the cord again. He took a few steps, smiling and bowing to the audience. Then he came crashing down for the second time. He ran off the stage and did not reappear.

By this time the audience were in no mood to take anything seriously and when an actress uttered the line – whether in the course of her part or out of sheer mischief was never clear – 'He is indeed a wonderful performer', the house disintegrated into uproar. The cast entered into the spirit of the thing and what had been intended as a vehicle for Henrietta Hodson's beauty and talent became a frenzied burlesque. The author – and Labouchere – had certainly provided a feast of material: gladiators, Christians facing lions in the arena; the eruption of Vesuvius. Even by Victorian standards it was a night of excess.

Henrietta Hodson was in tears, but before the Lewises left – embarrassed for their hosts but still inwardly quaking with laughter – they realized that no one had enjoyed the evening more than Labouchere himself.

11

Between Liphook and London Bridge

One cold morning in January 1873, Lewis's father, James Graham Lewis, arrived at Ely Place at his usual time, just after ten o'clock. He went into his office and started work immediately – a slight departure from routine, as it was his habit to go into Lewis's office and chat for a few minutes before his son became totally submerged in the work of the day. This morning Lewis was not even aware that his father had arrived until he got a message from a clerk, asking him to drop down and see Mr Lewis Senior.

When Lewis entered the room, his father greeted him as usual and apologized for not coming up to say good morning. He didn't actually feel very well. Lewis expressed concern. His father never complained of anything, although he had been suffering from rheumatism during recent months.

'I'm going home,' James Lewis said. 'No – don't worry. Don't fuss about it. I'll get a cab home.'

Lewis said he would accompany his father. It wouldn't take long to Euston Square. He would see him home and then wait till the doctor arrived.

'Nonsense. No doctor,' the old man said. 'No need for you to come with me. I shall be all right.'

Later, Lewis thought he should have ignored his father's objections and insisted on accompanying him home. As it was, Lewis's clerk called a cab and James Lewis went off in it.

When he arrived at his house, the old man went up to his bedroom. He rang for a servant, a middle-aged woman called Higgins, and asked her to run a bath for him. While the bath was running he lay on his bed, fully clothed, his eyes closed.

When Higgins returned and told him the bath was full, he asked what the temperature of the water was. She went away and tested it with a thermometer and came back with the answer: 70 degrees. 'Not hot enough,' James Lewis murmured. 'Raise it . . . At least another 10 degrees.'

Higgins went away again and when the thermometer registered 80 degrees she returned and told her master. He did not appear to hear her. He seemed to be asleep, lying on his back, his expression peaceful. He was dead.

Lewis, of course, was shocked by the suddenness of his father's death. James Lewis had been in his seventieth year; unlike his wife, he had always had such good health that his son had somehow expected him to live to a great age. Now he was gone. He would live on for a little in his children's hearts; in the gratitude of the hundreds of often wretched people he helped without hope of reward; most strangely, perhaps, in English literature as the reality behind Mr Jaggers.

Now Lewis was virtually alone in the practice. Uncle George still went to his office upstairs, but his work load was much lightened: anything of importance came to Lewis. Fortunately, his energy seemed boundless. The more he demanded of himself, the more he was able to do.

It was said around this time that few of the Prince of Wales's circle escaped trouble of one kind or another. Not surprisingly, perhaps, for many of them had the reputation of being arrogant coxcombs, spendthrift gamblers, or insatiable lechers.

The member of the Marlborough House set who stood in the dock at Guildford police court in July 1875 was none of those things. He was – at a time when the description still meant something – an officer and a gentleman.

Colonel Valentine Baker was a professional soldier. He had served in the Crimean War and the Kaffir War. He had been made a colonel at the age of thirty. He commanded the Tenth Hussars – the Prince's own regiment – and he was a personal friend of the Prince. There was a touch of Buchan's Sandy Arbuthnot about him: he was an Orientalist who had travelled widely in Persia and then written a book on his journeys. To top it all, he had a rich wife.

On a sunny afternoon in June 1875 he stood on the railway platform at Liphook, in Surrey, waiting for the London-bound train. The train arrived and he got into a first-class carriage.

An attractive girl of twenty-two, Miss Rebecca Kate Dickinson, was already in the carriage. She and Colonel Baker were strangers to each other, but after a few minutes they began to chat. Baker was a handsome man of fifty, educated and well-bred. Miss Dickinson presumably felt there was no need to rebuff his conventional pleasantries, and responded with polite small talk. They chatted away as the train sped on. Then she noticed a change in the colonel's manner. They passed Woking, the last stop before London. Now the colonel was suggesting that, after they had arrived at their destination and parted, they should somehow keep in touch. Correspond perhaps? By now she could see he was getting (as she later put it) 'excited'.

'Of course not,' she said. 'What an extraordinary idea.'

Then, according to Miss Dickinson, the colonel jumped across the carriage, sat down beside her and grabbed her by the waist. He started to kiss her, repeatedly. She screamed, but it was useless. This was not a corridor-train. And she could not reach the communication cord.

She managed to struggle to her feet and broke free. Desperate with terror, she put her hand through the open window of the carriage, grabbed the door handle and managed to turn it. The door swung open, with the colonel hanging on to Miss Dickinson to prevent her falling out. She was screaming loudly and the colonel told her, 'If you get in, I will get out by the other door. Then everything will be all right.'

But she stayed where she was, screaming. A platelayer working on the track saw her and the train was signalled to stop. When it did, Miss Dickinson fell off the footboard and collapsed on the line. The guard came up to see what had happened. According to the evidence the guard gave later, the colonel was heard to say, 'Don't tell the guard anything. If you do, you don't know what trouble you'll get me into. Just tell him you were frightened.'

The guard ordered Colonel Baker into a carriage occupied by two male passengers; then he locked the door. He put Miss Dickinson into the charge of a clergyman. Then, when the train reached London, Colonel Baker had to give his name and address to the railway authorities. That night he went back to his regiment at Aldershot. The next day he was arrested by the Surrey police on a charge of indecent assault.

The Prince of Wales was appalled when he heard of Baker's arrest. Inevitably, he asked Lewis to act for the colonel.

The case attracted enormous public attention. There was considerable sympathy for Colonel Baker, not only because most people saw this as a sudden tragic aberration on the part of a distinguished man, but also because there was a good deal of doubt about Miss Dickinson's story. Not so much the question of her giving the colonel any encouragement – the 'she led me on' defence that confused cases of this kind, then as now – but the extent to which the whole incident could be a projection of Rebecca Dickinson's own hysteria or frustration. (And of course the account already given of the events in the railway carriage is her version, which Colonel Baker neither confirmed nor denied.) Miss Dickinson's terror had been real enough – but had the colonel's behaviour been such as to inspire terror on that scale? Who *was* this Miss Dickinson, anyway?

Unfortunately for the colonel, she was 'respectable'. This drama would have been less of a tragedy – more likely outright farce – if this had been a third-class carriage and (to choose appropriate nineteenth-century stereotypes) the colonel a pork butcher and Miss Dickinson a little dressmaker. This was how this sort of person behaved and who could know the truth of the matter? But Miss Dickinson had one brother a doctor, another a lawyer, and a third a subaltern in a line regiment. She therefore had to be taken seriously.

Lewis suggested an apology, and the colonel offered one: 'If I have caused Miss Dickinson annoyance I beg to express my most unqualified regret. Still I solemnly declare that what she has told you has been under the influence of exaggerated fear and alarm.'

That would not do. Miss Dickinson wanted revenge. She was determined to press charges. From the police court at Guildford, Baker was remanded to the summer assizes at Croydon on 30 July.

Lewis had briefed Serjeant Ballantine for the defence.

His junior was Henry Hawkins, later the famous 'hanging judge'. But Colonel Baker effectively tied the hands of those defending him: he refused to allow his counsel to cross-examine Miss Dickinson or to pursue any line of defence that might be thought in the least critical of her. So, at his own insistence her damaging testimony against him – to say nothing of the evidence of the other passengers, her screams, and the spectacle of her clinging to the carriage-door – all went unanswered. Hawkins called the colonel's attitude 'Quixotic' and wrote many years later:

> As a gentleman and a British officer, he preferred to take on himself the ruin of his own character, the forfeiture of his commission in the army, the loss of his social status and all

> that made life worth living to casting even a doubt on the lady's veracity in the witness-box.

Their tongues thus tied in advance, Ballantine and Hawkins could only suggest that Miss Dickinson's account was too 'highly coloured' and that she had tragically misunderstood the colonel's intentions.

The jury took ten minutes to find Colonel Baker guilty. Before sentencing him, Mr Justice Brett seized the opportunity to pontificate on the subject of kissing: 'Some kisses are entirely proper. Thus the kiss of a daughter by her father is a holy one and the kiss exchanged among a playful assembly of young people may be perfectly harmless. But a kiss that gratifies or excites passion is undoubtedly indecent.'

He then gave the colonel twelve months' imprisonment, fining him £500, and making him pay the total costs of the case.

Jailed and ruined, Baker asked to be allowed to resign his commission. The Prince of Wales and the Duke of Cambridge (commander in chief of the army and the Queen's cousin) tried to persuade Queen Victoria to accept this. Unyielding as usual, Victoria refused, insisting that the unfortunate Baker go through the savage pageantry of being brought from jail, paraded before the regiment he had once commanded and, standing on the square, to the beat of muffled drums, stripped of all the insignia of rank: an exercise in calculated humiliation that certainly gratified the Queen. She had always disliked Colonel Baker – his friendship with her son was calculated to arouse her animus – now he could be excluded from English society altogether.

Baker served his time and, after his release, joined the Turkish army. (They were delighted to have a soldier of such proven courage and experience.) He commanded a division against the Russians; then, as Baker Pasha, he commanded the Egyptian gendarmerie – Egypt was then part of the Turkish empire. Later, when the British invaded Egypt and the Egyptian army deserted to a man, the Prince of Wales tried to get Baker appointed commander in chief of the British army of occupation. Vindictive to the last, the Queen refused; and it was as Baker Pasha and not Colonel Baker that Valentine Baker died in Egypt in 1887.

It is tempting to see the fate of Colonel Baker as a kind of reversal of Mrs Borradaile's in the Madame Rachel trials (although Baker suffered much more: his humiliation was more lasting). While Mrs Borradaile had been derided and brought down for daring to cherish a fantasy about the ageing rake Lord Ranelagh, Baker – handsome, gallant, the very beau ideal of a British officer – was crucified for some kind of indiscreet behaviour towards a young woman whose character and mentality (thanks to the colonel's selfless delicacy) must remain a mystery. Clearly the colonel did or said something to alarm her, but why the absolute frenzy of terror? One can only speculate about the state of mind that could produce such a violent reaction. Little is known of Miss Dickinson's subsequent life, except that she never married, had no friends, and never worked. She lived, however, to a ripe old age.

12

The Torturer

1876 WAS AN EVENTFUL YEAR for the Lewises. This was the year they left Taviton Street and took a long lease of 88 Portland Place. It was also the year that Lewis became famous. He had been well known, successful, for a long time, but fame – solid, indisputable fame – came to him in 1876.

The move from Taviton Street had been inevitable for some years. They could have found a suitable house in Kensington or Belgravia, but Elizabeth preferred to wait for one in central London. Now she had what she wanted – an appropriate base for Lewis's ever-advancing professional career and her own ever-burgeoning social success.

It took Elizabeth some time to get the house right. From the first she had seen its great potential and was determined to develop it to the full. She had been particularly delighted by the huge dining-room. It deserved – it demanded – a ceiling to match its noble proportions; and the ceiling designed by Basil Champneys (a friend and neighbour of the George du Mauriers at Hampstead, who had introduced him to the Lewises) was of appropriate grandeur.

Over the next thirty years this house was to be thronged with painters, sculptors, musicians, actors, writers, lawyers, politicians – indeed, from at least the 1880s almost to the time of Lewis's retirement shortly before his death, to be invited to 'Lady Lewis's' was to enter a social milieu at once fluid and eclectic. If you had talent – for almost anything – it would be noticed here (had, in fact, already been noticed by Elizabeth Lewis or you would not have been invited). Her entertaining was free from the obsession with rank that often lays a dead hand on 'Society'; at the same time, Lewis's friendship with the Prince and with figures from the wider scene of finance and politics saved the Lewises' parties from the bitchery and narcissism that attends the social life of 'artists.' At Portland Place one had the best of both worlds. Here the establishment and Bohemia had to embrace – because Elizabeth told them to.

She was not, of course, 'Lady Lewis' when she came to Portland Place. Lewis would not be knighted for another sixteen years. But life itself seems to have ennobled her in advance of the official accolade. If the young and beautiful hostess already carried a hint of the *grande dame* she would one day become, then her own lively sense of humour would take care of that.

The guests who came to 88 Portland Place that first year were few in comparison with the numbers that would come later; but they still represented a distinguished sampling of London life. The du Maurier's came. George du Maurier was just settling down to the long years as a *Punch* illustrator; he would write his bestseller *Trilby* only at the very end of his life. James McNeill Whistler (whom du Maurier disliked) came. He was painting brilliantly, but already hard-up and embroiled in his strange relationship with his patrons the Leylands that would culminate in the Peacock Room and his bankruptcy. George Washburn Smalley and his wife came. Smalley was the London correspondent of the New York *Tribune*: a friend of Henry James and an ubiquitous figure in the memoirs of the time. He was to write several pieces on Lewis almost gushing in their appreciation. W. S. Gilbert and Arthur Sullivan came, accompanied by that shrewd midwife of their joint talent, Richard D'Oyly Carte. Here social life began to merge with business for, at the time the Lewises moved to Portland Place, Carte was floating the Comedy Opera Company, with the express intention of putting on works by Gilbert and Sullivan; and Lewis was handling the legal aspects of the venture – a venture involving three very different men: the irascible Gilbert, the gentle, melancholy Sullivan, and the shrewdly twinkling Carte. And, like Carte, Henry Labouchere – most volatile of the Lewises' friends – was that year entering into the project that would forever be associated with him: he was planning his weekly *Truth*, which would first appear in January of the following year.

Hardly of this company, because so much closer to their hosts, were Edward and Georgiana Burne-Jones. Burne-Jones was still relatively obscure, depending largely on sales of his paintings to a single collector, William Graham. But like Lewis himself, he stood on the brink of a larger fame: his highly acclaimed exhibition would take place at the Grosvenor Galleries the following year, establishing him as the peer of Millais and Holman Hunt.

1876, then, was memorable for lifting the curtain at 88 Portland Place; and for enshrining within the Lewises' new home the essence of their next thirty years.

Lewis's involvement in the case that was to make him famous began on 1 May 1876 when a Mr Joseph Bravo called at Ely Place. Mr Bravo was an elderly man of mixed blood – he had been born in Jamaica of negro–Jewish parents; and a newspaper later described him as 'having moist, thick-lidded eyes, old-fashioned Dundreary whiskers, and a coffee-coloured skin'. The name 'Bravo' was familiar to Lewis from the press reports. This man's stepson, a young barrister called Charles Bravo, had died under rather strange circumstances and the case had been widely reported. As Lewis and Lewis were pre-eminent in all criminal business, it had only been a matter of time before one or other of the parties came to Ely Place in order to retain the services of the firm.

We do not know what Joseph Bravo said to Lewis. We do know that Charles Bravo had died on 21 April 1876 and that an inquest had taken place on 25 April. The inquest had not only failed in its purpose – that of eliciting the truth; it had also blown up a black cloud of suspicion around the unfortunate Bravo's death.

The death of Charles Bravo – often called 'The Balham Mystery' – lacked no theatrical element to make it the *cause célèbre* it turned out to be. For once, at least, the cast of characters deserved the publicity they enjoyed.

Throughout the case everyone's attention was focused on the dead man's widow, Florence Bravo. She was young, rich, and beautiful. Born in 1845, the daughter of a rich landowner called Robert Campbell, Florence came from a background where maids and valets, a tutor and a governess were expected, routine appendages.

A husband – appropriately wealthy and well placed – had to be found for Florence Campbell. The matrimonial machine duly furnished one: Captain Alexander Ricardo, grandson of David Ricardo, the political economist. At the time of their marriage he was twenty-one, Florence nineteen. Love was buttressed by a substantial marriage settlement. The bridegroom gave Florence a life interest in £40,000; her father one of £20,000. The Bishop of Oxford married the young Ricardos; and a honeymoon on the Rhine – Lewis's own favourite venue for holidays – was followed by a stay in Norfolk. But Ricardo liked London and they soon went back there.

By this time it was evident that young Ricardo was not just a heavy drinker – fairly usual for a young man of his class and background – but an alcoholic hell-bent on destroying himself. Within a year he had suffered his first attack of delirium tremens. Between these alcoholic bouts of his the young couple appeared happy enough – indeed, Florence said they were happy – but the bouts got more and more frequent. After five miserable years Florence, desperate, turned to her mother for advice.

Mrs Campbell's advice was to go to Malvern and see Dr Gully.

For the last twenty years people had been flocking from all over England to consult this remarkable man. Today, Dr Gully would be described as a medical hypnotist. His cures were legendary and it was hoped he might be able to help Captain Ricardo. Florence took her husband to Malvern and they rented a furnished house there.

Dr Gully did his best. At first the treatment had some success, but after a while Ricardo was drinking as much as ever. Delirium tremens started again.

But, if Dr Gully could do little for the husband, his effect on the wife was profound. A friendship of extraordinary intensity sprang up between Florence and the sixty-two-year-old physician. One cannot help feeling that the dreary, alcoholic Ricardo got pushed into the background: Gully and Florence had eyes only for each other. Florence was fascinated by the doctor – rotund, authoritative, but with the gift of making any woman feel that she, and only she, was beautiful enough and intelligent enough to capture his heart.

Meanwhile, Ricardo's health deteriorated fast. His behaviour became so impossible that Florence left him, vowing she would seek a legal separation. Her parents supported her; her mother took her to the family estate at Buscot in Oxfordshire. Not long afterwards, Ricardo succumbed to a final attack of delirium tremens. Florence was a widow: she was free.

Free, of course, to marry Dr Gully; and there is no doubt that, if Florence had married him, her story might have ended happily. Unfortunately the doctor had a wife still living, though he was separated from her.

When Lewis first heard the story it was at once apparent to him that the most important person in Florence's life was not her first husband, Captain Ricardo, nor even her second husband, Charles Bravo, but Dr Gully.

Who was he? What was the secret of his power, particularly his power over women?

Born in 1808 in Jamaica, of wealthy planter stock, he had been educated in Edinburgh and in Paris and was a pioneer of homeopathy and hydropathy. Selecting Malvern as a British equivalent of the great continental spas, he had set about developing it. With great success, for within a few years 'everyone' was going to Malvern: Tennyson, Thomas Carlyle, Bishop Wilberforce, Charles Dickens – all undergoing the ritual of the spa with its diets and douches, sulphur baths, and wet sheets wrapped around the sufferer taking the cure. By the time Florence met him, the doctor had added hypnotism to hydropathy.

Certainly Dr Gully had the power to fascinate, to dominate. He has still aroused enthusiastic championship a century after his death; he merits an entry in the *Dictionary of National Biography*. It has been claimed that he saved the life of Florence Nightingale when she underwent a course of treatment at Malvern in 1857.

With Ricardo dead, Florence was a rich woman in her own right. The £40,000 settled on her at her marriage became hers absolutely, and this made her parents all the more concerned when she appeared to be totally under the influence of Dr Gully. They brought pressure on her to give him up. Florence refused. Estranged from her family, she spent some months at Malvern (which Dr Gully was about to leave), and then took a house in Streatham directly opposite one rented by Dr Gully.

And now Florence acquired a lady-companion, once described by Thackeray as 'an article as necessary to a lady as her brougham or her bouquet'. Florence's companion was called Jane Cannon Cox. Born, like Dr Gully, in Jamaica, Mrs Cox was described as of 'mixed French and Asian blood, with coarse black hair and skin the colour of old ivory stretched over high cheekbones'. She was in her early thirties when she first met Florence Bravo. Like her, she was a widow, but with three sons and very little money with which to educate them. She managed to get the boys into a private charity school, but life was a struggle; she was delighted to find herself a resident of Florence's luxurious home in Streatham.

By this time, Florence and Dr Gully were – by her own admission – lovers. In 1873 they went together to the German spa, Kissingen, in Bavaria. Some weeks after they returned, Florence realized that she was pregnant. In November she had a miscarriage, presumably induced by Dr Gully. After that, all physical intimacies ceased between them, although they still remained close friends. Dr Gully took a house in Balham in South London and, clearly still under a compulsion to be near him, Florence bought an impressive, Gothic-style mansion called the Priory closeby. There she took up residence with Mrs Cox, who soon afterwards introduced her to two people who were to become her implacable enemies: Joseph Bravo and his wife Mary.

Mrs Cox knew Joseph Bravo through some business transactions that had passed between them. He professed to be her benefactor, but the impression emerges that benevolence was not much in Joseph Bravo's line: he must have profited in some way. What is not in doubt is that both Joseph Bravo and his wife were intrigued by this beautiful – and so rich! – young widow living alone at the Priory.

Joseph Bravo was rich himself. He had made a fortune in his native West Indies, and now he lived at 2 Palace Green, Kensington (previously Thackeray's house and later the Israeli embassy). But, whatever his motive, he wanted his stepson Charles to meet the young widow.

Charles Bravo was described as fat and 'effete-looking'; his mother was an Englishwoman, a widow, who had married the rich mulatto, Joseph Bravo, after her first husband's death. This first husband, Charles's father, was said to have been English too; but nothing was known about him and Charles had taken his step-father's surname. Joseph appears to have been fond of Charles, but to have enjoyed a kind of cat-and-mouse relationship with him in money matters (Charles depended on his stepfather: he was not yet making an adequate income at the bar). Joseph supported his stepson financially, but kept him short most of the time, making him sit up and beg when he, Joseph, felt like it.

He may have suggested to Charles that the rich young widow was worth cultivating; possibly Charles Bravo arrived at that conclusion himself. In any case, very soon after they first met, Charles was pursuing Florence relentlessly, subjecting her to that obsessive, round-the-clock wooing some women find irresistible. Like her, he was just over thirty, and, although he had none of Dr Gully's charisma, he was suave and self-assured, a sharp young barrister on his way up.

It is hard to avoid the impression that, despite the intelligence attributed to her by her friends, Florence was impressionable, almost naive. Hardly out of the aura of Dr Gully, she seems to have fallen at once under the influence of Charles Bravo. His whirlwind courtship succeeded quicker than he could possibly have hoped. Bravo's motives were depressingly clear. If he married Florence, he would escape from the financial domination of his disagreeable stepfather; he would be master of that fine house, the Priory; he would be in effective control of £40,000.

And money meant a great deal to Charles Bravo: everyone agrees on that. He is said to have been 'obsessed' with money, and moreover he had political ambitions. With Florence's money behind him, he could get into Parliament.

Clearly, Florence was attracted to Bravo; and no doubt, in courting her, he had presented himself in the most attractive light possible. Although he had no money of his own, he could offer Florence one thing she wanted: respectability. By Victorian standards and, one suspects, most acutely in her own eyes, Florence was a fallen woman. She had indulged in illicit sexual congress with Gully, a married man. She had allowed him to abort the child that had resulted from that criminal intercourse. She was besmirched, degraded. Any man, however humble, who married her would be extending the hand of forgiveness to a poor magdalen. And Charles Bravo was not any man. He was well educated, poised, a rising barrister.

Florence may well have thought along these lines, although she had not yet forgotten Dr Gully. How would he react if she married Bravo? She wrote, mentioning the possibility.

He reacted with shock and distress and immediately came to call on her. Her nerve failed her – perhaps she felt she might not be able to resist her elderly lover, even now? – and, avoiding a meeting, she wrote to him saying that their attachment had to be brought to an end.

Florence could see that Charles Bravo was about to propose to her, and now she suffered more qualms of conscience. How could she accept Charles's honourable proposal of marriage without revealing the hideous fact that she had been Dr Gully's mistress?

When Charles did propose, she accepted him. And then, almost immediately, told him of her affair with Gully.

With hindsight, it is possible to see that Charles Bravo reacted to the confession with his usual shrewdness. Florence, in her innocence, had offered him a dagger aimed at her heart. He did not use it – why should he? – but cherished it for future use, as required.

As Florence was later to testify:

'He said I had acted nobly and generously in telling him, and that he was still more certain from my having told him that I was still less likely to err again.'

"I am satisfied to make you my wife," he said, "but of course you must never see Dr Gully again."

'He made me swear a solemn oath that I would not divulge to any human being what I had told him.'

Florence was much relieved at Bravo's reaction. She was reassured, too, when Charles told her – as a kind of cosy *quid pro quo* – that he had been keeping a mistress who had given him a child. (No one ever knew where he got the money for this. In fact, at his death, Charles Bravo had financial resources that neither his stepfather nor anyone else could account for.) They made a mutual agreement: he would never mention Dr Gully to her; she would never mention mistress or child to him.

At this point Florence's companion, Mrs Cox, chose to involve herself in the matter of her employer's forthcoming marriage. A ruthless survivor, Mrs Cox probably judged this a good moment to switch allegiance from Florence to the new lord and master, Charles Bravo.

Mrs Cox knew all about Florence, Dr Gully, and the abortion. Without saying anything to Florence, she approached Charles Bravo. Would it not only be right and proper, she wanted to know, for him to tell his mother the whole truth about Florence and Dr Gully?

He replied that, if his mother were told, 'this marriage would not take place'.

Bravo and Mrs Cox understood each other perfectly. By keeping his mother ignorant of the fact that he was marrying a 'fallen woman', Charles retained the power to destroy Florence any time he chose. Mrs Cox knew she had to propitiate the husband, not the wife. Florence might have the money, but Charles was the master now.

Even before the marriage there were problems. Charles created a row over the marriage settlement. He demanded that all Florence's horses, carriages, and personal effects became his on the wedding day. When Florence's lawyer protested, Bravo said, 'I cannot bring myself to sit at a table or on a chair that does not belong to me.'

When told of this, Florence said, 'It looks as if you are marrying me for my money, not for myself.'

But she ignored all these warning signs and the marriage duly took place at All Saints, Ennismore Gardens, in Kensington. The newly married couple went to the Campbells' estate at Buscot for a few days; then they returned to the Priory, where, after a few weeks, gradually, steadily, things began to go wrong.

Bravo had dropped the mask of the attentive, sympathetic lover even before he got to the altar. Now he set in motion a cleverly devised, long-planned war of nerves.

His extraordinary meanness was a major weapon in this war. Up to her marriage Florence had run the Priory on gracious lines, with gardeners, a coachman, a groom; and, indoors, a butler, a footman, a lady's maid, two housemaids, a cook, and her companion Mrs Cox. From the wedding day onwards, Bravo nagged Florence about her 'extravagance' and the need for 'retrenchment'. It was useless her protesting that, after all, she *had* the money – more than enough for them to live as they pleased. Bravo went on nagging, and he even involved his mother and stepfather in the row, quoting 'Father Joseph' (his name for his stepfather) on the necessity of getting rid of the coach and horses.

It is not clear how much of this was genuine miserliness, how much part of a deliberate plan to break Florence down. If it was a plan, it was working. Her parents noticed that she was becoming addicted to large quantities of wine-and-water at all times of the day, and over a few months Florence's relationship with her husband and his parents deteriorated sharply. When she suffered a miscarriage, Charles was brutally unsympathetic. And – a sinister sign – he began to refer to Dr Gully (thus breaking the pact made before their marriage). When Florence went to St Leonard's for a day with her brother's wife, Augusta Campbell, Bravo jeered, 'Is Dr Gully going too?'

At last Florence could stand no more and fled to her parents' estate at Buscot. Charles Bravo realized he had gone too far. He turned on the charm again; started to woo her with letters decked out with flowery phrases. As he expected, this worked: the unfortunate Florence could never hold a grudge for long. By now she was pregnant again; she returned to him.

The date was 11 March 1876.

Things are moving towards a climax. There is Charles Bravo – crafty, obsessively mean, pursuing a carefully planned scheme of behaviour towards his wife, the real thrust of which will only become apparent after his death. There is Florence – rich and beautiful, but essentially credulous and weak, quite unable to stand up to the brutal Bravo: a born victim. There is Mrs Cox bent on looking after herself at any cost, who has already turned against Florence – although Florence has no inkling of this.

And on the periphery there are others. Dr Gully: old and wrinkled but still gallant and, one surmises, still in love with Florence, although now he can do nothing to save her. There is the repulsive 'Father Joseph' – Joseph Bravo – and his wife, Mary Hougham Bravo: hysterical and vindictive, still beside herself with anger that *any* woman could imagine herself good enough to marry her son Charles.

Around the middle of March, Charles told Mrs Cox that he had received several anonymous letters referring to Florence's affair with Dr Gully. He professed great indignation, but this must have been feigned because everything points to his having written the letters himself as part of the war of nerves against Florence.

She herself was again far from well. On 6 April she had another miscarriage, and, curiously, her husband did not call a doctor, although he was something of a hypochondriac himself.

During the Easter weekend Charles was in a particularly bad mood: irritable, restlessly moving from room to room about the house. On the night of Easter Monday he complained of neuralgia and told the head housemaid, Mary Keeber, that he was rubbing his gums with laudanum (this was important in view of what was soon to happen).

The Tuesday after Easter, 18 April, Charles and Florence drove up to London. They did some shopping – contriving to quarrel in the course of doing it, as they so often did – and parted, amicably enough by this time, for Charles to have lunch with the head of his chambers in the Temple. They made their separate ways back to Balham; she by her coach, he by train.

When Charles got back from London, in the afternoon, Florence was not feeling well and was resting on the sofa. When Charles arrived he remarked that he had had 'a jolly lunch'; he appeared to be in good form. He told Florence he would go out riding, and would take the worse of the two cobs: an ill-tempered beast called Cremorne.

The coachmen was in the stableyard when Charles came back. Charles climbed down from the saddle with difficulty. He looked pale and haggard and was in evident pain. He said the cob had bolted with him: 'I'm all of a shake.'

He went straight up to bed. A hip-bath of boiling water was brought up.

Later, he came down to dinner about half past seven. They had 'fish, roast lamb, and anchovy savoury'.

After dinner, around nine o'clock, Charles Bravo told Florence she ought to go to bed. Since Mary Keeber, the housemaid, was having her supper, Mrs Cox went up with Florence to act as lady's maid. At the foot of the stairs Florence paused and asked Mrs Cox to bring her up a little wine and water. Going into the dining-room, Mrs Cox half filled a small tumbler from a decanter of Marsala on the sideboard, added water, and took it upstairs.

About a quarter of an hour later, when Mary Keeber went up to Florence with a copper can of hot water, Florence held out the tumbler Mrs Cox had brought her, which was now empty, and asked Mary to bring her some more Marsala.

When she was getting the wine from the dining-room, Mary Keeber saw Charles Bravo come out of the morning-room opposite. He did not speak and she thought he looked pale and angry. She took the wine up to Florence. Then Mrs Cox told her to put out the two Skye terriers that were still in her mistress's bedroom. Mary had some difficulty persuading the dogs to leave the warmth of the bedroom and, as she was trying to get them downstairs, she saw Charles come out of his room. He was wearing his nightshirt. His face was grey and beaded with sweat and his voice rose to a scream: 'Hot water! Hot water!' Then he opened the window and leaned out of it, vomiting.

Mary Keeber ran to the kitchen and got the water. When she came back, Charles was sitting on the floor and Mrs Cox was massaging his chest. Then, on Mrs Cox's instructions, they tried to give him an emetic with mustard and water, but he could take very little of it. Soon afterwards he lost consciousness.

Mrs Cox told Mary Keeber to get some spirits of camphor from her (Mrs Cox's) bedroom. After running downstairs to tell Rowe, the butler, to fetch Dr Harrison from Streatham, Mrs Cox returned to Charles's room. Mary saw her continuing to massage his chest. Having looked for the camphor, Mary decided that Florence should be told what was happening. She went up and woke Florence, who at once ran in to see Charles.

She was appalled by what she saw. He was lying in his own vomit, soaked in sweat, his face greenish-grey and death-like. According to everyone who saw her (Mary and the other servants), Florence appeared distraught. Her unrestrained grief, in fact, contrasted very strongly with the cool, matter-of-fact demeanour of Mrs Cox.

Florence insisted that another doctor be sent for: a Dr Moore, who lived much nearer to the Priory than Dr Harrison. Florence then went back to Charles. The three women had to manoeuvre him into an armchair – he was too heavy for them to lift into bed.

Dr Moore was the first of the two doctors to arrive. He examined Bravo, but could find no symptoms of poison. Florence asked the doctor if he thought Charles would recover. He feared not, he said. 'Her grief seemed to me entirely natural,' the doctor said later.

Mrs Cox had little to say to Dr Moore. And yet, when she heard Dr Harrison arrive, she rushed downstairs to intercept him before he was half in the door, saying, 'Dr Harrison, I am sure he has taken chloroform!'

But neither doctor could find any trace of chloroform or anything else. They wondered if Bravo had suffered some kind of seizure.

Then, at 1.00 a.m., without regaining consciousness, Bravo vomited. Blood in the vomit suggested some irritant poison but, incredibly, the two doctors permitted the vomited matter to be thrown away. Nor – another blunder – did either of them think of examining the roof directly under the window through which Bravo had been sick. Two days later the slates were still seen to be covered with vomit – which might have provded indisputable evidence of the kind of poison he had taken, if indeed he *had* taken poison. As the *Lancet* put it: 'They [the two doctors] acted with a blatant disregard for all the rules of forensic medicine.'

Charles Bravo lingered on for two more days. Other doctors were called in. Never had there been so many medical experts invoked in a case of suspected poisoning – and never had a case been shrouded in so much rumour and doubt. A friend of Bravo's, a Mr Royes Bell, came from London; so did a Dr George Johnson from King's College Hospital. Throughout these visits Bravo (who had by now recovered consciousness) remained calm and self-possessed to an extraordinary extent, for he must have known he was facing death. When the doctors questioned him, he gave careful, controlled answers. When Dr Johnson asked him what he had taken, Bravo replied, 'I rubbed my gums with laudanum – I may have swallowed some.' Johnson said laudanum would not account for his symptoms. 'If it isn't laudanum I don't know what it is,' Bravo said.

Meanwhile Mrs Cox had taken Royes Bell aside. She said she had something important to tell him. He called the other doctors. She then said, 'When I answered Charlie's cry for help, he told me, 'I've taken some of the poison; don't tell Florence.'

Dr Harrison wanted to know why she hadn't told him that when he first arrived at the house. She said she had. He replied that she had spoken of *chloroform*.

Now he knew he was dying, Bravo's attitude to Florence seemed to have changed. Although she was exhausted, she stayed at his bed-side; and he acted more affectionately towards her than ever before. When she took his hand, he exclaimed, 'What a lot of trouble I'm giving you, Florrie . . . Kiss me. You've been the best of wives.'

'Oh, Charlie, Charlie,' she cried. 'What is the matter with you? What have you taken to make you so ill?'

He did not answer. Then he said he wanted to make a will. They fetched pen and paper and he did so, leaving all he had to Florence. The surgeon, Royes Bell, and the butler, Rowe, witnessed Charles's signature.

Over a period of more than twenty-four hours his condition appeared more or less stable. His mother and stepfather were sent for.

With the arrival of the elder Bravos the atmosphere changed. For Florence, the nightmare was rendered even more hideous by the hostility and suspicion they exuded. She had kept up a constant vigil at the dying man's bedside; now she was made to feel an intruder. With the Bravos came a grim-faced woman called Amelia Bushell (Mrs Bravo's personal maid for many years), who was stationed at the door of the sick-room like a prison warder.

By Thursday morning, everyone realized that Charles Bravo was on the point of death. For two days a strange stalemate had held in the master-bedroom at the Priory. Here was a man dying of a dose of some irritant poison who yet refused to admit he had taken poison at all; who stonewalled the questions of the doctors with talk of rubbing his gums with laudanum. And yet he was dying – and he knew it.

Desperate with grief, wounded by the smouldering hatred of Joseph Bravo and his wife, Florence sent for a man who was probably the most famous physician of his time, Sir William Gull. A diagnostician of genius, he had been made a baronet for identifying the typhoid that nearly killed the Prince of Wales in 1871.

On his arrival Sir William immediately ordered the vomit that was still lying on the slates to be taken up and analysed – something that had never occurred to the bevy of inferior doctors who had been in and out of the house for two days. Then he went up to the sick-room. Again, the bluntness of his approach contrasted with the equivocation of the other doctors.

'This is not disease. You are poisoned,' Sir William told Bravo. 'Pray tell us how you came by it.'

Later, Sir William was to say how amazed he was at Bravo's calm. 'It could only be the laudanum,' Bravo reiterated.

Sir William went over the ground already covered by the other doctors, but Bravo continued stonewalling; he kept repeating that he had only taken laudanum.

Then Dr Johnson uttered a warning that could have served as a prophecy: 'If you do not tell us more than we know at present, someone may be accused of being the cause of your death.'

'I am aware of that,' Bravo said, 'but I can tell you nothing more.'

Before he left the house, Sir William Gull had made a final appeal to the dying man: what poison had he taken?

'Before God, it was only laudanum,' Bravo insisted. 'Is there really no hope for me?' he asked. When Gull shook his head and told him he had not many hours to live, Bravo was silent. To Sir William, it appeared that Bravo was locked in a conflict – between his determination to keep his secret and his fear of death.

He was to hold that secret till the last. The whole family were assembled round his bed. He kissed Florence and his mother and bade everyone farewell. Weak as he was, he led them in the saying of the Lord's Prayer. Then, at 5.30 in the morning, he died.

After her husband's death Florence showed her usual talent for stage-managing events to her own disadvantage. She wrote a tactless letter to her already hostile father-in-law Joseph Bravo about Charles's belongings. And – a major error – she suggested that the inquest on her husband be held at the Priory itself.

This represented a departure from normal procedure large enough to arouse the curiosity of the press and the public. Rightly or wrongly, the impression was given that the coroner was wholly complaisant, ready to oblige the charming young widow in anything, and this was compounded by the fact that he did not choose to notify the press.

When it did take place, the inquest was conducted in a manner so perfunctory as to deepen the suspicions already burgeoning in several minds. The coroner did not even take proper notes. Dr Johnson, who had been in attendance when Bravo was dying, wanted to give evidence but the coroner cut him short. He had heard enough, he said. The verdict of this travesty of an inquest was at least written down: 'that the deceased died from the effects of a poison – antimony – but we have not sufficient evidence to show under what circumstances it came into his body'.

Antimony is a poison that crops up frequently in Victorian murder cases. It was used extensively in stables; it had the property of improving the glossiness and general condition of horses' coats.

If the way the inquest was conducted had been intended to avoid publicity, the reverse had been achieved. The dead man's friends told the press the way the inquest had been conducted and several papers took up the cause with enthusiasm. The *World* headed its report 'A Tragedy?' and the *Daily Telegraph* began a campaign to have the verdict of the inquest quashed and a new inquest held.

Meanwhile, Florence went off to Brighton to recuperate. Joseph Bravo went to Ely Place.

When Joseph Bravo went to Lewis after the inquest, Lewis would have been aware from press reports of the main facts – in so far as they could be separated from the fog of rumour and surmise. No doubt Bravo told Lewis of his suspicions about his daughter-in-law, probably even denouncing Florence in crude terms as Charles's murderess, with perhaps Mrs Cox cast as accomplice.

Hardly a man to inspire sympathy or liking, Joseph Bravo seems to have persuaded Lewis of the justice of his cause. Certainly from the moment Lewis took on Joseph Bravo as his client, he gave him all his skill and support. 'My client, right or wrong,' would certainly have applied to his conduct of the Bravo case.

The *Daily Telegraph* was successful in its lobbying for a second inquest. On 19 June 1876, in the court of Queen's Bench, the Lord Chief Justice, Mr Justice Mellor, and Mr Justice Field in effect quashed the first inquest and set up another.

Everything about the second inquest was in contrast with the first. Instead of the dining-room of the Priory, the court was to sit in the billiard-room of the Bedford Hotel in Balham, near the railway bridge. A more uncomfortable venue could hardly be imagined. It was a very hot summer with the sun blazing down, and yet, except for a narrow gap at the top, the windows had to be kept closed against the roar of trains crossing the nearby railway bridge. After a few hours the atmosphere grew stifling. It was to be described as a 'torture chamber'; the conflict between Lewis and Florence Bravo as 'gladiatorial' in its cruelty.

Lewis was, of course, representing Joseph Bravo and his wife. Arrayed against him were, for the Crown, Sir John Holker (the Attorney General), John Gorst, QC, and Harry Poland; Sir Henry James, QC, and John Biron for Florence Bravo; Serjeant Parry for Dr Gully; and John Murphy, QC, for Mrs Cox.

Once before, at the Mansion House, when he prosecuted the directors of Overend Gurney, Lewis had confronted a similar phalanx of learned counsel. His performance on that occasion had convinced everyone that, had he chosen the senior branch of the law, he could have risen as high as it was possible to rise. This time he was to enjoy an even greater triumph – at the expense of the unfortunate Florence Bravo.

The proceedings began in a macabre way. The jury were taken to Lower Norwood Cemetery to look at the exhumed body of Charles Bravo. A kind of window had been inserted into the coffin so that, as the jury filed past, they could see his face – three months buried, but firm and fresh-looking as in life (antimony has a preservative effect). Unfortunately, some muscular contraction had drawn back Bravo's upper lip in a hideous snarl.

Joseph Bravo was the first witness to be called, and Lewis examined him. He agreed that his wife had not approved of Charles's marriage. Lewis then asked him about Mrs Cox's allegation that Charles had told her he had taken poison. Bravo vehemently denied that his stepson could have taken anything – 'I have disputed it all through' – and said he had told Mrs Cox as much.

He said that Florence and Charles were always 'affectionate' with each other, although his bitterness against Florence showed when he added that after Charles's death she 'did not appear much grieved in any way; the dinners at her table were served as usual, with several courses'.

Then came the doctors, Dr Moore and Dr Harrison, who had been first on the scene. Dr Harrison said he had no doubt that, if Charles Bravo had thought he had been poisoned by someone else, he would have said so.

Sir William Gull gave evidence next: 'I told him he was dying of poison. There was no expression of surprise – and that surprised me . . . that induced me to think he knew it already. I saw not the slightest indication in his manner that he had suspicions against anyone else of having administered poison to him.'

A toxicologist, Professor Redwood, gave evidence confirming that Bravo had died from poisoning by antimony. He also discussed antimony briefly. A little-known slow poison, it had at one time been subject to an interdict by the French Government. The most famous of all medical murderers, Dr Palmer of Rugeley in Staffordshire, had killed his wife with antimony.

So far, all the witnesses had largely repeated or endorsed what had been known at the time of the first inquest. Now a number of Bravo's friends gave evidence. Among them a Mr Jepson Atkinson made the greatest impression. He reiterated what a number of people had said already: that Charles Bravo was the last man in the world to commit suicide. He also said that it was Bravo's invariable custom to drink a deep draught of water last thing at night before going to sleep. The implication was clear. How easy for anyone who was aware of this to slip into Charles's bedroom and drop a fatal dose of antimony into his water carafe. And, of course, this implication was of deadly import for Florence Bravo and Mrs Cox. They had been alone together on the first floor of the house while Bravo and the servants were still downstairs.

Florence's mother, Mrs Campbell, was the next witness. She told the story of her daughter's unhappy marriage to Captain Ricardo and how she had left him; described her relationship with Dr Gully and her marriage to Charles Bravo. She also mentioned Florence's excessive fondness for wine.

When Lewis rose to cross-examine Mrs Campbell, he came straight to the point. What did Mrs Campbell know of her daughter's relationship with Dr Gully?

'I am under the impression,' Mrs Campbell answered, 'that my daughter's infatuation with Dr Gully commenced after the death of her first husband, Captain Ricardo.'

Lewis did not press her beyond that.

Next morning, Mrs Cox gave evidence: a small figure, her back held poker-straight, a black silk mantle draped across her shoulders.

Examined by her counsel, she gave her history and background; told how she had gone to Florence Bravo as companion; described how the contact between her and the Joseph Bravos had brought about the marriage between Florence and Charles.

The Attorney General, John Holker, rose to cross-examine. He began by asking her what was the oath she had taken at the first inquest. She repeated it: 'To tell the truth, the whole truth . . .' He then quoted the evidence she had given at that first inquest. She had testified that Bravo had said, 'I have taken some of the poison; don't tell Florence.'

Holker paused. Then he quoted a later statement she had made – and this came as a surprise to practically everyone in court – in which Bravo's words had become: 'I have taken poison for Dr Gully; don't tell Florence.'

There was silence. 'Then,' Holker said deliberately, 'you did not tell the whole truth?'

Mrs Cox did not answer. The hostility against her seemed to thicken, coalesce. But she appeared calm. This was the moment, Lewis always believed, when Mrs Cox decided to betray Florence Bravo – if it became necessary.

Holker pressed her about Florence's relations with Dr Gully. Mrs Cox hedged. Dr Gully's attitude was one of 'gentlemanly familiarity'. Was Dr Gully Florence's lover? What did Sir John mean by 'lover'?

Mrs Cox continued to be evasive and the Attorney General handed her over to Lewis.

A newspaper report of the time says that 'the Attorney General had put his questions in a somewhat persuasive style, but Mr Lewis adopted a sharper tone and more aggressive methods'. In fact, most of the accounts of the inquest are frankly hostile to Lewis: 'His "answer my question, Madame!" came like a crack of a whip at the least hesitation.'

The nub of these criticisms is that an inquest is simply an enquiry into the manner of a particular person's death, and that Lewis exploited the weakness of the coroner (one writer describes him as 'cowed'), transforming this second inquest into a trial at which Florence Bravo and Mrs Cox stood in the dock.

Lewis certainly played ruthlessly to win. The accepted rules of court procedure did not apply to a coroner's inquest. Lewis saw his chance and grabbed it. He attacked Mrs Cox head-on. 'Would it not be true to say,' he demanded, 'from the conversation you had with Mr Bravo before his marriage, that you believed he knew she had had criminal intercourse with Dr Gully?'

'No, not then,' she replied.

'Was it your impression from his conversation that he believed her to be a perfectly chaste woman?'

'I believe,' Mrs Cox answered slowly, 'that before the marriage he knew everything but not at that time.'

This was a most important moment. Suddenly the threat implicit in Lewis's severe demeanour released some check or censor in Mrs Cox's mind and the words began to pour out:

'At that time [before the marriage] I had spoken of her to Mr Bravo in the highest terms – of her disposition, her kindness and her being able to make him happy. He believed her to be a chaste woman and I did not create any suspicion that was different from that. I had spoken to him of Dr Gully and he told me that Mrs Ricardo [Florence] had told him all about Dr Gully. I did not keep anything back before the marriage – *well, I did*, but let me understand fully what you mean?'

Everyone saw what was happening. Terrier-like, Lewis pressed on: 'What was it you kept back before the marriage, Mrs Cox?'

'I kept back from him what Mrs Ricardo had told me after giving up her acquaintance with Dr Gully.'

But Lewis was not satisfied. He kept pressing her for definitions and Mrs Cox kept trying to escape into generalities. He went on, trying to force her into a corner. 'Did Mr Bravo let you know,' he demanded, 'that he knew his wife's intimacy with Dr Gully had been of a criminal nature?'

'Yes,' Mrs Cox replied. 'At Palace Green [Joseph Bravo's house] he told me.'

And so it went on. At one point Mrs Cox's counsel, J. P. Murphy, jumped up and approached Lewis. He thrust a piece of paper under his nose. It was a drawing of Mrs Cox dangling from a gibbet with a bottle labelled 'Poison' in her hand: she had received it anonymously through the post. Murphy denounced Lewis's cross-examination as a 'continuation of this self-same torture'.

The thrust of Lewis's questioning was now clear. He wanted to discredit Mrs Cox as a liar and a perjurer and to show Florence Bravo as a 'fallen woman'. The inquest had heard that Bravo had kept a mistress at Maidenhead and had given her an illegitimate child: this was hardly worthy of mention. But, as one report put it, 'When it was learned that Mrs Bravo had been guilty of fornication, a shiver of excited horror ran through the room.'

Lewis's cross-examination of Mrs Cox had already done Florence Bravo enormous harm; but, if she revealed tomorrow that Dr Gully had performed an abortion on Florence after her return from their holiday at Kissingen, then the results could be hideous. Judges in the 1920s and after liked to warn jurors, 'This is not a court of morals' – but Victorian courts were, all too often, just that, and no judge would have dreamed of saying they were not.

The next day Florence's counsel, Sir Henry James, took Mrs Cox cautiously over the evidence. He ended by asking, 'Had you any reason to suppose that Mrs Bravo had any antimony in her possession, or that she ever used it in any way?'

'I never did,' Mrs Cox said.

Lewis suddenly stood up. He held a small bottle labelled 'Antimony Tart', turning it in his hand so that everyone could see it. 'Have you ever seen any bottle like that?' he demanded.

Mrs Cox replied coolly, 'I have seen many bottles like that.'

This particular bottle had been found in Mrs Cox's own medicine cabinet, one of many homeopathic remedies she kept there. It contained antimony but in so weak a solution as to be harmless.

The next day Florence herself was to testify. The reporters were thrown into a fever of description:

> A handsome lady of about thirty years of age, with large expressive blue eyes, chestnut hair tinged with gold, and having a graceful figure. She was in deep mourning, enhanced by a *fichu* arranged around her shoulders. She wore little jewellery except a valuable emerald ring on her finger . . . Beside her had been placed a glass of sal volatile and water which she sipped now and again . . .

Gently, Sir Henry James took her over the familiar, unhappy ground. Her first marriage; her 'attachment' to Dr Gully; the story of Charles Bravo's last days.

Lewis stood up to cross-examine.

Florence had answered her own counsel's questions frankly and to the point. She had created a good impression. Now, coldly and deliberately, Lewis set out to destroy this. Florence had admitted her involvement with Gully, but Lewis demanded more. He set out to analyse every detail of their affair.

The *Saturday Review* was to write indignantly:

> The gloating zest with which the audience in court, including even so-called ladies, gave themselves up to enjoy the spectacle of a woman, to whom reputation was dear, having wrung from her by questions as cruel as the rack an open confession of dishonour, not only a general impression but in precise detail.

Having obtained the letters Charlers Bravo had sent to Florence, Lewis began to question her about them. Quoting phrases of Bravo's like 'I only want your love', Lewis demanded, 'Do you mean to tell the jury that your late husband was always jealous of Dr Gully?'

Florence said she did.

Lewis then held up a letter, which Florence admitted she had written, dated 16 November – no year given, Lewis said, but obviously written during the lifetime of her first husband. Lewis read the letter to the court. Addressed to a housemaid called Lawdon, it stated that she, Florence, was sorry she had to dismiss Lawdon and she promised her a good reference. Then came these words:

> I hope you will never allude in *any way* to *anyone* of what passed at Malvern. Let it all be buried in the past, and if *anybody* questions you, please refuse to answer any enquiries. I shall remain here till January and then think of buying a house at Clifton.

'What was it?' Lewis asked, 'that was never to be alluded to by anyone? What was to be buried in the past and no enquiries answered?'

'It was my attachment to Dr Gully,' Florence said, 'but it was not a criminal attachment then.' Then, speaking with great emotion, she added, 'That attachment to Dr Gully has nothing to do with this case – the death of Mr Bravo. I have been subjected to sufficient pain and humiliation already – and I appeal to the Coroner and the jury, as men and Britons, to protect me.'

Although, according to the *Saturday Review*, 'the audience moved their feet as if applauding', these particular men and Britons ignored her appeal.

Lewis pressed on to the kill. 'Now, Mrs Bravo, what passed at Malvern?'

'It seems to me,' Florence retorted, 'that you and such as you think it impossible for a woman to love a man without what is wrong occurring.'

Lewis ignored that. '"Not to say anything of what passed at Malvern." What passed?'

'I have explained it.'

Lewis quoted from a letter of Florence to her mother, dated 16 April, in which she said, 'Charles is walking about with a book under his arm, as happy as a king.' Then he said, 'Mrs Bravo, is it not strange that two days later he is alleged to have committed suicide?'

That, in effect, was the end of Lewis's cross-examination.

The modern reader may well consider Florence Bravo's liaison with Dr Gully and the way Lewis dragged out every detail for the delectation of prurient, mock-shocked spectators to be entirely trivial: much ado about nothing. And so it was, of course, by the criteria of the 1980s. But in 1923 Edith Thompson was hanged because her young paramour Frederick Bywaters murdered her husband: the love-letters she had written to Bywaters were thought to have incited him to do so. It has often been said that she was executed for adultery, not for murder.

Florence Bravo was never put on trial. The verdict of the second inquest was that Charles Bravo had been murdered, but that there was insufficient evidence to fix guilt on any person or persons. But in the popular mind she had already been tried – with Lewis as prosecuting counsel.

For some weeks the newspapers cast Lewis as a ruthless bully who had hounded a young widow, forlorn and beautiful, into despair. For that season, at least, he was The Man You Love to Hate. They dubbed him 'The Torturer' or 'The Avenging Angel', lacing fame with obloquy, although, strangely, as the weeks became months, the hostility evaporated and the fame remained.

Florence never saw the inside of a prison cell but her life was ruined. No one could ever be quite sure that she had not poisoned her husband; and she would be known forever as a 'fallen woman', which in 1876 was to be cast into the outer darkness. So, through Lewis, Joseph Bravo did win a kind of backhanded revenge.

Who did poison Charles Bravo? Most writers on the case answer: Mrs Cox. She had the opportunity; her actions on the night of the poisoning were calculated to arouse suspicion. And the way she turned on Florence Bravo, her friend and benefactor, indicated that she had something to hide. Jane Cox was a schemer and an opportunist: in every way the most likely suspect.

Lewis thought her guilty. In an interview he gave in 1893 he said, 'At an inquest the advocate is not allowed to make a speech to the jury. Had I been able to do so, I should at once have relieved both Dr Gully and Mrs Bravo from any suggestion that they in any way participated in the crime. I then – and still do – believe them: Not Guilty.'

The interviewer then asked Lewis who he thought *had* poisoned Charles Bravo; '"Who?" repeated Sir George – and he told me the name.' Dr Gully was never suspected by anyone. Florence having been eliminated by Lewis, there remains only Mrs Cox.

But, although Lewis may have had access to information denied to the inquest, there are grave objections to Mrs Cox as the murderess. Did she have a strong enough motive?

The motive usually attributed to her is a desire to keep her job as Florence's companion – a comfortable job, and one, it is argued, that she could have never got anywhere else. She killed Bravo, this argument runs, because being the miser he was (urged on and supported by another super-miser, Joseph Bravo), he would sooner or later have sacked Mrs Cox as part of his economy drive.

But then this theory conflicts with Bravo's extraordinary behaviour over the two or three days prior to his death. He knew he had been poisoned and yet he pursued a policy of obstruction and denial even unto death. Why? If he had known himself to be the victim of someone in the household, why should he shield them? He clearly did not think Florence had poisoned him – his affectionate, even remorseful attitude to her is sufficient indication of that, and the fact that he left her all his property. If he thought Mrs Cox had poisoned him, why did he not denounce her or at least voice his suspicions?

Why did this hitherto rather irascible young man display such superhuman restraint during the last hours of his life?

In her book *How Charles Bravo Died*, published in 1956, Yseult Bridges advances a theory which answers all these questions – and exonerates Mrs Cox. Her explanation is very plausible. She suggests that Bravo, having married Florence for her money, was, at the time of his death, in the process of poisoning *her*. This would indeed account for Florence's persistent ill-health. Her symptoms would be consistent with being poisoned by antimony. (In fact, after the second inquest it was revealed that Bravo, under an assumed name, had been buying antimony from a chemist in a south coast town.)

If he were poisoning Florence, how did Charles Bravo come to be poisoned himself? Yseult Bridges believes it was by accident. The white crystals of antimony he was using to poison his wife closely resembled the white crystals of the Epsom Salts he was in the habit of taking – and he kept both jars on the same shelf in his bedroom. Fuddled by wine, he had taken the antimony by mistake, thinking it was Epsom Salts. That would account for his rushing out of his bedroom when he realized what he had done, shouting for 'Hot water!'

When he recovered consciousness, Bravo found himself in the ultimate dilemma. If he revealed the nature of the poison – antimony – then he would have to admit to possession of it. At the worst, suspicions about Florence's health might be aroused and investigations made. At the best, he would have to abandon his attempts to kill her. He decided to gamble. With luck, if he recovered (and his possession of antimony was not suspected), he could start poisoning her all over again. He badly wanted the Priory and £40,000 free of strings.

He lost his gamble – and by the time he knew he had lost, it was too late. Perhaps, from the first moment he staggered out of his bedroom, it had been too late.

Florence Bravo lived for about eighteen months longer. Socially ostracized, she abandoned herself to that fondness for wine her mother had mentioned and died of chronic alcoholism. Her ancient lover – and unwitting Nemesis – Dr Gully lived on till 1882.

With their incorrigible gallows-wit the writers of broadsheets had poor Florence pinned down just as surely as they had Lady Mordaunt a few years earlier:

THE TORTURER

When lovely woman stoops to folly
And finds her husband in the way,
What charm can soothe her melancholy
What art can turn him into clay?

The only means her aim to cover,
And save herself from prison locks,
And repossess her ancient lover
Are Burgandy and Mrs Cox!

13

Libel and Labouchere

FAR FROM DAMAGING Lewis's practice, the mood of public hostility aroused by his conduct in the Bravo case actually enlarged it. Coinages like 'The Torturer' and 'The Avenging Angel' fascinated newspaper readers. 'Ruthlessness' always evokes an ambivalent reaction in the public mind. Anyone romantic enough to believe in this Lewis of the public prints – cold, tenacious; driving and efficient as a machine – would be inclined to want him on their side, so that he could deploy these qualities against their enemies. This attracted a number of small litigants but, in due course, some big ones too.

The year of 1877 was to bring another *cause célèbre*, but first there was an interlude involving one of Labouchere's friends, the actress Clare Rousby (known in the manner of the time as 'Mrs Rousby'). She was twenty-five in 1877 and had only two more years to live. She had bought a play from an actor and dramatist called Daniel Bandmann for £100. £50 of this was due on the delivery of the script and a further £50 on the first night, when the play was to be presented at Labouchere's Queen's Theatre. Playing the traditional role of a playwright – a peevish ghost haunting rehearsals to everyone's annoyance – Bandmann objected to the way the Fifth Act was being played. Cursing, he grabbed Mrs Rousby's script. She fought to get it back and her arm got bruised in the struggle. 'Mr Bandmann,' she said, 'this is not the first time you have struck a woman.' To which he replied by calling her a lying bitch.

The beautiful and hot-tempered Clare Rousby had already met the Lewises socially through Labouchere and Henrietta Hodson. It was inevitable that Lewis should act for her.

Lewis interviewed all the witnesses, as he always did, seeking some common truth to unite their testimonies. There was general agreement that Bandmann had struck Clare Rousby. There had been cries of 'Shame!' from the other members of the cast; no one had interfered, though, except for one man who had called out to Bandmann as he made his exit, 'Thank God I am not a wife-beater!'

The case duly came up before the Lord Chief Justice. Bandmann's defence was that he had not struck Mrs Rousby at all. As to the bruising on her arm, that had happened when she had been playing Joan of Arc in another production a month earlier. Mrs Rousby was a heavy drinker, Bandman further alleged; and, as she was 'in an unhealthy state', the marks of the bruises showed larger on her than they would have done on a healthy person: she had decided to exploit this fact in her row with Bandmann. As Joan of Arc, she had been so drunk that she had fallen from her horse. Bandmann called witnesses in an effort to prove this, but their evidence was inconclusive – almost farcical.

The judge had at first appeared to favour Bandmann but after hearing these witnesses his sympathy shifted to Mrs Rousby. Summing up, he pointed out that it was really she who had been put on trial, since Bandmann had accused her of drunkenness and of making a false allegation against him. Both of these were more serious charges than the one before the court. In a private criminal prosecution, which this was, it was sufficient to show that, even if a blow was struck by the defendant, it was delivered unintentionally.

After an hour's absence the jury acquitted Bandmann. Lewis realized he had made a tactical error by not making this a civil action for assault. In that case, as defendant, Bandmann would have had to go into the witness box, where he could have been cross-examined and, Lewis believed, totally discredited.

Later that year, the lovely Rousby was involved in another farcical episode, this time in the company of Labouchere himself.

Several years earlier, Labouchere had started contributing a weekly series of articles to a new paper, *The World*. Labouchere had chosen to deal with City matters: the articles were mostly exposés, lifting the lid off company-promoters, share manipulators, crooked financial tipsters, and the like. The articles were written in a straightforward, hard-hitting style that has since become familiar but which was then quite new. Labouchere's first campaign had been the exposure of Sampson, city editor of *The Times*, as a corrupt tipster. He had accused Sampson of receiving pay-offs from various financial magnates – not so much for promoting their projects as for ignoring them. Within a month Sampson had resigned.

Remembering Overend Gurney and the suffering that had followed it, Lewis was very sympathetic to Labouchere's activities. Others were less so. They might not be swindlers themselves, but they were of the establishment and they hated anyone who threatened to disturb the status quo.

Now, since the beginning of 1877, Labouchere had been running his own journal, *Truth* ('A new and better *World*,' as he told a friend). As Labouchere was naturally even freer writing for his own paper than for someone else's, he was soon plunged into litigation; and this is how Lewis, already a friend, became vitally important to Labouchere. He acted in all the libel actions in which Labouchere was involved. Many years later he was to say, 'Let me tell you that all Mr Labouchere's libels have been connected with cases for the public good. No litigant has ever been more successful than he.'

Something Labouchere had written in *Truth* led to the incident in which Mrs Rousby was implicated. Labouchere had formerly been chairman of the Westminster Aquarium and when it had got into difficulties he had been characteristically blunt, writing in *Truth*, 'The affairs of the company are under the control of Mr Wybrow Robertson, a manager already dismissed for dishonesty.'

A month or two later, in August 1877, Labouchere had gone to the annual fair at Boulogne with a group of friends which included Alexander Henderson, the actor-manager, and the beautiful but doomed Mrs Rousby.

They were gambling happily in a booth. After expending hundreds of sous, Mrs Rousby at last won a butter-dish on a glass pedestal. For Labouchere, this was success. Carrying the butter-dish but with Mrs Rousby on his arm, he made his way through the crowds. Then he noticed something less than pleasing. Weaving his way towards them in an unsteady manner which suggested drunkenness, came Wybrow Robertson.

Labouchere ignored him.

But Robertson wanted a fight. 'If only your hands were empty, I'd knock you down,' he growled.

Still holding the butter dish and still squiring Mrs Rousby, Labouchere continued to move through the crowd.

Robertson had now been joined by his brother and they both started to shout insults at Labouchere and his party. Labouchere threatened to call the gendarmerie and then Robertson struck him in the face with his glove. Enraged, Labouchere hurled the butter dish at Robertson. It missed him, so Labouchere struck out with his stick.

Robertson's brother threw himself bodily on Labouchere, but a second later Alexander Henderson came to the rescue and the fight broke up.

Back in England, Robertson issued a writ for libel. Although Lewis had warned him that the matter was *sub judice*, Labouchere insisted on repeating the alleged libel in further articles in *Truth*, giving more details of Robertson's frauds at the aquarium. Serjeant Ballantine was representing Robertson and he advised him to get Labouchere committed for contempt. Having flouted Lewis's advice – something that was to happen again and again during their long friendship – Labouchere asked Lewis what to do.

Lewis suggested Labouchere should apologize, thus gaining time till the case came on. Labouchere was reluctant. He didn't like apologies.

'All right,' Lewis said. 'We'll take counsel's opinion.'

He took Labouchere to see Edward Clarke at his chambers in Garden Court in the Temple. Clarke had been present at the manic first night of *The Last Days of Pompeii* but he did not know Labouchere. Lewis, for his part, had great faith in Clarke, a young barrister soon to make his name when Lewis briefed him to defend the Stauntons.

But Clarke's advice today was not what Lewis had expected. He agreed with Labouchere. It would be wrong to apologize.

Lewis still thought an apology the best tactic – no more than that, he reminded them. It would be a way to gain time. If Labouchere didn't apologize, he could find himself in jail.

Clarke said, 'That is so. But I still advise you not to apologize, Mr Labouchere. On the other hand, if I am wrong and Mr Lewis is right, then you're the one who will go to jail.'

Labouchere said nothing would suit him better. It was a pity, though, that the contempt hearing had been set for Tuesday: 'For that's the day I write my libels.'

Lewis was not used to being flatly contradicted by counsel, but he respected Clarke for his independence and said no more. In the event Labouchere was not cited for contempt, as the two judges hearing the cause disagreed.

The case of *Robertson* v. *Labouchere* was heard before the Lord Chief Justic and a special jury three months later. Naturally Lewis briefed Clarke for Labouchere.

The proceedings lasted for several days, and were mostly concerned with the financial position of the Westminster Aquarium company. The nub of the case was: had Robertson been dismissed? If so, why? For dishonesty?

Everything was halted when, after three days, Serjeant Ballantine (appearing for Robertson) collapsed in a fit. He recovered, but the Lord Chief Justice then went sick and the court was again adjourned.

Eventually the court sat again. In due course it fell to Edward Clarke to examine Labouchere who – headstrong and self-opinionated as usual – insisted, again against Lewis's advice, in testifying that Serjeant Ballantine had attended a directors' meeting at the aquarium; and at that meeting had remarked that Robertson (now his client!) was a trickster who had behaved in a thoroughly dishonest manner.

This caused an angry scene in court, but Labouchere stood behind this allegation, challenging Ballantine to go into the witness box and deny it. Ballantine not unnaturally refused to do this (he would almost certainly have created legal history: counsel going into the box to testify against his own client).

As a witness Labouchere proved altogether too tough for Serjeant Ballantine – as he was to prove too tough for at least two generations of learned counsel in the years to come – and Robertson lost the case. It was the occasion for mutual congratulation between Clarke, Labouchere, and Lewis himself.

Now occurred an event that made 1877 an *annus mirabilis* for Edward Burne-Jones, bringing full public recognition of his talents, to the great joy of Lewis and Elizabeth. He had his first big exhibition, at the Grosvenor Gallery. There his paintings made what was described as 'a prodigious impression', with three paintings in particular – 'Chant d'Amour', 'Days of Creation', and 'The Beguiling of Merlin' – attracting particular attention.

There were predictable criticisms that these were 'literary' paintings, but Burne-Jones had achieved his breakthrough at last.

Speaking with the authority of one who had in a long lifetime known a great variety of artists – sculptors, painters, writers – Elizabeth always maintained that Edward Burne-Jones represented the artist in his purest essence. All he asked of life was to be allowed to go on painting. In temperament no one could have been further removed from what proper Victorians defined as 'Bohemian' behaviour. Equally, he lacked the aggressive or missionary drive of a trail-blazer in any of the arts. Burne-Jones could never have fought the battles that Millais and Holman Hunt had fought twenty years earlier; but, without their pioneering, he would have been dismissed as a merely literary painter. The master of an intricate line, perhaps, but 'great'?

Naturally Lewis and Elizabeth were delighted. No one could have been less affected by fame than Burne-Jones, whose grave and oddly childish spirit always appeared to walk a different path from the rest of humanity.

Scarcely a week passed without the two families exchanging visits. As they grew older the Lewis children were to grow to love the Grange; meanwhile Edward and Georgiana were indispensable guests at the parties – increasingly grand and celebrity-orientated – that Elizabeth was giving at Portland Place.

14

Starvation?

LEWIS HAD NOT BEEN a player of the legal game for long before he discovered that, like most fields of human activity, the law has its lions and jackals, its heroes and villains. To his chagrin, most of the villains appeared to belong to his own branch of the profession. For years he complained about the low standards of many solicitors – as deficient in legal ethics as in knowledge of the law – but it was difficult to know how to set about improving them. He fought hard against corrupt practitioners and sometimes helped bring about their downfall.

Heroes were harder to find. But, had Lewis been asked, at the end of fifty-five years in practice, to name the man who most deserved the title of hero, he would have replied, Edward Clarke. Not for nothing was he, Clarke, called the Bayard of the Bar. He really did possess all the virtues of chivalry – and he carried them with a total absence of self-righteousness or self-regard. The secret was that he did not realize that these qualities were in any way exceptional. Courtesy, kindness, and fairness were to Clarke so normal and expected that he took them for granted – in himself, if not in others. In his fifty years at the bar he became the subject of a hundred stories – and not one of them unfavourable. His immediate offer to defend Oscar Wilde without fee after the fiasco of his Queensbury prosecution is well known; in fact, Clarke gave his services on many other occasions – moved always by compassion, never by mere ambition.

He was, however, ambitious by nature; and his rise to fame and wealth had a touch of Smilesean self-help about it that was very rare at the nineteenth-century bar. His father was a silversmith and Clarke was born in King William Street in the City of London. Largely self-educated, he won a clerkship at the India Office by competitive examination. This was only a stepping-stone; he studied at night and got a Tancred Studentship at Lincoln's Inn. During his years of study he maintained himself as law reporter for the *Morning Herald* and by casual journalism. Briefless after his call to the bar, he soon attracted attention by his tenacity and thoroughness.

Not tall, with a square face framed in side whiskers, this was the young man that, in 1877, Lewis found himself briefing more and more. Now, quite unexpectedly, was to come the major case that every advocate needs to make his name – and it was Lewis who gave Clarke his chance.

Lewis had just arrived at Ely Place on the morning of Monday, 16 April 1877, when a messenger called with the urgent request that Lewis might act for four people who had just been arrested at Penge in South London. They had been charged jointly with the murder of Mrs Harriet Staunton.

The group consisted of two brothers, Louis Staunton, aged twenty-six, and his brother Patrick Staunton, aged twenty-four; and two women, Patrick Staunton's wife Elizabeth Ann Staunton, aged twenty-eight, and Alice Rhodes, mistress of Louis Staunton, aged twenty. The murdered woman had been married to Louis Staunton.

None of these names meant anything to Lewis, but after a little hesitation he agreed: he would act for them. Accompanied by his clerk, George Daintrey (who himself lived in Upper Norwood, not far from Penge), Lewis set off for South London.

Harriet Staunton came from a curious, even tragic family, but nothing in their history equalled the horror that was to overtake her.

Her grandmother had been the celebrated Regency courtesan Nelly Holmes, who had married a Colonel Pitt who had later succeeded to a peerage, becoming Lord Rivers. (Apparently bride and groom parted at the church door, never to meet again.) Lady Rivers had a daughter, who passed as her niece, and this daughter later married a coachman called Richardson. Harriet Richardson, later Staunton, was the child of this marriage.

Her elder sister, who had the beauty and intelligence Harriet lacked, married William Howard, Lord Wicklow's heir. They had no children, as far as anyone knew, but, after Howard died in a Dublin brothel in 1864, his widow claimed there was one. This led to a long-drawn-out legal imbroglio, which ended up before the Committee of Privileges in the House of Lords in 1870. Mrs Howard's claim was eventually disallowed, and she married a man named Casabianca.

Her mother (and Harriet's) had also married again, this time a parson named Butterfield, and in 1877 he was Rector of Longney in Gloucestershire.

When the notorious Lady Rivers (Nelly Holmes) died in 1872, she left her two granddaughters £2000 each. Harriet was therefore (in terms of the 1870s) an heiress. She was described as being 'of rather weak intellect'. Her mother, Mrs Butterfield, was terrified that she would fall victim to a fortune-hunter – and of course she did.

The ruthless, fortune-seeking husband was a familiar figure in the earlier part of the nineteenth century. He had always been encouraged by the fact that from time immemorial the common law had maintained that, as regards property, a husband and wife became, on marriage, one person at law. As one nineteenth-century legal writer put it:

> The Creator took from Adam a rib and made it Eve; the common law of England endeavoured to reverse the process; to replace the rib and re-merge the personalities.

A wife could be protected by recourse to the Chancery court, and this involved elaborate settlements drawn up before her marriage (usually her property was conveyed to trustees 'for her own exclusive enjoyment', and she was further shielded against a man who might try to charm her into dissolving her settlement by what was called a 'restraint on anticipation').

In practical terms all this amounted to one law for the rich and another for the poor. A rich young woman usually enjoyed the protection of a marriage settlement; a middle-class girl had to take her chance. As for the poor – they often lived so near actual destitution that the use of the word 'property' becomes meaningless in connection with them.

Of course a settlement had to be agreed by the future husband's solicitor and he would naturally fight the husband's corner. A badly-executed settlement could be disastrous. Miss Fairlie's unfortunate marriage settlement is pivotal to the plot of Wilkie Collins's *The Woman in White*, first serialized in 1859.

Lewis had always believed that a woman should keep her own property after she married – that she should be something more than a mere chattel of her husband. But not until 1870, when the first Married Women's Property Act was passed, did the law recognize a woman's claim to retain what was justly hers; and the 1870 legislation only dealt with a married woman's earnings. Not till the act of 1882 was her property protected.

But that was too late to help poor Harriet Richardson. She met Louis Staunton in 1875. Staunton was an auctioneer's clerk, glib and flashy: the archetype of the predator who exploits foolish women and, occasionally, murders them.

Harriet's mother recognized him for what he was and did her best to stop the marriage. She went to the Court of Chancery to have her daughter declared a lunatic and her money placed in trust. Unfortunately this failed and Harriet married Louis Staunton in June 1875.

The Stauntons showed their hand immediately. From the first day of her marriage Harriet was treated cruelly by all the Stauntons – their hatred for her venting itself in a range of brutalities that took in everything from a savage indifference to actual blows. Louis Staunton had married her for money – and, when he got his hands on that money, he had as little regard for her as for an animal conveyed to a slaughterhouse to yield up its meat and hide.

In March 1876 Harriet gave birth to a son, and this soon added to the horror of her situation, for the Stauntons were apparently able to treat a baby-in-arms with the same gratuitous cruelty they vented on its mother. From now on, Harriet was kept confined, at a sub-animal level, with her sickly baby boy.

Even before the birth of the child, Louis Staunton had started living with Alice Rhodes; and this strengthened his resolve that, as soon as he got his hands on Harriet's £2000, both mother and child would be eliminated.

Louis worked in collusion with his brother Patrick. Psychopaths, lacking normal human emotions, they appeared to have a certain affection for each other. They arranged for Harriet and her son to be taken down to a house in the village of Cudham in Kent that was occupied by Patrick Staunton and his wife. Patrick Staunton was an artist, singularly lacking in talent, according to contemporary accounts; before the brothers got Harriet's money, he used to hawk his water colours around neighbouring villages.

In October 1876 Louis Staunton came down to Cudham and set up house with Alice Rhodes at a farm called Little Grays. His first act after arriving was to take Harriet up to London. There she executed a deed assigning to him her entitlement under her grandmother's will.

This done, there was no point in keeping her alive any longer.

She was taken back to Woodlands (Patrick's house) and there

Patrick and his wife Elizabeth set about starving Harriet and her baby to death. This was done systematically. Mother and child were kept locked up in a garret. Not only was Harriet denied food; she was often also deprived of water to drink. She was never given water to wash herself or the baby, with the result that they both became verminous and afflicted with sores. (After Harriet's death the dirt on her body was so thick that it was described as being 'like the bark of a tree'.)

Louis Staunton wanted his wife and child out of the way, but he was not living under the same roof and he was happy to let his brother Patrick and his wife engineer their deaths: something they enjoyed, anyway. Patrick would work himself into a frenzy as he inflicted savage beatings on both mother and child, covering them with kicks and blows as he shouted curses and abuse.

Meanwhile, Harriet's mother, Mrs Butterfield, was in a state of great anxiety about her daughter. (She had been rudely rebuffed when she tried to see Harriet soon after her marriage.) In January 1877 she had met Alice Rhodes by accident at London Bridge station and noticed that she was wearing a brooch belonging to Harriet. Alice had been sullen and aggressive; at last she told Mrs Butterfield that Harriet had been ill and was staying at Brighton. Naturally this incident intensified Mrs Butterfield's fears. She managed to find out that the Patrick Stauntons were living at Cudham, and went down there in search of her daughter. When she arrived there, she was met by Patrick Staunton who shouted, 'Damn your daughter! Come here again and I'll blow your brains out!'

Now she tried the farm at Little Grays, to meet with similar, if less frightening, abuse from Louis Staunton and Alice Rhodes. She went to the local police and they took her seriously enough to watch the farm at Little Grays – because Mrs Butterfield naturally assumed Harriet was being kept there, rather than at Woodlands where she actually was. Of course, the police saw nothing. In great anguish, Mrs Butterfield returned to Gloucestershire.

As might have been expected, Harriet's baby boy was the first to die. He had been kept with his mother in the garret, and, seeing that he was dying, his father decided that it would be safer if the child could be got into hospital before it actually expired. That way, there could be no problems with death certificates, or – if they did not call a doctor – with disposing of the body. So, on 8 April, Louis Staunton took him to Guy's Hospital and left him there under the assumed name 'Harris'. He died that night, and Louis, still calling himself 'Harris', arranged with an undertaker for the child to be buried as quickly as possible.

By now Harriet, too, was near death. On 12 April Louis Staunton and Patrick's wife Elizabeth took lodgings at Forbes Road, Penge, 'for a lady inclined to be paralysed'.

That evening the whole group brought the dying Harriet to London by train. She arrived at Forbes Road speechless and barely conscious. At ten o'clock the next morning a surgeon called Longrigg was summoned to the house, but by 1.30 p.m. Harriet was dead. Curiously, considering the state of her body, he gave a death certificate without question.

The murderous quartet must have felt enormous relief. Mother and child had both been disposed of, and in the one case the slackness of the hospital authorities, in the other that of Mr Longrigg, had relieved them of legal responsibility for the crimes. They had, it seemed, literally got away with murder.

But, as Frederick the Great said, 'His Majesty King Chance does three-quarters of the business of this miserable universe,' and the Stauntons certainly had reason to echo his remark.

It will be remembered that Harriet's sister had married a Mr Casabianca. By chance he happened to be living not far from Penge. On the evening of Friday, 13 April, he had occasion to go to a shop at the corner of Forbes Road. It happened that Forbes Road was on the boundary between Kent and Surrey – with the division running right down the centre of the road: the houses on one side in Kent, those on the other in Surrey. While Casabianca was in the shop, a young man came in and began talking to the shopkeeper. He wanted to know where a death should be registered, in view of the fact that this road straddled the county boundary. Yes, the death had only taken place around one o'clock that day.

Of course there was no reason for Casabianca to feel suspicious as he listened to this snatch of dialogue; he had never seen Louis Staunton before (who was the young man making the enquiry). But when Staunton went on to say that the lady whose death they were registering had been brought from Cudham in Kent, Casabianca was at once alert. Cudham? That was where his mother-in-law had gone in search of Harriet and been so brutally rebuffed.

Next morning Casabianca went to the police. The surgeon Longrigg had the wit to have second thoughts about the death certificate:

he withdrew it immediately. An inquest was ordered. On 19 April a post-mortem examination of Harriet's body was made by four doctors, all of whom confirmed that death was due to starvation.

The body was emaciated to an extent one associates with Belsen or with Indian famine victims. The post-mortem report disclosed a complete absence of fat and an abnormal smallness of the liver, kidneys, and heart, indicating starvation over a long period. There were also some changes in the body that might suggest poisoning, but these were not confirmed on subsequent analysis. And the dirt on the body was incredible: thick and horn-hard, like the shell of a crustacean.

The three Stauntons and Alice Rhodes were arrested and charged with murder.

The annals of crime show no clearer case of premeditated and cold-blooded murder than that of Harriet Staunton. There was no room for any doubt about the facts – there was even an eye-witness available to testify to the imprisonment of Harriet and her baby: a sixteen-year-old orphan called Clara Brown who was employed as a 'slavey' at the Patrick Stauntons. Harriet Staunton and her son were imprisoned, then starved and maltreated until they died. That was murder. Just as much murder as if they had been shot or stabbed to the heart. Moreover, murder carried out with a particular coldness and cruelty. Murderers much less certainly guilty were hanged for killings carried out in rage or in a frenzy of jealousy. Yet the Stauntons escaped the gallows. How?

Because they were represented by George Lewis and Edward Clarke. A less imaginative solicitor and an advocate lacking Clarke's genius for creating a mood in which blind emotion transcended reason must almost certainly have failed and then this sinister quartet would have gone to the gallows. Clarke's advocacy, backed by Lewis's meticulous groundwork, saved them.

Clarke brilliantly exploited two basic emotions in what one might term the collective psyche. First, an instinctive distrust on the part of the public for 'experts' of any kind – in this case the four doctors who conducted the post-mortem on Harriet Staunton – coupled with the public's delight in seeing expert contradict expert, displaying the intense jealousy and dog-eat-dog attitude everyone knows is rife among learned men. Everyone knows, too, that, when an expert pronounces on his speciality, another expert can always be found to contradict him and the public will often believe the rebuttal, however absurd.

The second emotion Clarke exploited goes much deeper, and could be defined as the transference of public sympathy from the innocent victim to the guilty tormentor. When they were arrested at Penge, the Stauntons had to be protected from angry crowds; after their trial, poor Harriet was forgotten and there was a hysterical backlash in their favour.

From the moment the judge entered the court and the trial began, Clarke followed the strategy he and Lewis had devised. The judge was Mr Justice Hawkins, and his conduct of this trial was to earn him the nickname of 'Hanging Hawkins' – easily remembered but an unjust summation of a long career. Hawkins was too hard-headed to respond to the line Clarke took for the defence – and so intense was Clarke's commitment to the Stauntons, that he never forgave the judge, even refusing to attend a farewell dinner on his retirement.

The Crown (the Attorney General, Sir John Holker, and Hardinge Giffard) faced a phalanx of junior counsel, without a Queen's Counsel among them. This was Lewis's decision and it broke with tradition but was amply justified in the event. Clarke defended Patrick Staunton; Montagu Williams, Louis Staunton; Douglas Straight, Mrs Patrick Staunton; Percy Gye, Alice Rhodes.

Counsel had all met together at Ely Place in the middle of July, with Lewis in the chair. It had been decided then that Clarke would carry the main thrust of the defence, which had to be against the medical evidence. Now, some six weeks later, on 19 September 1887, the strategy was to be put to the test.

The Crown outlined the story of Harriet and the Stauntons: the defence could hardly deny the facts, but, the medical evidence was a different matter. Knowing that no *odium theologicum* can equal the detestation one medical specialist can feel for another, it had not been hard to find a doctor to challenge all the findings of the post-mortem. He was a Dr Bristowe of St Thomas's Hospital. Without ever seeing the body of Harriet Staunton or getting nearer to Penge than Harley Street, this gentleman was ready to go into the witness box and affirm that the four doctors who had conducted the post-mortem were wrong – hopelessly wrong! There were four of them and they had spent several hours on their examination of the body, but that was of no consequence. They were wrong.

Upon what did Dr Bristowe base *his* opinion? On reading a copy of the post-mortem report. A document written by the very men whose professional knowledge he was ready to dismiss with contempt was sufficient for him to pronounce his own verdict: Harriet Staunton died, not of starvation, but of Addison's Disease (a form of tubercular meningitis).

Clarke had also been able to draft a tame pathologist called Dr Payne to support Bristowe; and such was Clarke's almost hypnotic power of persuasion that with such slender arguments – Bristowe and Payne were, after all, expressing opinions unsupported by evidence, as they might have done in the correspondence columns of a newspaper – he was able to raise considerable doubt in the public mind as to the cause of Harriet Staunton's death.

None of this weighed with the judge, nor indeed with the jury. Found guilty, all the prisoners were sentenced to death.

But a climate of opinion had been created. Then, as now, there were journalists who made a speciality of whipping up controversies. One of them was Charles Reade, who also wrote novels with titles like *Hard Cash* and *It's Never Too Late to Mend.* Another was Clement Scott, George du Maurier's brother-in-law, a considerable lecher who liked to write in moralistic vein. Both these men were experts in manipulating public hysteria – rather as was James Douglas in the 1920s – and they orchestrated the campaign for the Stauntons. Plenty of doctors could be found to sign a petition attacking the post-mortem findings; and the Home Office bowed to the storm. Alice Rhodes was pardoned and the other sentences commuted to penal servitude. Public sympathy had been successfully transferred from the murdered to the murderer.

This was a great success for Clarke – indeed it can be said to have 'made' him at the bar – and to a lesser extent for Lewis. For both of them there would be occasions when a passion for justice would transcend their zeal as players of the legal game; but this time they simply played to win – and played brilliantly: justice had nothing to do with it. A huge hot-air balloon of hysteria and false sentiment was blown up and launched and it carried the great British public along with it. As the caption to a *Punch* drawing of Edward Clarke had it, 'There is no need to be hanged when you can get me.'

15

La Comtesse and the Detectives

THE STAUNTON CASE took a great deal of Lewis's time and energy in 1877 – not only the trial, but the aftermath of lobbying and argument that led to the prisoners being reprieved. Elizabeth was pleased with his success but Lewis suspected that she might prefer that Lewis and Lewis continue the shift in direction, away from an almost exclusively criminal practice, that had begun around the time when Lewis first met the Prince of Wales.

Meanwhile the drawing-room at Portland Place was on its way to becoming a salon. Everyone agreed that George and Elizabeth made a perfect social team: Elizabeth with her wit and brio blowing up the ordinary stuff of gossip into exaggeratedly swollen balloons and then puncturing them with sharp self-mockery. Lewis himself did not lack his own quieter brand of mockery. Deceptively mild, but with the steel of authority behind the mask of the monocle and the fur coat, worn even on the warmest days. Everyone had laughed – but approvingly – when W. S. Gilbert had played a private joke in public, going to great lengths to give the Lewises a surprise at the first night of *Trial by Jury*. The actor playing the solicitor was made up to look exactly like Lewis. At the first night George and Elizabeth had been sitting in the stalls of the Royalty Theatre – and then up there on the stage had appeared the familiar monocle, the Dundreary whiskers, the fur coat. The Lewises had pretended not to see the joke, coyly ignoring the whole thing, but of course they knew that the applause that swelled around them was really for Lewis, endorsing him as a celebrity.

If anyone was ever cut out to be a celebrity's wife it was Elizabeth. She had the ability to create exactly the kind of private background a public man required. Her powers of organization enabled her to run the household at Portland Place with the efficiency of one of Her Majesty's men-of-war, although she never lost her humanity when dealing with her staff – and that was at a time when servants depended on the goodwill of their employers to an extent unimaginable by anyone born in this century.

On moving to Portland Place, the Lewises had to employ a complete staff, so they needed a butler. After seeing nearly a hundred applicants, they engaged a Yorkshireman called William Parkes. He was a man of solid temperament whose traditional north country bluntness was always kept in check by Elizabeth. She made it clear to him at the beginning that, while he might be a formidable figure below stairs – indeed, was expected to be – above stairs he deferred to her in everything. She did not expect him to proffer advice unless she asked for it – which from time to time she did. They soon established a perfect mistress-and-man equipoise that was to last for more than thirty years. Elizabeth knew how to delegate, and Parkes appreciated the fact that she would never foul up the lines of authority laid down for the household. For her part, Elizabeth recognized Parkes's ability to function on his own initiative, unless some altogether exceptional crisis arose.

They also needed a chef, although sometimes this post was vacant for months at a time and they made do with female cooks. For many years one man held the post – a Swiss named Charles Gramecy – but on a rather now-on-now-off basis. Gramecy's work pattern was to cook impeccably – indeed brilliantly – for six months, and then disappear. His disappearances coincided with alcoholic bouts of fearful intensity. At the end of such a bout he would return to Portland Place and ask for his job back. When this happened there was a clash of principles, which always ended the same way. Each time Lewis maintained that Gramecy should not be taken back; each time Elizabeth wanted him back because, she argued, he was quite simply the best chef they had ever had. Once, when Lewis was adamant that the Swiss should not return, Elizabeth resorted to a stratagem that was not really in character. She appeared to accept Lewis's decision without further argument. Then, a week or so later, she told him that she had taken on a new chef. Only after he had pronounced the dinner he had just eaten to be magnificent did she reveal that it had been cooked by Gramecy, who had slunk back below stairs.

*

When number 1713 of the racing paper *Sport* appeared it carried a particularly interesting item:

> Mr Montgomery is the unluckiest man alive. A short time ago he hit on a scheme of backing horses which has since proved infallible. He has, in addition, exceptional means of obtaining information about horses, with the result that he has already won over a quarter of a million pounds.
>
> Our readers may wonder why he is the unluckiest man alive therefore. The answer is that bookmakers, realizing that Mr Montgomery can always beat them, refuse to take his bets. He has, however, found a way of still making bets without the risk of them being refused. Many of his friends are making bets for him with the bookmakers. They find no money, take no risks. They merely forward the money to Montgomery and receive 10 per cent commission.
>
> Of course, many of his friends are adding money of their own to the bets. But Mr Montgomery is afraid that they will soon be prevented from betting, as he has been himself, and he needs a large number of people to put money on for him.

This was an unusual suggestion, but then *Sport* was itself an unusual publication. Only one issue of it ever appeared – number 1713 – and this was entirely written by two fraudsmen, Harry Benson and William Kurr.

Benson had enjoyed a remarkable career. Born in Paris of English parents, he was well educated and intensely plausible. In 1871 he had engineered his first big swindle. Posing as the Comte de Montague, Mayor of Châtendun, he had persuaded the Lord Mayor of London to open a relief fund for the victims of the Franco-Prussian war (Benson was to act as 'trustee' for the fund). Ultimately this was revealed as a fraud and he was sentenced to a year's imprisonment. In jail he made a desperate attempt to commit suicide by setting fire to his bed and remaining in it till he was so badly burned that he was crippled for life. At the time that unusual issue of *Sport* appeared, he was living in luxury at Shanklin in the Isle of Wight under the name of Yonge.

Kurr was a villain of more ordinary fibre, but still a man of cunning and determination. He was the active junior partner, carrying out plans masterminded by Benson.

For a few years prior to 1877 the partners had been operating a number of fraudulent enterprises. The most profitable of these was a bogus betting firm called the Systematic Investment Society. Benson and Kurr were just congratulating themselves on having devised a swindling-machine of almost unlimited potential when they realized that the law was on their trail – in the person of Chief Inspector George Clarke of Scotland Yard.

Clarke had joined the police as early as 1840 and had gained promotion slowly but now, nearly forty years later, he was a chief inspector and the Yard's acknowledged expert on the turf and the criminals who made a living from it. No less than ninety race course swindlers had gone to jail through his efforts.

Benson knew Clarke well enough by reputation to take the threat seriously. Clarke was the archetype of the dogged, plodding sleuth-hound. Not a Dupont, from Poe's coldly intellectual detective stories; more like Sergeant Cuff from Wilkie Collins's *The Moonstone*. He could be relied on to stay on their tail, Benson thought.

The Systematic Investment Society could be abandoned if necessary – the ingenious Benson could always come up with something new – but now that the Yard was aware of their existence, no future enterprise could ever be safe.

Benson's solution was to buy into Scotland Yard. In other words, hire an informer who would watch Clarke and tip off Benson and Kurr whenever the chief inspector appeared to be getting too close for comfort. Neither Benson nor Kurr doubted that they would be able to find a suitable informer among Clarke's colleagues. Detective officers were wretchedly paid at that time; it would not be difficult to find one who was ready to jeopardize his career for ready cash.

Even so, the response they got must have surprised them. The first detective they approached was a quiet, rather sly man called William Meiklejohn, an inspector. He found it hard to manage on his wretched salary and was quite willing to report on Clarke in return for the money Benson offered.

The conspirators soon found, however, that one observer was not enough. Clarke was a wily old bird. They had to have several spies watching him.

In a short space of time other detectives were drawn into the net. The most remarkable of them was Chief Inspector Nathaniel Druscovitch. Still under forty, he had been born of Russian-Polish parents (his grandfather was said to have been a secret agent of Napoleon against the Tsar). He was a brilliant linguist, speaking French, Polish, Russian, German, and Yiddish.

Benson and Kurr approached him at a vulnerable moment. He owed £60 and did not know where he was going to find it. Benson offered him £60 immediately, and so harassed was the detective that he agreed to put his whole career at risk for this sum. The fraudsmen agreed that Druscovitch was a valuable acquisition. His talents as a linguist would come in particularly handy, for they were planning an operation in France.

A third detective was approached and successfully bribed. This was a chief inspector called William Palmer. He, too, was in debt and succumbed to the same kind of offer. Benson and Kurr congratulated themselves. Now they must have good notice if Clarke moved against them. But he continued his enquiries, plodding on, terrier-like. Despite the detectives they had suborned, he was still a threat. Benson wondered if Clarke himself might not be susceptible to the same kind of persuasion, but decided it was too dangerous to try – for the moment, anyway.

Meanwhile, Benson and Kurr prepared number 1713 of *Sport*, a once-off publication that, the partners hoped, would make more money in a week than some more conventional organs made in twenty years. The magazine was produced by a backstreet printer in Edinburgh and the same man printed a thousand cheques for Benson. These cheques purported to be issued by the Royal Bank of London, Charing Cross – a bank which did not exist.

Using names and addresses taken from a directory, the gang now sent hundreds of copies of *Sport* to people throughout France. Accompanying each copy was a translation into French of the item about Mr Montgomery, the unluckiest man alive, and also this letter, signed by 'Andrew Montgomery', and written in Benson's impeccable French:

> Dear Friend,
>
> Your name has been favourably mentioned to me by the Franco-English Society of Publicity, and thus I repose in you the highest confidence.
>
> What I request of you is most simple. I will send you for each race the amount which I wish to put on the horse that I know, under my system, will win. It will be necessary to send the money in your name but on my account to the bookmaker for otherwise you would not get the real odds – which it is impossible for me to get because of my previous success and admitted knowledge.
>
> On settling day the bookmaker will send you the sum I

> have won, plus my original stake. Please forward this amount to me and I will send you a cheque for 10 per cent of the amount as commission.
>
> It is essential that you keep this matter quite secret, whether you wish to help me or not.

Perfidious Albion notwithstanding, an overwhelming number of French punters jumped at this. It was too good to miss. Merely posting off a cheque and then getting 10 per cent of the winnings!

Those who accepted got back courteous letters of thanks accompanied by cheques on the Royal Bank of London made out for impressive round sums and signed by a nominee of Mr Montgomery. The dupes then fowarded these on to the bookmakers named in the letter of acceptance: either a 'Mr Jackson' or a 'Mr Francis', both described as 'Sworn Bookmakers' – a meaningless phrase that sounded impressive. (The 'bookmakers' were, in fact, dummy concerns operated by Benson and Kurr.)

In due course the punters got back from Mr Jackson or Mr Francis even larger cheques for their winnings, plus the original stake. As this cheque was made payable to the nominee who had signed Mr Montgomery's cheque in the first place, the French dupe could not endorse it and thus had to return it to Mr Montgomery.

Now it is obvious that, so far, Benson and Kurr had made nothing out of all this. Indeed, they were heavily out of pocket on the printing and postage.

But at this point human greed – the essential hinge of all swindles – began to surface. The mugs, seeing all this money passing through their hands, wanted something more than a 10 per cent commission. They began to send their own cheques to the bookmakers, along with those of Mr Montgomery.

This was the expected pay-off for Benson and Kurr. They reacted to these extra cheques in one of two ways. Either the punter never heard from the bookmakers or Mr Montgomery again; or, if the punter's cheques were large enough, they were sent their 'winnings' in the hope that they would plunge still deeper.

Now the money began to flow in. £15,000 in the first three weeks; within six weeks £80,000 (ten or twelve times those amounts in 1981 terms).

One of the biggest plungers was a wealthy French widow, the Comtesse Marie de Goncourt. Her enthusiasm for Mr Montgomery knew no bounds. Having 'won' £1,000, she sent £10,000 to be put

The younger Lewis, already successful but with his greatest cases still to come.

'A unique backwater.' Ely Place in 1932, little changed from Lewis's time.

Elizabeth Lewis, painted by her friend John Singer Sargent at the peak of her fame as a hostess and patron of the arts.

Katie Lewis as a young girl by Sir Edward Burne-Jones.

The Pelizzioni case, as imagined by a contemporary artist.

A mind untroubled or the iron composure of a murderess? Adelaide Bartlett at the time of her trial.

'The Torturer': George Lewis cross-examines Mrs Cox at the Bravo Inquest.

Courtier in exile: Valentine Baker as inspector general of the Egyptian Constabulary.

On pleasure bent but with the glint of authority in his eye. King Edward VII when still Prince of Wales.

The Baccarat case: Sir Charles Russell cross-examines Sir William Gordon-Cumming.

The mask of innocence. Virginia Crawford at the time of her marriage.

'I was deprived of the one great safeguard of my life.' Oscar Wilde in 1892, when he was already becoming estranged from George Lewis.

The Chief. Parnell around the time he first met Lewis.

'The Bayard of the Bar':
Sir Edward Clarke QC.

Sir Charles Russell QC
(later Lord Russell
of Killowen,
Lord Chief Justice).

Lewis in caricature. Drawings by 'Spy' of *Vanity Fair* and Max Beerbohm.

'He knows all about us'. Lewis at work, portrayed by Sir Philip Burne-Jones, Bart. (*Mrs Elizabeth Wansbrough*)

George Lewis by John Singer Sargent.

on a horse running in the Ayrshire Handicap.

At this point Benson and Kurr fell victim to their own greed. Not content with the £10,000, they wrote urging the Comtesse to increase her stake to £30,000. This was the best opportunity she would have to make a large fortune, Benson wrote, and, if she were unable to raise the whole amount herself, he, Mr Montgomery, would even be prepared to add to it.

Benson was all too persuasive. More enthusiastic than ever, but running short of money, the Comtesse went to her bank, the Crédit Lyonnais, with the idea of borrowing the £30,000. The manager was concerned that so solid a customer should need to borrow so large a sum, and feared some kind of swindle. He got in touch with the bank's London branch, who consulted their solicitor, a man called Michael Abrahams. Abrahams immediately went to the Yard to see Chief Inspector Druscovitch. The wheel had come full circle.

Druscovitch's first action was to go to the offices used by Benson and Kurr in Northumberland Street, Strand. He realized that crunch-time had come. The best he could do was to alert his paymasters to what was happening.

Scotland Yard's first task was to find out the numbers of the £10,000 of banknotes issued by the Crédit Lyonnais on behalf of the Comtesse. Benson and Kurr's first task was to unload the banknotes before they could be traced.

Eventually Benson and Kurr decided – after consultation with Druscovitch and the other bent detectives – that the best plan would be for Benson and one of his henchmen called Charles Bale to go up to Glasgow and change the money into Scottish banknotes (which the gang believed would be impossible to trace, as Scottish notes then had no numbers). Kurr would remain in London, in constant touch with Druscovitch.

A warrant was issued for Mr Montgomery's arrest and – of all the officers at the Yard! – Druscovitch was ordered to execute the warrant. All he could do was play out a charade of trying to do this; the situation was deteriorating by the hour. Kurr saw that Druscovitch's nerve was going: he brought Meiklejohn back from Birmingham (where he had been working on a case) to oversee the crumbling Druscovitch. At this point Benson paid the three detectives £500 apiece as a refresher – little enough compared with what the partners had made.

Now Benson and Kurr disappeared. Druscovitch was pretending to chase the non-existent Mr Montgomery. On 10 November the two fraudsmen were in Scotland, at Bridge of Allan, and it was there that they received a telegram of warning, followed by a letter, from Inspector Palmer (the least active of the three corrupt detectives). Druscovitch was on his way to Bridge of Allan with instructions to arrest Mr Montgomery there (his superiors at the Yard had somehow been tipped off).

By the time Druscovitch arrived, Benson and Kurr had left. Druscovitch had to go back to London to face superiors who were growing a little puzzled at this hitherto brilliant officer's non-performance in this case.

Kurr went to another part of Scotland. Benson – who, it must be remembered, was crippled and therefore more noticeable in a crowd – went to Holland. There his luck finally ran out. He gave the hotel proprietor a Scottish banknote. The Dutchman had never seen one before and thought it counterfeit. He called the police. Benson was arrested on suspicion.

The Dutch police had Benson's particulars as a wanted man. They telegraphed Scotland Yard. Realizing that Druscovitch still held the warrant for 'Mr Montgomery's' arrest, Meiklejohn suggested sending a telegram to the Dutch police, and this was done. It read:

> MEN YOU HAVE IN CUSTODY NOT THOSE WE WANT. LIBERATE THEM. OFFICERS WILL BE SENT OVER LATER.
> LETTER FOLLOWS.

When Superintendent Williamson (their superior) duly ordered Druscovitch to Rotterdam, Druscovitch felt confident that the Dutchmen would have acted on these instructions. To his horror, he found Benson and two of his henchmen still under arrest in Rotterdam, waiting for him to convey them back to London. The police there had received the telegram but with Dutch caution had decided to wait for the letter of confirmation before releasing the trio. Druscovitch had no choice but to arrest Benson and the others and take them back to London. On arrival there he heard that another detective (unconnected with the plot) had arrested Kurr in Scotland.

The trial of Benson and Kurr attracted a good deal of attention. Coming before Baron Huddleston at the Old Bailey, Benson got fifteen years' penal servitude; Kurr and a brother of his associated with the swindle, ten years' penal servitude; Murray (another accomplice), eighteen months' hard labour.

Scarcely had Benson and Kurr arrived at Portland, the grim jail where they were to serve their sentences, when they made statements accusing the three detectives they had bribed – Druscovitch, Meiklejohn, and Palmer. They also alleged that their solicitor had been in the plot. He was a dubious character called Froggatt, well known to Lewis as one of the jackals of the law. They also accused Chief Inspector Clarke, alleging that, although the other three detectives had not been aware of it, he had been involved in the plot and had visited Benson at his home in the Isle of Wight.

Clarke's response to these accusations was to go to see Lewis at Ely Place.

Lewis had known Clarke for many years. He would no doubt have described him as a solid workhorse of a man, far from brilliant but almost certainly honest. He had in fact suggested to Joseph Bravo that he hire Clarke to gather additional information against Florence Bravo after the first inquest on her husband (Scotland Yard detectives were allowed to undertake private engagements in their off-duty hours at that time). Bravo had done so, but it appears that, off the turf, Clarke was less effective: he found out nothing.

Lewis knew that there had been rumours about corruption at the Yard going around for a long time. But Clarke? That rather surprised him.

Clarke had been arrested after the other three. In fact, he had arrested the solicitor Froggatt and given evidence at the police court against him.

The evidence against Clarke himself, Lewis believed, was of rather an equivocal nature. There was nothing against him comparable with the case levelled at his wretched colleagues, who had damned themselves again and again during the three months in which they had struggled to avoid arresting Benson and the rest of the gang.

But Clarke's visits to Benson were suspect, although he maintained that he had not known who Benson was. The 'Mr Yonge' he had visited at Shanklin was a wealthy man of leisure, living out a curious exile on the Isle of Wight. But, assuming that Clarke had been fooled by Benson's persona of a rich eccentric, attended by a housekeeper, two housemaids, a footman, and a French valet, the acquaintanceship between them appeared unlikely and had to be questioned.

What had this mysterious nobleman – rumoured to be a close friend of the Emperor of Austria – got to offer the veteran detective?

The answer had to be information. Clarke was investigating an earlier Benson-Kurr swindle deriving from a bogus company called 'The General Society for Insurance Against Losses on the Turf'. While he had not got as far as Benson and Kurr themselves, he had actually arrested two of their underlings, Edward Murray and Charles Walters. According to Clarke, he had reached a point of frustration in the case: he had evidence against Murray and Walters but not against those bigger criminals he suspected of being behind them. It was then that he received an invitation from Mr Yonge to visit him at Shanklin. Mr Yonge regretted that he could not come to London because he was a cripple and unable to travel. He could assure Inspector Clarke, however, that his journey would not be wasted. He, Yonge, had some remarkable information to impart concerning Charles Walters, recently arrested by Inspector Clarke, and at this moment on remand in the jail at Millbank.

Having very properly reported this odd invitation to his superior, Superintendent Williamson, Clarke went off to Shanklin.

But, if Clarke was to be believed, Yonge had little information to give. Apparently he had invited Clarke to his home merely to ask him not to let the prosecution call him (Yonge) as a witness in the forthcoming case against Murray and Walters. Clarke objected that there seemed to be no good reason why Yonge be called at all. Yonge gave no clear answer to that. He continued to beat about the bush, telling a curious story about how Walters had come to him with a request to translate racing advertisements into French.

An odd and pointless interview as Clarke described it. The prosecution at the trial would say that this was simply the occasion of Clarke's enrolment in Benson's gang; and that he had not been fooled by the 'Yonge' disguise for a second. But Clarke swore that he had not been bribed; he maintained that, if he had visited Yonge–Benson again – and he had done so – it was simply in the hope of getting more information. Later, Clarke told Lewis, Benson did indeed try to bring pressure on him by threatening to show Clarke's superiors a note he had written settling up a meeting in London. Clarke showed Lewis the note: it was discreetly phrased but inconclusive as proof either way. As Lewis later put it, he accepted Clarke's story, basing his acceptance on what he knew of the man's character – but an element of doubt remained in his mind.

*

Lewis gave the brief for the defence of the old detective George Clarke to the young barrister Edward Clarke, who at that time appeared to be riding a crest of success that made him almost irresistible. At the trial, which took place at the Old Bailey on 24 October 1877, before Baron Pollock and with John Gorst, QC, leading for the Crown, Clarke fought hard to prove that Inspector Clarke *had* been totally fooled by Yonge, the rich eccentric, and had never connected him with Benson, the master fraudsman. He instanced Clarke's successful pursuit of so many other racecourse swindlers – like all successful detectives, he had to take risks: he could not confine his acquaintanceships to the kind of solid citizens his lordship might wish to see sitting on a jury! A detective could not afford to be too particular; he must meet and talk with all sorts and conditions of men. Some would lie to him – that was inevitable – even try to compromise him, just as Benson was trying to compromise Inspector Clarke. But these were risks that had to be taken in the public interest.

And so Clarke went on, carefully building up the picture of his namesake as a solid, tenacious policeman entrapped by a smooth and cunning villain. Unfortunately, the Benson he was presenting to the jury appeared to bear no resemblance to the man who was waiting to go into the witness box to testify against the detectives. Benson sat, utterly dejected, his hair cropped convict-style, looking more like a bum lining up for a hand-out than the proprietor of a mansion in the Isle of Wight. But, with great patience and tact, Clarke set about building up a persona for Benson very different from the physical reality the jury could see before them.

Clarke's first words to Benson were, 'Now, Mr Benson, I have a few questions to ask you.'

The effect was remarkable. As Clarke wrote many years later, Benson responded at once to this courteous approach. His face lit up; he rose and bowed his acknowledgement, awaiting Clarke's questions. These were all designed to lend credibility not to the convict in the witness box but to the wealthy dilettante who had dazzled Inspector Clarke. He was asked about his fine house at Shanklin, about the wide cross-section of society he had entertained there, about his education, his interest in the arts. Flattered, pitiably glad to escape, if only for a few moments, from the hideous present to the luxurious past, Benson responded as Clarke had hoped he would. By the time the cross-examination was over, it was easy for the jury to believe in the man Edward Clarke conjured up for them.

Having succeeded in this, Clarke concentrated on Inspector Clarke's character: his thirty-seven years of unblemished service as a policeman, the latter part of it as a detective. There was no reason why Clarke should have allowed himself to be corrupted at the end of a long and honourable career: 'He has for a number of years been connected with cases involving turf frauds, and has been in constant communication with men who by means of these frauds have accumulated large sums of money, but of whom he was a vigilant and persistent foe. Can it be doubted that the swindlers of whom he was the enemy would have filled his hands with gold if he would only consent to aid them in diverting the pursuit of justice?'

Clarke's persuasive magic worked again. Chief Inspector Clarke was acquitted. The three other detectives were sentenced to two years' imprisonment, joining their former paymasters at Portland

As Edward Clarke saw it, he was the only one of the counsel engaged who had any chance of winning; his colleagues 'could only jump in and splash about'. For his part, although Lewis was a passionate advocate of the right of a prisoner to go into the box and give evidence on his own behalf, he was always to believe that in this case the prohibition against this worked to the advantage of the accused. For, if Inspector Clarke had been able to go into the witness box on his own behalf – and what excuse could counsel have found for keeping him out of it? – he might have been cross-examined to deadly effect about his relationship with wealthy 'Mr Yonge'.

16

Opera Bouffe

EARLY IN 1878 Katherine Elizabeth Lewis was born, the youngest of Lewis's children – always to be known to everyone, inside the family and out of it, as 'Katie'.

She resembled her mother more than did either of her sisters, and not only in appearance. From early childhood she displayed the same audacity and directness, but she was essentially different. As Max Beerbohm was to say years later, when Katie was a beautiful young woman and he was hoping to marry her, she had all her mother's charm and wit but also a softness her mother lacked. Katie, he said, was even prepared to concede that fools might have been created with *some* purpose in the divine scheme!

Now she was a baby in a cot in the upper part of the house in Portland Place, the subject of intense concern and interest to the other children, particularly to her sisters, Alice, now thirteen, and Gertrude, now seven. George ('George the Second') also showed interest, but in a more subdued fashion: boys were not supposed to enthuse over babies. All three elder children were being taught by a governess; and had also begun to have occasional lessons from a brilliant young man called Joseph Jacobs. Born in Sydney, Australia, Jacobs had come to England to study at St John's College, Cambridge. At the time he met the Lewises, he had recently graduated as Senior Moralist – that is, he had come first in the Moral Sciences Tripos in the whole university.

Jacobs could stand for many young men and women whom George and Elizabeth befriended at the most crucial stage of their lives – the point when they become aware that they possess unusual abilities but find it difficult to assert themselves without appearing brash or aggressive. This actually applied much less to Joseph Jacobs than to most of the Lewises' protégés – especially those who were struggling to establish themselves in one or other of the arts. Jacobs had arrived from the antipodes already well equipped to scale the social and cultural stockades of London town.

Joseph Jacobs had been introduced to the Lewises by Edward Burne-Jones. Young as he was, he had already written articles championing the painter before it was fashionable to do so. Jacobs shared the Lewises' satisfaction in the fact that Burne-Jones had 'arrived'. He had in common with Burne-Jones a passionate love of medieval legend, especially Jewish legend, which was to result in his publishing collections of fairy tales and editing for a time the journal *Folk Lore*.

Although Alice, Gertrude, and George were still very young, Elizabeth was delighted that they were coming into contact with a mind as sensitive and well stocked as Joseph Jacobs's. 'I wouldn't care if they were only half their present ages,' she said. 'They must still benefit.'

If the pleasure they got from his lessons was any criterion, they did benefit. They certainly loved gentle 'Mr Jacobs', as they always called him. And for him the drawing-room of 88 Portland Place was to prove a launching-pad into the world of literary success.

The course of almost anybody's friendship with James McNeill Whistler followed a course that showed harsh and jagged as a fever chart: the fact that the Lewises managed to keep him as a friend for over thirty years represented a triumph of diplomacy on their part – especially as Elizabeth was hardly the hostess to turn the other cheek.

The year 1878 had been a disastrous one for 'the Butterfly'. (Like Dickens, Whistler liked to refer to himself in the third person.) His patrons the Leylands had commissioned him to create the Peacock Room. Now he had quarrelled with them and he was barred from it for ever; never again would he see the Bacchanalia of gilt and gold he had created. He was enraged. And he was soon to be granted an opportunity to vent that rage on an enemy – Whistler often spoke of his 'enemies': clearly he was one of those to whom enemies are a necessity.

Appropriately enough, the enemy Fate proffered at this juncture was a man who was himself of a dangerously cyclical temperament. In 1878 John Ruskin began to tread out a new circle of madness. He was in a mood to attack everything and everyone, from the newly perfected technique of lithography, to Rembrandt's 'licentious' paintings, to Goya's 'hideous' work – which should be burned! Such was Ruskin's mad-dog mood when Whistler put his 'Nocturne in Black and Gold: the Falling Rocket', a study of fireworks, on exhibition at the Grosvenor Gallery.

Ruskin's abusive judgement of the painting is famous: 'Cockney impudence . . . I never expected to hear a coxcomb ask two hundred guineas for flinging a pot of paint in the public's face.'

The details of the lawsuit that followed are equally well known. Although he was friendly with Lewis and Elizabeth, Whistler did not ask Lewis to act for him. His volatile temperament dictated his conduct in this as in everything. A number of different lawyers had acted for him since he had come to London. Up to the time of his action against John Ruskin, he had relied mainly on an amiable and competent man called Anderson Rose, who had already seen him through a number of financial scrapes and Whistler turned to him now.

The Butterfly had no doubt enjoyed his tourney in the witness box with Ruskin's counsel, Sir John Holker. Holker had asked Whistler if he did not ask two hundred guineas for two days' work and the painter had flashed back: 'No, I ask it for the knowledge of a lifetime.'

He got a farthing's damages. Lewis considered – anticipating the opinion of Bernard Shaw – that Whistler had made a mistake in not asking for damages in respect of commercial earnings lost through Ruskin's condemnation rather than injury to 'artistic reputation': an intangible the court could hardly be expected to understand. If Whistler had said he had lost £2000 in lost commissions, he might have been awarded £1000 damages.

Burne-Jones was a friend of Ruskin's – Ruskin had written of his Arthurian canvases in ecstatic terms – and Ruskin dragooned him into giving evidence against Whistler. Slow and gentle as usual, Burne-Jones's manner protested the repugnance he felt at what he was having to do. (He had in fact been subpoena'd but, in view of Ruskin's patronage, he could anyway have done nothing to avoid giving evidence.) Reluctantly, he had to pronounce against Whistler's work: 'Mr Whistler gave infinite promise at first, but I do not think he has fulfilled it.'

Pictures of night, he went on, were rarely successful: 'This is only one of a thousand failures artists have made in their efforts to paint the night.'

Whistler was incensed at Burne-Jones for thus enlisting himself among Whistler's enemies. He had some cause, for Burne-Jones also joined a consortium to help Ruskin find the costs of the case. Given Whistler's temperament, it is strange that his friendship with the Lewises survived – knowing, as he did, what close friends they were of Burne-Jones. Typically, he might have argued that George and Elizabeth were friends of Burne-Jones, his enemy, ergo, they too were his enemies. But perhaps he was motivated by cautious self-interest, for he ignored the Lewises' perfidy in continuing to know Burne-Jones; and by the time he was officially declared bankrupt – for £4641 9s 3d (a very large sum in 1878) – Lewis was acting for him.

On being declared bankrupt, Whistler immediately called on all his friends. As one of them said, he arrived 'in his long overcoat, longer than ever, swinging his light, thin cane, laughing his defiance'.

He asked his friends to put in their claims against his estate. Many were reluctant, feeling embarrassed. But Whistler told them to ask for every penny. There was good reason for this, and he was acting on instructions from Lewis. The more friends he had among his creditors, the greater their say would be in the administration of his estate.

The meeting of Whistler's creditors was held at the Inns of Court Hotel. Sir Thomas Sutherland (one of Whistler's most powerful patrons) was in the chair, flanked by Whistler on the one side and, on the other, George Lewis. The biggest creditor was Frederick Leyland, formerly Whistler's most generous patron. Among the assets with which he would be concerned was a savage caricature of himself entitled 'The Gold Scab: Eruption in Filthy Lucre', which showed Leyland as a repulsive-looking peacock covered in sovereigns.

Sir Thomas Sutherland made no attempt to control Whistler when the artist attacked Leyland as 'the quintessence of plutocratic putrefaction'. Nor did Lewis. They may have disliked Leyland. More probably, they saw the futility of trying to put any curb on Whistler.

Perhaps in the hope of intimidating them, Whistler had told all his creditors that the great George Lewis was 'acting for me in this matter of my bankruptcy'. No doubt Lewis did his best for Whistler with individual creditors, and negotiated on his behalf with James Waddell, the receiver, but the main advantage in Lewis's stewardship must have lain in his refusal to be bullied by Whistler. All too often Whistler got his own way – to his own ultimate disadvantage.

With regret, Lewis had to advise a kind of scorched-earth policy.

Whistler would have to sell everything by auction – his house and its furnishings, his own paintings – everything.

But then, Lewis told him, he would be free. Lewis almost certainly gave Whistler to understand, with all the subtlety he could command, that there was no reason why those friends of his who were also creditors should not 'claim' selected canvases against money they were owed. Later, canvases thus claimed could be returned to Whistler as a 'gift'.

Whistler did as Lewis advised. Many important canvases were 'claimed'; and in addition Whistler told stories of making bailiffs tipsy and then removing valuable paintings from under their noses. At least, Whistler's biographers concede, the bankruptcy gave him a fresh start. His house was sold and a week later he went to Venice.

During the period that Whistler was involved in his ruinous quarrel with the artistic establishment, Lewis acted in another row: this time among the practitioners of a very different and, in Whistler's estimation, vastly inferior art form.

For several years, Richard D'Oyly Carte had been one of the most regular visitors to the Lewises, though they did not feel the affection for him that they did for Arthur Sullivan. Despite the joke of the Lewis look-alike in *Trial by Jury*, they never got close to W. S. Gilbert. Elizabeth perhaps sensed the anger in Gilbert, masked by hearty Victorian 'fun'. There is a jovial sadism evident in the *Bab Ballads* and *The Mikado*; and there was the lewd play that circulated in typescript around the better West End clubs for many years after Gilbert's death – although there was no way Elizabeth could ever have seen that.

Later, of course, differences were to arise between Gilbert and Sullivan; but now the enormously successful triad they formed with D'Oyly Carte was threatened by purely external factors. The trouble blew up during the run of their new hit, *HMS Pinafore*, which opened in May 1878 to rapturous notices and large audiences. Then in the summer of 1879 things began to go wrong.

It will be recalled that in 1876 Carte had founded the Comedy Opera Company, to give the musical and theatrical genius of Gilbert and Sullivan a permanent home. At first Carte had encountered some difficulty finding a suitable theatre but had eventually secured a lease of the Opéra Comique (long since vanished). The Comique was actually a subterranean theatre hidden away beneath the (also long since demolished) Holywell and Wych Streets. The auditorium of the Opéra Comique was reached through a long tunnel which was entered just off the Strand.

The trouble began when Carte went off on a visit to America. He had overlooked the fact that the lease of the Opéra Comique was due to expire during the time he would be away. The official lessee of the theatre and holder of the Lord Chamberlain's licence to perform was a man called Richard Barker, then stage manager for D'Oyly Carte. When Carte left for America, he appointed a friend of his and Barker's called Michael Gunn to act as manager in his absence, naming him by power of attorney.

This set off a row among the directors of the Comedy Theatre Company. Meeting after Carte had left, they passed a resolution dismissing Michael Gunn. A notice was posted in the theatre saying that D'Oyly Carte was no longer in charge.

A frantic Richard Barker came to Ely Place to see Lewis. And Lewis began to receive a series of anxious telegrams from Carte in America.

Lewis had no doubt that this had all been planned by Carte's fellow directors long before he had left. This was a palace revolution intended to be enacted in his absence. On 21 July 1879 a motion was heard in the Chancery Division of the High Court to restrain Michael Gunn from remaining in possession of the Opéra Comique Theatre. This was opposed by Lewis. The motion failed and Gunn continued in charge in Carte's absence.

Then, on 31 July, the date on which the company's lease of the theatre expired – and also the three hundred and seventy-fourth performance of *HMS Pinafore* – trouble erupted in the theatre itself.

The second act had just begun. Someone in the wings shouted 'Fire!' There were sounds of scuffling and cries of pain. Some of the actors on stage reacted with anxiety and alarm, bringing the performance virtually to a stop. The audience got restive; people stood up.

Alfred Cellier, the conductor, standing on his podium in the orchestra pit, turned his back to the proscenium and addressed the audience: 'Ladies and gentlemen – there is no cause for alarm. Please remain seated!'

But they ignored him. A rush for the doors began. Cellier continued to appeal for calm, but his voice was soon drowned in the mounting uproar.

Then George Grossmith, star of the show, came forward to the footlights and announced that the performance had been broken up by a gang of roughs, hired by the anti-D'Oyly Carte directors. Their aim was to wreck any further performances of *Pinafore* and also to seize the scenery and props.

Grossmith could hardly be heard through the uproar, although on seeing him a few people did sit down again.

Backstage, a battle was raging. A contemporary report says:

> The gallant crew of *H.M.S. Pinafore*, assisted by loyal stage hands, proved too much for the enemy, and the invading boarding-party was soon driven off the ship. During the engagement several of the First Lord's sisters and cousins and aunts had fallen in a swoon, but 'Little Buttercup', the stoutly-built bumboat woman, distinguished herself greatly in repelling boarders.

Eventually the police arrived and order was restored. The performance was resumed.

Lewis was not altogether displeased: now Carte's enemies had gone too far. The hostile directors were summoned to appear at Bow Street magistrates' court to answer a charge of assaulting Richard Barker and creating a disturbance at the Opéra Comique Theatre.

Not actually being directors of the company, neither Gilbert nor Sullivan played any active part in all this. But when Carte returned – having cut short his American tour – he instructed Lewis to bring an action against his co-directors. This he won. Then, on Lewis's advice, a manifesto was drafted and issued to the public, making known all the facts of the case.

17

A Prince and his Pleasures

LEWIS'S FRIENDSHIP with the Prince of Wales had begun with Lewis advising him on matters concerned with the royal mistresses; it was to be confirmed – and deepened – by Lewis's support for him throughout a scandal about cheating at cards. But, several years before that, Lewis had to deal with difficulties arising from another of Edward's passions – horse racing. It need hardly be said that the so-called sport of kings was just as repugnant to his mother, the Queen, as all his other pursuits.

Whatever might be thought about his exercising his *droit de seigneur* among the young wives of the Marlborough House set, the Prince could at least have argued that his appearances at Epsom or Aintree enhanced his popularity – and therefore that of the throne itself. His worst enemy would have conceded him an intense capacity for enjoyment. Sir Edward Grey said of him, 'He combined bonhomie and dignity: a rare ability. He had a capacity for enjoying life which is always very attractive – particularly so when it is combined with a positive and strong desire that everyone else should enjoy life too.'

At any of the classic race meetings the Prince would walk around, saluting everyone, shaking hands with all and sundry – clearly loving every moment.

Naturally, he wanted to own horses himself. At first he ran them under other people's names because the Queen objected to his using the royal colours for racing.

The Prince's colours – purple, gold braid, and scarlet – were first seen at Newmarket in July 1877. Lord Marcus Beresford, who had first brought the Prince and Lewis together, advised the Prince on everything concerning racing and the turf. In 1883 he suggested that the Prince send his horses to a trainer called John Porter.

The first to go to Porter were two fillies named Geheimniss and Junket and they were leased from Lady Stanford. Apparently Porter arranged all the details. It was agreed that the Prince would pay for the fillies' upkeep for as long as they were racing; that they would run under the royal colours; and – very important – that Lady Stanford would receive half of any winnings. She professed herself delighted with the whole arrangement.

Unfortunately, reflecting on the deal afterwards, the Prince began to have misgivings. Perhaps he thought of what his mother's reactions would be. He discussed the matter with friends he considered knowledgeable about racing – and finally decided that it would not be wise for him to run Geheimniss and Junket under either his own name or a pseudonym. So he requested Lord Alington and Sir Frederick Johnstone to take the two fillies off his hands.

Lord Alington at once wrote to Lady Stanford, explaining the reasons for the Prince's decision. He said that the Prince proposed to ask the Exchquer to increase the amount of money allowed to him. The keeping of race horses might, HRH suspected, diminish public sympathy for this request. 'But all this,' Lord Alington rather naively concluded, 'is between you and me.'

Lady Stanford was infuriated. The Prince had reneged – behaved like a common racecourse welsher! No gentleman went back on his word, especially his word to a lady. As for Lord Alington's 'explanation' – well, that only added insult to injury. She instructed her solicitor, Thomas Wright of Leicester, to reply to Lord Alington in threatening terms. Wright did so, saying that in the preliminary negotiations, the trainer, John Porter, had clearly stated that the fillies Geheimniss and Junket were to be run in the name and colours of the Prince. That was the bargain – and Lady Stanford intended to see that HRH stuck by it. If agreement could not be reached quickly, Wright added, his client would have to seek redress in the courts and – playing his ace – HRH would of course be the party proceeded against.

The Prince sent for Lewis at once. What was he to do? This damned woman appeared to mean what she said. What could *Lewis* do?

Not much, Lewis must have reflected. Nothing, in so far as turning the tables on Lady Stanford was concerned. She was right: the Prince had gone back on his word. He was vulnerable to any action she chose to bring; he had no legal leg to stand on. Lewis had to placate

Lady Stanford, no matter how much humble pie he had to eat on behalf of the Prince.

He set about eating it: a long, and one suspects, disagreeable process. Lewis usually understated the qualities of both friends and opponents, so, when he describes Lady Stanford as 'capricious', it must come from the heart. No sooner had they got one obstacle out of the way, Lewis said afterwards, than Lady Stanford created another. At last Lewis wore her down to the point of agreeing that, if she did bring an action – which she still swore she was resolved to do – it would be against Lord Alington and Sir Frederick Johnstone, not the Prince.

Lewis knew her vanity craved a royal apology. He knew, too, that it could be dangerous even to suggest this to the Prince, who was renowned for his explosive temper. But he did suggest it and the Prince took the suggestion well. He wrote to Lady Stanford in very conciliatory terms, expressing 'deep regret' at what had happened: it was all a misunderstanding. Finally, displaying a humility that astounded Lewis, he thanked her for not bringing the action she had threatened.

This time, Lewis had not merely advised the Prince; he had been engaged in long and even humiliating negotiations on his behalf. The Prince was duly grateful – even though expressions of gratitude, like apologies, did not come quickly to his lips.

As Lewis's social and professional lives began to interact more and more, as he numbered more aristocrats and artists, actors and company promoters among his clients, so the house at Ely Place reflected this changed emphasis. No longer did Lewis and Lewis's offices merit Montagu Williams's description: 'A dull, dirty, and depressing place.' Clients passed from the noise and bustle of Holborn Viaduct into Ely Place – described as 'a cul-de-sac of intense tranquillity'. Coming to number 10, one passed through the great double doors bearing the famous name. Polished silk hats shone in the hall; shaded lights twinkled under green canopies; the atmosphere was sober, full of a subdued bustle, a quiet urgency. A clerk would meet the client in the entrance hall and usher him or her into a waiting-room. Then a discreet Ting! of a little bell would summon them into Lewis's presence. If it was winter, a cheerful fire would be burning in the grate. The room itself was of a calculated ordinariness: a wide mahogany desk, furniture upholstered in a dark sage green, and a round Chippendale table.

Lewis would be standing in the centre of the room. He would grasp his visitor's hand firmly; then invite him to sit down. Draped across a chair would be the famous fur coat; on the table would repose his tall silk hat, its polished surface reflecting every flicker of the fire. After a little preliminary chit-chat Lewis would work around to the matter in hand – gently but with a steely insistence, coming to the point very quickly. If this were a first visit, a client might have to suffer some very precise and searching questions: Lewis did not taken on everyone who came to him. But, if the would-be client passed the test, he never left Ely Place without a feeling of renewed confidence – this despite Lewis's determination never to raise false hopes. (Irving once told him that he must early in life have adopted the principle of Croaker in *The Good-Natured Man*: never to expect anything but the worst, the more to be agreeably surprised if the best did transpire.) But he would often see a way through the clouds later on. Better Lewis's realism than the facile optimism of a lesser man.

Occasionally Lewis might have occasion to summon his confidential clerk, George Daintrey. Taller than his employer but about the same age and a kind of softened facsimile of Lewis with his moustache and sidewhiskers, he lacked only the monocle. Daintrey might be required to bring in a document or even a cutting from a newspaper. Evidently he was always there, lurking just offstage, because he appeared immediately at the Ting! of Lewis's bell.

But if you were an established client, the black deed-box personal to you would already be waiting on Lewis's desk before you entered. Your name would be painted in white on the lid. When the interview was over, your box would be returned to the strong-room, to sit with hundreds of others, its owner's name turned to the wall.

The client who called in the afternoon would be offered tea, served on the round Chippendale table. If the client happened to be a beautiful woman, she would probably be offered tea – or some other refreshment – at any time of day.

And of course many beautiful women did sit in that office in Ely Place and sip tea in the intervals of pouring out their troubles to Lewis. Ellen Terry, Lady Warwick, Lady Colin Campbell, Virginia Crawford, Mrs Patrick Campbell, Lillie Langtry, Katharine O'Shea – all of them beautiful and all of them asking Lewis's advice.

It was inevitable that Lewis should have acted for Lillie Langtry, granted her association with the Prince of Wales. On the whole Lewis's professional connexion with her lacked drama: it mainly concerned her marriage with her uneasily complaisant husband, Edward Langtry – a marriage that, doomed from the beginning, took twenty years to die. Her troubles brought Lillie to tea at Ely Place quite often. A break had to come – but when?

Lewis counselled caution. No doubt because he knew it would be better for such a break, with its attendant publicity, to come after her relationship with the Prince had ended (Lewis had no difficulty in setting a term on *that*, in his mind).

Until the Prince did tire of Lillie though, the situation had to be contained – and with delicacy. There were some disquieting rumbles in 1879 when a man called Adolphus Rosenberg fired a warning shot in a scandal sheet called *Town Talk*, which he owned. He speculated about the husbands of some of the 'beauties of society' being only 'dummies'. Some of these beauties, he considered, had too many husbands. The innuendo was there, for those who wanted to see it. Two months later Rosenberg was more specific. The 'warmest' ever divorce case was about to be heard. The co-respondent, he gloated, was a big pot, the biggest: 'The poor husband is almost frantic. "Darn this country," he says. "Nothing belongs to a fellow here. Even his wife is public property."'

Over the next months Rosenberg worked himself up into a frenzy of innuendo, which grew more and more offensive and more and more obviously aimed at the Prince. Lewis had urged Lillie to hold off – again, to safeguard the Prince – but he discerned a worrying aspect of these attacks. Most of the scandal sheets – *Paul Pry*, *Puck*, *Tomahawk* – knew exactly where to stop. But Rosenberg appeared to be obsessed. A note of pain, almost of personal jealousy, began to sound through his articles. Lewis feared that such a man might be undeterred by the prospect of going to jail.

In the next few weeks Rosenberg went so far as to say that the Prince was to be named as co-respondent in the forthcoming Langtry divorce (no petition had been in fact filed). By this time Lewis wanted to act, but it is thought that the Prince ordered him and the Langtrys to hold back, so fearful was he of another Mordaunt affair.

Fortunately for the parties involved, Rosenberg's preoccupation with society beauties caused him to libel someone else. He had seen a picture of Mrs Cornwallis-West, another often-photographed beauty. He started by saying that it was presumably all right for women of a certain type to be photographed and then displayed in shop windows, but, when a 'woman of position' like Mrs Cornwallis-West allowed this, she has to be considered to be 'in the same street'. He went on: 'After having received her commission, she returns home to assume fresh positions, put on other costumes, and be taken backwards, full face, in profile . . .'

Rosenberg was undoubtedly obsessed. The innuendo of 'fresh positions' and 'taken backwards' was gross even for the scandal sheets. The lady's husband, William Cornwallis-West, Lord Lieutenant of Denbighshire, sued Rosenberg for defamatory libel – thus pulling the chestnuts out of the fire for Lewis and the Prince.

When Rosenberg appeared at the Guildhall court, Montagu Williams at once rose to announce that he was instructed by Messrs Lewis and Lewis to proceed against Rosenberg in respect of libels against Mr and Mrs Langtry which had been published in *Town Talk*. The Prince had changed his mind.

The magistrates set bail for Rosenberg at £2000; he could not raise it, so he had to stay in jail till the case came up at the Old Bailey. Until then, he was silenced. But what if Rosenberg's counsel chose to subpoena the Prince? Poor Lady Mordaunt and her lovers must have cast a long shadow in Lewis's thoughts that night.

No one called the Prince. Nothing much, indeed, happened at Rosenberg's trial. It seems odd, reflecting on his temperament, that he did not choose to turn the occasion into an orgy of mud-slinging, but his counsel probably refused to go along with this. The defence mounted on his behalf was strangely tame. If a plea of justification had been advanced, Rosenberg could have dished up a good deal of dirt. But this was not attempted. The defence put forward by Mr Willis, QC, excused Rosenberg's remarks about the alleged Langtry divorce by claiming that it would be unethical for him to reveal his sources (words which have a somewhat modern ring). Indeed, Rosenberg hauled down his flag, inexplicably pleading guilty. He was sent to jail for eighteen months for the Langtry libel and got another six for his remarks about Mrs Cornwallis-West. Lady Mordaunt's sad ghost had not walked. Everyone could breathe easily again.

Lewis's satisfaction that the Prince's affair with the Lily had not blown up in everyone's face was obscured by a personal grief. On 13

March 1879 his uncle, George Coleman Lewis, died at his house in Woburn Place. Death did not come quite as suddenly to him as it had to Lewis's father. Uncle George had been ill for some days, but the old man's passing still came as a great shock to Lewis. Unlike his brother, James Lewis, George Coleman Lewis had relinquished a good part of his workload in recent years. Lewis and Lewis still acted in bankruptcies, of course, but could no longer be described as specializing in them. Uncle George had, however, continued to act for the Dramatic Authors Society.

Now Lewis was finally alone. He *was* Lewis and Lewis: the only partner. And, although the firm got busier and made more money and Lewis's fame spread across the Atlantic and around the world, alone he would remain for the next fifteen years.

It was through Lillie Langtry that the Lewises met the young man who became the most remarkable of all their protégés – although he would most certainly have denied being anyone's protégé. Oscar Wilde was in the truest sense a self-made man – and the same qualities that enabled him to conquer London within a few years were also available to destroy him.

At this time Wilde was a big clumsy young man with the kind of tallowy skin that sometimes goes with freckles. He wore a shabby frock-coat, which he left open to show a flowered waistcoat, and carried lavender gloves.

But something must have shone through this fat boy's show of dandyism, for Elizabeth asked him to come to tea. And then, later, to dinner. He had wit, even then, and no doubt Elizabeth and Lewis detected it – though behind what Lillie Langtry called 'those great, eager eyes', anxiety and insecurity lurked.

It is tempting to conclude that it was Elizabeth who managed in a few months to transform Oscar from an Irish hobbledehoy to a polished 'aesthete' (an expression then unknown, which he was to make famous). The rather grubby frock-coat had gone: he wore a velvet jacket edged with braid, knee breeches, buckle shoes, a shirt with a wide turn-down collar, and a large flaring green tie.

A year or so later, in 1881, Wilde was still playing the same role. *Punch* published a cartoon of him looking out of a sunflower. The caption read:

Aesthete of aesthetes
What's in a name?

The poet is Wilde
But his poetry's tame.

Best of all, Gilbert and Sullivan – ever attuned to the *Zeitgeist* – wrote *Patience*, a clever satire on the aesthetic movement. This opened at the Opéra Comique on 23 April 1881. It was a great hit and its promoter, D'Oyly Carte (knowing that Wilde was *the* aesthete in the public mind) was soon writing:
'I have suggested to him [Wilde] that it would be a great boon for him if he were to go one evening to see *Patience* and were to let it be known beforehand so that he would be recognized.'

Wilde took the hint, came to the theatre, and was identified at once with the absurd Bunthorne in the play: splendid publicity! But his ultimate intentions were more serious. He was contributing to the *World*, and his brother Willie (also a journalist) helped him to place articles elsewhere from time to time.

It was Elizabeth who suggested to their friend D'Oyly Carte that Wilde might go on a lecture tour of America. It would make him known and it would be good publicity for the forthcoming New York production of *Patience*. Carte liked the idea and suggested it to Wilde. Wilde agreed and left for New York on Christmas Eve.

By this time Wilde was very close to the Lewises. There is a letter from him to twelve-year-old George, sending him a pencil-case. Below his signature Wilde asks, 'Who is this?' There is a sketch of Henry Irving wearing a top hat. When young George wrote to thank him, Wilde responded with another charming letter.

Early in January 1882 he writes to Elizabeth from New York. He has not yet started his lectures and says: 'Without Mr Lewis to consult I feel a little at sea!' And then, a fortnight later: 'When I go to the theatre the manager bows me in with lighted candles and the audience rise. Yesterday I had to leave by a private door, the mob was so great. . . . Loving virtuous obscurity as I do, you can judge how much I dislike this lionizing which is worse than that given to Sarah Bernhardt, I hear.'

But an enemy had appeared on the horizon. This was an English journalist called Archibald Forbes who had recently covered the Zulu War as a correspondent at the front. Like Wilde, he was on a lecture tour of the United States and chose to project a very different image from Wilde. He wore a huge guardee moustache and medals acquired in various wars. He was intensely jealous of Wilde's success, and began to make sneering references to him in his lectures. Angry letters were exchanged between the two men and it is clear that Wilde feared that Forbes would wreck his tour. He wrote to Lewis from Niagara Falls, 'His [Forbes's] attack on me, entirely unprovoked, was one of the most filthy and scurrilous things I ever read.'

In fact, the playwright Dion Boucicault (famous as the author of *London Assurance* and *The Colleen Bawn*) had already written to Elizabeth at the end of January, blaming Carte as well as Forbes for ill-treating Wilde. He accuses Carte of merely using the Irishman. When Wilde could be displayed simply as a laughing-stock to advertise *Patience*, Carte was happy enough. What he had not reckoned on was Wilde making a success in his own right. Quite apart from the link with *Patience*, he had triumphed in America through sheer force of personality. As Boucicault put it to Elizabeth, 'When he [Carte] found he was astride of a live animal instead of a wooden toy, he was taken aback!' And he ends his letter: 'I cannot tell you with what admiration and gratitude Wilde speaks of you both. . .'

Lewis ended Forbes's harassment of Wilde with just fourteen words. He cabled Forbes on 28 January (before Elizabeth could have received Boucicault's letter, which was dated 29 January):

LIKE A GOOD FELLOW DON'T ATTACK WILDE.
I ASK THIS PERSONAL FAVOUR TO ME.

And that was that. There was no more trouble. Nothing could demonstrate more effectively the power Lewis wielded in the world of men and affairs in the early 1880s. Neither Forbes nor Carte wished to offend Lewis. So they left Wilde alone.

Wilde never forgot this intervention by Lewis; and there is no doubt that the admiration and gratitude Boucicault spoke of were enhanced by the Forbes incident. George and Elizabeth had entertained and encouraged Wilde all though his first years in London; they watched and applauded his ascent to fame. And then, Wilde himself always believed, by his own folly he forfeited their love.

18

Mademoiselle de la Tremoille

ALTHOUGH HE RESEMBLED Charles Bravo little as a man, Edwin Bartlett had certain things in common with him as a murder victim. Both were relatively young when they died; both were difficult in their personal relationships. Both died of poison; both left young and beautiful widows who were suspected of killing them.

This said, as many points of difference between the two men spring to mind. But the Bartlett and Bravo cases were both classic Victorian murder mysteries with every necessary ingredient – intrigue, jealousy, and questions that must remain for ever unanswered. In each case the attendant circumstances were odd to the point of being bizarre; and in each case a great deal of hostility was aroused against the widow.

For Lewis, the difference was that, while he acted against Florence Bravo, he acted *for* Adelaide Bartlett. She did not come to him directly. When she was accused of murder, her own solicitor, a Mr Wood, had told her she must approach Lewis and Lewis. (For some time past, Lewis had found himself acting as a consultant in cases brought to him by other lawyers.)

Florence Bravo came from a long-established English landed family; but there was some mystery surrounding the origins of Adelaide Bartlett.

She was born in France and the name she was given was Adelaide Blanche de la Tremoille. At her trial she was described as the 'unacknowledged daughter of an Englishman of good social position', her mother being French. But, if her nameless father did not acknowledge her, he never abandoned her. Although his identity was not revealed, he was always there to provide his daughter with apparently unlimited funds whenever she needed them. Thus, when she was charged with murder, Mr Wood was able to go straight to

Lewis and Lewis, in his turn, could brief the barrister he wanted for her defence without giving any thought to the cost.

In 1875 the beautiful Adelaide was in England (presumably her father was paying her expenses). In London she met and married a successful grocer, Edwin Bartlett. At first glance he appeared solid and conventional enough but, from the moment he married Adelaide, a streak of eccentricity manifested itself. He sent his young wife back to school – to complete her studies! – first in the London suburb of Stoke Newington and later in a Protestant convent in Belgium. And – another odd fact – bride and groom had only met on one occasion before their wedding day.

The explanation given for Adelaide being sent back to school was that she was as yet too immature to give Edwin Bartlett the kind of intellectual companionship he craved – although there was never any indication, then or later, that he had any intellectual interests of any kind.

The root of the matter was no doubt financial. Adelaide brought a substantial dowry from her father, money which immediately became available for the further expansion of Bartlett's chain of grocery shops in south London. The fact that the Bartletts were almost strangers when they married suggests that the marriage was arranged. Adelaide's father bought his daughter a solid English husband, while at the same time the husband got some working capital.

The marriage may be said to have really begun in 1877, when Adelaide came back from Belgium, and the couple settled in Herne Hill. They lived an isolated life. Bartlett was interested only in business, but Adelaide was apparently happy with her embroidery and her dogs. Both were in good health, and in 1880 Bartlett was accepted by the British Equitable Insurance Company as a first-class life.

Also living in the house in Herne Hill was Bartlett's father, a speculative builder who had gone bankrupt, which perhaps accounts for his sour attitude to Adelaide: he was financially dependent on his son, and he may have felt his daughter-in-law threatened his position. Certainly he tried to set Edwin against her.

He did not succeed. When there was some suspicion that Adelaide might be having an affair with her brother-in-law, Fred Bartlett, Edwin defended her loyally. Fred went off to America, and old Bartlett settled down into grumbling acquiescence.

In 1881 the apparently calm pattern of the Bartlett's lives was disturbed. Adelaide decided she wanted a child. At her trial, it was revealed that there had been an agreement, arrived at before she and Bartlett married, that their union should not be consummated physically till Adelaide considered herself 'ready'. Now, in 1881, she was ready.

In big things and in small, Adelaide Bartlett always got her way. Clearly she possessed an extraordinary power over men. Let her name her wish and Edwin would rush to fulfil it, like a genie out of a bottle.

This was proved by the way he pandered to her restlessness. Adelaide had no sooner settled in one place than she wanted to be in another. And so, at the mercy of her whims, they moved from Herne Hill to Merton and then on to Pimlico – all within the space of a few months.

Adelaide had the child, but it was stillborn; and this was enough to persuade her that she would never have another – or so she told a woman called Annie Walker, who had acted as midwife at the birth and had since become something of a confidante. Soon Adelaide told Annie that Edwin had made a will leaving her all his property, but only on the condition that she did not remarry. According to Annie, 'this made her angry'.

Immediately after the loss of the child, the Bartletts made their move to Merton in Surrey; and it was there that they met the man who would constitute the apex, so to speak, of an extraordinary triangle.

The Bartletts met the Reverend George Dyson at the local Wesleyian chapel. He was minister there; and the Bartletts, or at least Adelaide, were delighted by his preaching, which was in the florid, pluck-these-brands-from-the-burning style then popular.

Dyson does not sound prepossessing in a physical sense: 'His face is pudgy and the lower half of it is almost obliterated by a heavy black moustache.' But, pudgy or not, Dyson exerted a powerful magnetism over the ladies of the congregation. As a graduate of Trinity College, Dublin, he was particularly impressive to the Bartletts.

A strange three-way relationship developed. Not only were the Bartletts and Dyson soon on christian name terms – very unusual for people of that social class at that period – but it was soon clear that Edwin Bartlett was throwing Adelaide and Dyson together. And, although Dyson was said to be a hypnotist – indeed, at the trial it was alleged that he had taught Adelaide how to hypnotize her husband – it was soon evident that it was Adelaide who was doing the hypnotizing: he was completely under her spell.

The subject of Adelaide's education came up almost immediately. Edwin suggested that 'George' should act as her tutor. So it was arranged that Dyson should come to the house each morning at eleven and remain there until Bartlett returned home in the evening.

When the Bartletts decided to go to Dover for a holiday, Edwin wanted Dyson to go with them; he even offered to pay the reverend gentleman's fare. Dyson accepted the offer and stayed in the same rooms as the Bartletts.

On 19 September 1885 Dyson was back in his lodgings in Putney when Bartlett called on him. This interview was important in view of the defence at Adelaide's trial. According to Dyson, Bartlett said that Adelaide liked Dyson's preaching; that she found it a joy and inspiration that could remake her life. Immediately after this meeting George Dyson wrote to Adelaide. That letter has been lost, but whatever was in it stirred Bartlett into writing back:

> Would that I could find words to express my thankfulness to you for the very loving letter you sent Adelaide today. It would have done anyone good to see her overflowing with joy as she read it whilst walking along the street, and afterwards as she read it to me. I felt my heart going out to you. I long to tell you how proud I feel at the thought that I should soon be able to clasp the hand of the man who from his heart could pen such noble thoughts.

Dyson replied in more restrained terms, but now the triad was firmly established. Bartlett asked Dyson whether, as a minister of the Christian religion, he considered that there was any justification for his, Bartlett's, view that a man should have two wives: one for companionship; one for sexual gratification. Dyson gravely replied that he did not think there was anything in Holy Scripture to justify such a view.

Later Adelaide was to say that Edwin was a man who derived the keenest pleasure from watching 'the effects of her charms upon other men'. He had done everything to throw her and George Dyson together: Bartlett had asked Dyson to kiss her and had been 'beside himself' with pleasure as he watched them embracing again and again. By the end of 1885 George Dyson and Adelaide Bartlett were in the throes of a passionate affair – and Edwin Bartlett was enjoying every minute of it!

He appeared to be in perfect health and spirits, quite apart from his delight in Adelaide's adultery. And yet – and for the first time this unlikely imbroglio passes from the merely unusual to the sinister – it was around this time that Adelaide told Dyson, 'Edwin has not more than a year to live – and he knows it.'

Now the Bartletts decided to make yet another of their moves. They took rooms in Claverton Street, Pimlico, where the landlord was a man called Frederick Doggett. By chance, Doggett happened also to be the local registrar of births and deaths.

Once the Bartletts were settled in these new lodgings, Edwin Bartlett began to feel ill. His normally ruddy complexion faded; his face acquired a muddy, greyish tinge. He became depressed, and this depression developed into a chronic fatigue.

Over the next two months his health steadily deteriorated. The affair between Adelaide and George Dyson went on, scandalizing the landlady, Mrs Doggett; but, more importantly, Adelaide captivated a new man, a man who could play an important part in her future plans. This was a local doctor, called Alfred Leach. He was young, only recently qualified, and – from the way he behaved – appeared somewhat naive. Adelaide consulted him and cleverly planted the idea in Leach's mind that Edwin was a hypochondriac – this was before the doctor had ever seen Edwin. Edwin suffered from vomiting and diarrhoea and Dr Leach diagnosed gastritis. Later – probably because he was highly suggestible and already in thrall to Adelaide – Dr Leach thought Edwin had been taking mercury, then the treatment for syphilis (a disease which Edwin had never had).

Meanwhile, Adelaide was keeping Edwin's family, especially his father, whom she hated, from seeing him. Old Bartlett wanted a second opinion; eventually Dr Leach brought in another doctor, a Dr John Dudley. But Leach did not give Dudley a fair chance. He did not mention his idea of mercury poisoning; in fact he did not put forward the theory of poisoning at all, and thus Dudley considered Edwin's to be a case of gastritis.

But now Leach opposed Adelaide's wishes. He wanted Edwin to go away 'to recuperate', at Torquay.

This did not suit Adelaide at all. She managed to thwart the proposal by pretending that Edwin had worms – this threw Leach off course and Torquay was forgotten.

At this point Edwin had a strange conversation with Dr Leach in Adelaide's presence. He started to discuss mesmerism (hypnotism). Edwin put forward the idea that someone might be mesmerizing him; that he was under the mesmeric control of someone else – presumably Dyson. Adelaide called the idea 'absurd'. As for Dr Leach, it merely confirmed his growing conviction that Edwin was mentally abnormal. Did Edwin hear voices? he wanted to know.

After this, Adelaide had to move fast. Dyson was still as besotted with her as ever; they had even discussed the question of their marriage after Edwin died. Dyson only got a pittance as a minister, and Adelaide told him that they would be able to live in luxury on the income from the Bartlett grocery chain. It was in the course of one such conversation about the future that she asked, quite casually, if Dyson would get her some chloroform. She wanted it to quieten Edwin, so that he could get some sleep.

Dog-like in his obedience, Dyson went off to get the chloroform. Adelaide had asked for a large quantity. He had to go to three different chemists to accumulate enough. All three served him because they knew him as a clergyman – and in the nineteenth century that commanded instant respect.

Meanwhile, Dr Leach had diagnosed Edwin as suffering from necrosis of the jaw, as the result of either mercury or lead poisoning. At Adelaide's trial the defence would maintain that he had been so depressed at this that he committed suicide.

At about 4.00 a.m. on 1 January 1886 Adelaide woke the maid in the house and sent her to get Dr Leach. She also woke the landlord, Frederick Doggett, and his wife. Edwin was dead. When Leach arrived, he showed that he was still highly responsive to anything Adelaide suggested: he accepted that Bartlett had taken a lethal overdose of *chlorodyne* rather than the chloroform that had actually killed him.

Adelaide hoped that she could get Dr Leach to write the death certificate. (Not till 1925 did it become law that no death could be registered without a certificate of death from natural causes or a coroner's order for burial.) Unfortunately for Adelaide she was, unknown to her, living under the roof of the local registrar for births and deaths.

This was a coincidence comparable with Mr Casabianca's meeting Louis Staunton in the corner shop in Penge. Dr Leach had finished examining Bartlett's body and was about to leave when Doggett confronted him. He told Leach that he could not, in his official capacity, register Edwin Bartlett's death. He would have to inform the coroner.

Bartlett had died from chloroform poisoning, not later than 1.30 a.m. (Adelaide had called the maid about 4 a.m.) If – as the prosecution was to say at the trial – she was guilty of his murder, there was a reason for her waiting two and a half hours before giving the alarm. The delay would give her time to make up a big fire to create a strong draught. This, with windows thrown open, would dispel the odour of chloroform.

Adelaide sent for old Mr Bartlett, and made arrangements for the funeral. She was still hoping Dr Leach would issue a death certificate. She made Mrs Doggett suspicious by asking if the sheets on her husband's bed could be washed at once. But, suspicious or not, Mrs Doggett did as she asked, so that when the sheets were required after the post-mortem they had already been laundered. Adelaide sent telegrams to Bartlett's business partners, informing them of his death.

Strangely, considering how often he had been visiting Adelaide, her lover George Dyson had not called that New Year's Day. Now she wrote to him, telling him of Edwin's death. He came the next day and was with Adelaide and her father-in-law while the post-mortem took place.

The verdict was death by chloroform poisoning. There would have to be an inquest.

Suddenly Dyson realized the danger he was in. Slavish, blinkered in his devotion, he saw how he had been edged, little by little, towards the precipice. It was *he* who had bought the chloroform. That made him her accomplice. She had been using him all along.

In his panic he threw away the empty chloroform bottles on Putney Heath. Everyone who saw him that day thought him distraught. He lost his nerve entirely, babbling to anyone who would listen; he told one of Bartlett's business partners that he had been 'duped by a wicked woman'.

The inquest was opened; then adjourned for nearly a month.

Dyson threatened to tell the police about burying the chloroform. He was quarrelling furiously with Adelaide, saying he was a ruined man. She, for her part, had realized the danger she was in. Her solicitor, Mr Wood, had taken her to see Lewis, who from now on took charge of the case. At the same time Adelaide tried to strengthen her position by telling what was afterwards called a 'marvellous story' to Dr Leach.

She began by saying that she had married too young – 'too young to even understand what marriage meant'. She went on, 'We entered into an agreement that it [their marriage] should be entirely platonic and that no sexual intercourse should occur. Except on one occasion, we abided by this agreement. The solitary exception was to enable me to have a child.'

Now she reached the real point of these confessions: 'He [Bartlett] liked to show me off before his male acquaintances and the more admiration and attention I received from them the more delighted he was. Then Mr Dyson came along. My husband threw us together. He asked us to kiss in his presence. . . Then a strange thing happened. During his illness he began to show signs of wanting to exercise the rights of a husband. I resented it and reminded him that he had given me to Mr Dyson. He agreed with me. Nevertheless, as he began to get better, his desires became more urgent and I had to think of some way of preventing him from putting them into execution. I got some chloroform with the object of sprinkling some on a handkerchief, thinking that in that way he would go peacefully to sleep. I was worried, however, as to whether I was doing the right thing, and on New Year's Eve I showed him the bottle and told him about it. We talked seriously and yet in a friendly way. He looked at the chloroform and put it on the mantlepiece at his side. He turned over and pretended to go to sleep. Soon he was asleep and then I fell asleep in my chair at the foot of his bed. The next I knew was when I woke up and found him dead.'

Naturally, Dr Leach found the implication of Edwin's perversity bewildering, but Adelaide's main purpose was to get across the reason for the chloroform.

By now Dyson's nerve had cracked. The dignified clerical persona had disintegrated: he was a very frightened young man. He made a voluntary statement to the police about buying the chloroform. At the resumed inquest Dr Leach and Dyson both gave evidence. Adelaide did not – and that created a bad impresssion. Even before the jury arrived at their verdict, the foreman said that Mrs Bartlett should no longer remain at liberty. She was arrested. The next day the jury pronounced a verdict of wilful murder by Adelaide Bartlett with George Dyson as accessory before the fact.

Lewis knew that there was only one man to brief in this case: Edward Clarke. Not only had Clarke already shown himself to be a magnificent redeemer of lost causes, but Adelaide's fate hung on the medical evidence. It was Clarke's handling of medical evidence that had saved the Stauntons.

As soon as he received the brief, Clarke got to work. Just as he had studied the pathology of starvation for the Staunton case, he now studied chloroform, its chemistry and effects.

The case for the prosecution looked clear. Adelaide Bartlett and George Dyson were in love: they wanted to marry. However complaisant Bartlett was, he was alive: an obstacle.

If Adelaide had a motive, she had also had an opportunity. She had been alone with her husband on the night of his death; she was, on her own admission, in possession of chloroform.

There remained only the cause of death, established at the inquest as due to the administration of chloroform. Like lines drawn by a navigator on a chart, converging inexorably at a certain point, all the evidence indicated Adelaide. There was one technical difficulty, though.

The experts agreed that anyone swallowing chloroform by mistake would cry out in alarm and disgust. Similarly, someone *forced* to take it would cry out even louder. No one had heard Edwin Bartlett utter a sound.

Prosecuting counsel, the Attorney General Sir Charles Russell (for many years it was an unbroken tradition for a law officer of the Crown to prosecute in poisoning cases), brushed the difficulty aside. Bartlett had been lulled into a doze by the external application of chloroform; then, when he was semi-comatose, Adelaide had administered the fatal dose.

This was the theory outlined by Russell to a court 'packed with fashionably-dressed women' – as the *Pall Mall Gazette* has it: again and again that phrase recurs in contemporary descriptions of murder trials. Lewis himself once half humorously deplored 'the gladiatorial fires that burn so strongly in these tender breasts'. But as soon as he stood up the Attorney General had made an announcement that greatly weakened the case against Adelaide. The Crown had decided to offer no evidence against the Reverend George Dyson.

This was a great relief to Lewis and Clarke. At one stroke the most important element in the Crown's case had been removed: the suggestion of conspiracy between Adelaide and Dyson. It also offered Dyson as a witness for Clarke to cross-examine (not possible, of course, if he had had to stand in the dock); and thus Clarke could expose the strange nature of the Bartletts' marriage. And – a whole new strategy was opening up for Lewis and Clarke – it would now be possible to shift much of the suspicion from Adelaide to Dyson. He had motive enough. He was pitiably poor and Adelaide had dangled before him the prospect of living in luxury on the profits of the Bartlett grocery chain, while at the same time remaining the admired and charismatic pastor of Merton Wesleyian chapel. As Clarke himself put it, 'the more closely I could associate his [Dyson's] actions with those of Mrs Bartlett, the more I could strengthen the reluctance of the jury to send her to the hangman's cord while he passed unrebuked to freedom'.

Clarke was right. The defence called no witnesses. Clarke relied on cross-examination; in his own phrase, associating Dyson's actions with those of Adelaide to as late a stage of events as possible. He also had to reassure Dr Leach and elicit from him a description of Edwin Bartlett that would suit the defence: that of an eccentric, invalidish man – the kind of man, indeed, who might commit suicide.

But everything really hinged on the medical evidence. Clarke made great play with the difficulty involved in forcing a man to take a fatal dose of chloroform against his will. If Adelaide had tried to administer chloroform to her husband when he was asleep, then she would have awakened him and he would have protested, cried out – and the Doggetts must have heard him. Even assuming that he was drugged beyond any possibility of being wakened, an attempt to force the chloroform down his throat would have choked him: at the post-mortem chloroform would have been discovered in the air passages.

Then Clarke put forward his own theory of Bartlett's death. Having 'given' his wife to Dyson in a strange mood of renunciation, Bartlett has second thoughts: he desires to reassert his rights as a husband over her. He tells her this; he is rebuffed. On a sudden impulse he pours a fatal dose of chloroform into a wineglass and drinks it. (In fact an empty wineglass was found beside his bed. No attempt was made to analyse what it had contained.)

Within two or three minutes, Clarke said, Bartlett would have passed into a coma. Then Adelaide returns and goes to sleep. Bartlett's coma deepens into death.

Clarke's speech lasted six hours. According to a contemporary report, after the jury returned:

> The Judge took his seat, folding his flowing red robes about him, the gold chains and the violet costumes of the sheriffs helping to relieve the gloom. Once more the terrible silence was broken by the clicking of the dock handle as it turned to give passage to the prisoner, whose face was now livid, her eyes closed, her lips glued together – scarcely alive. Carried to the front of the dock, she stood supported on either side by women warders. Two spruce doctors and the grave chaplain stood on her left and behind her two sturdy policemen.

The Jury's verdict was framed in the most equivocal terms possible – equivalent, Lewis thought, to the Scots' 'not proven': 'We have considered the evidence and although we think grave suspicion is attached to the prisoner, we do not think there is sufficient evidence to show how or when the chloroform was administered.'

This said, a formal verdict of not guilty, was returned.

That night, Lewis and Elizabeth gave a party. Clarke and his wife went to the Lyceum where Henry Irving and Ellen Terry were playing in *Faust*. When the Clarkes took their seats in the stalls, they received a standing ovation from the assembled audience.

Despite the mass-hysteria that was generated on behalf of the Stauntons, there were a great number of people who deplored the fact that they had escaped the gallows. But no one minded Adelaide getting off, though she was generally believed to have been guilty. It was thought that she had somehow managed to get the chloroform down Edwin's throat without his protesting, though no one could imagine exactly how she had done this. Apparently, the broadsheets were silent about her, but Sir James Paget, the famous surgeon, had the last word over luncheon at his club: 'No doubt the lady was quite properly acquitted, but in the interests of science she should tell us how she did it.'

19

No Time for Adultery

SOON AFTER Uncle George died in 1879, the Lewises rented Ashley Cottage, Walton-on-Thames (they were to buy it a few years later). It had been Elizabeth's idea. For some time she had been telling Lewis how good it would be to have a country home. Not too far from London, though – near enough for Lewis to retreat to on a Friday and still be back at Ely Place on Monday morning without having spent too many tiring hours in a railway carriage. And then there were the children. Elizabeth pointed out that they needed to get some fresh air into their lungs after a week in smoky old London.

Ashley Cottage seemed ideal. Although the *Strand* magazine was to dub it 'the most picturesque little habitation imaginable', a modern estate agent would describe it as an elegant country residence standing in its own considerable grounds. The long building was surrounded by a variety of trees and shrubs; the garden path was an eighth of a mile long and lined with rose bushes. At the end of it, a sundial stood at the centre of a circular lawn – the sundial being older than Ashley Cottage itself, it was said. Not far away was a pond, heavy with water-lilies. A huge chestnut tree stood in front of the house, giving shade in summer, but robbing the chequerboard of small-paned, white-painted windows of necessary light.

Inside, the rooms were admittedly small compared with those at Portland Place. Like every house the Lewises occupied, Ashley Cottage reflected Elizabeth's eclectic and always admirable taste. The hall paid a tribute to her German ancestry with pictures of Goethe, Heine, and Beethoven. The dining-room was dominated by one of Burne-Jones's Arthurian scenes – Ashley Cottage was full of his work, as was 88 Portland Place – together with engravings by Frederick Leighton and Samuel Cousins. The furniture throughout was Chippendale, although Elizabeth made one or two concessions to this being a 'cottage' with a Welsh dresser of fine simplicity in the kitchen and a long brass fender in the dining-room.

Since Ashley Cottage had been taken with the children in the forefront of Elizabeth's mind, the school-room was an important place (it was kept unchanged for many years after they grew up). Now that the children were older, Joseph Jacobs was taking a larger share in their tuition. Both Lewis and Elizabeth were anxious that they should receive an education of wider scope than that usually accorded to English children of the upper-middle class. And they wanted this wider vision for the girls just as much as for George, who was soon to tread the establishment route denied to his father because of his Jewish blood: he was to go to Harrow and then to Balliol College, Oxford.

The Lewises' attitude might be described as 'progressive'. They believed that there were large areas of knowledge that should be accessible to a child as soon as he or she could understand them. Thus Alice, Gertrude, and Katie – to say nothing of George – had been allowed from an early age to meet the famous and not-so-famous who thronged the receptions at Portland Place. And they played an active part in social gatherings. They were not simply paraded under the surveillance of a nanny, patted on the head with an encouraging word or two, and then – silent, and pink with embarrassment – relegated again to the upper part of the house. (No doubt some of the guests, conditioned to a more typical Victorian attitude, thought George and Elizabeth were breeding little monsters.)

When the Lewises acquired Ashley Cottage, Alice was fourteen; still refusing to assuage the anxiety that nagged her father at odd moments, she remained, somehow, the odd girl out. Certainly everyone noticed that Alice entirely lacked the natural authority that should attend an elder sister. Everyone but Elizabeth, that is. To Lewis's exasperation, Elizabeth maintained a careful – and untypical – euphoria where Alice was concerned. If Lewis contrived never to quarrel, Elizabeth was expert at evading areas of possible conflict between them. The remarkable harmony they attained was achieved by their agreement as to separate areas of responsibility. Alice could not thus be tidily assigned. The question remained unsolved, to Lewis's increasing frustration. Elizabeth not only refused to discuss, she refused to recognize any degree of withdrawal on Alice's part – alienation would be too strong a word. Lewis, the victor of a hundred legal battles, confronted with these domestic nuances found himself at a loss. Gertrude, at seven, already appeared to have a more proprietary attitude to the new baby, Katie, than Alice did. George Junior held rather aloof, as befitted a young gentleman preparing to go to Harrow School.

Through the years – from about 1875 to the mid-1880s – the Lewises' social life continued to expand in ever-widening circles. Lewis was now personally as well as professionally a familiar of the Prince. On 19 February 1882 Edward entertained members of the theatrical profession for the first time at Marlborough House. Sitting down to dinner was a nicely contrived mix of actors and members of the set. Representing as it were the middle ground was Lewis, who naturally knew all the other thirty-six guests – whether they were actors like Squire Bancroft, George Grossmith, John Hare, and Henry Irving, or playboys like 'Sporting Joe Aylesford' (the Earl of Aylesford) and Charles Wynn-Carrington, who wrote, 'I sat next to Kendal [William Kendal], a good-looking bounder, who distinguished himself later in the evening by singing a very vulgar song which was not favourably received in high quarters. It was a dullish evening.' He added that the mummers were 'sandwiched in between ordinary mortals with more or less success'.

Elizabeth, of course, had already met and entertained all the 'mummers' of any note. This was the era of the great theatrical dynasties. Lewis had known most of these people since his childhood; his father had loved to relax with an older generation of Bancrofts and Kendals after a day championing the villains of Jacobs Island and Seven Dials.

But, while Elizabeth found the company of theatre people enjoyable, she remained more seriously concerned with painting, music, and literature. Apart from the Lewises' friendship with artists such as Burne-Jones, Alma-Tadema, Frederick Leighton, and Whistler, the 1880s saw Portland Place giving an equal welcome to musicians of executant genius like Anton Rubinstein and Ignace Paderewski. (The Lewises' was the first private house in which Paderewski gave a recital as a compliment to his hostess.) And in the early 1880s a number of writers began coming to Portland Place. The elderly Browning, long widowed and with only a few years to live, was among them. Henry James came: a dark-bearded, intensely serious man in his forties who bore little resemblance to the rotund, quasi-episcopal figure familiar to later generations. George Meredith came occasionally (he lived at Box Hill, in Surrey), bringing with him a breath of that mental athleticism, that sense of being 'alive with constant fire' that originally evoked the now-forgotten epithet 'Meredithian'. In his late forties, with his disastrous marriage to Peacock's daughter long behind him, he had to acknowledge Elizabeth's stature. The more so as she had been one of the first to recognize his *Tragic Comedians* as an extraordinary *roman à clef*. (It is based on a book by Princess von Racowitza, telling of her love affair with Lassalle, a German politician, killed in a duel because of her.)

Never a very frequent visitor to the Lewises – he was a lion already captured by another well-known hostess, Susan Jeune – Thomas Hardy could hardly have failed to respond to Elizabeth, given his obsessive admiration for women of poise and beauty and social position. His relationship with Florence Henniker typified this side of his character which has since been charted by his biographer, Robert Gittings: the preoccupation is perhaps best enshrined in the title *A Group of Noble Dames*.

Hardy had his only professional contact with Lewis in 1882, when the novelist was living at Wimborne in Dorset. In 1879, when he was in London and mixing to some extent in theatrical circles, Hardy had adapted his own novel *Far From the Madding Crowd* for the stage. This may have been intended for Lewis's friends, Henry Irving and Ellen Terry, who were then acting together at the Lyceum. If so, nothing came of it. Hardy then turned to a man called Comyns Carr, who had some experience of adaptation for the theatre. Carr rewrote Hardy's play, and in 1880 Hardy and Carr submitted the piece to the management of John Hare and Madge Kendal. They accepted it; then prevaricated; then finally rejected it. Madge Kendal said afterwards she had never seen the script. Whether this was true or not, either she or Hare gave the play's basic idea to a young man who was considered a promising dramatist. This was Arthur Wing Pinero who – like Lewis himself – came of a family of Sephardic Jews long settled in England. Pinero at once got to work and wrote a play called *The Squire*, which Hare and Kendal in due course produced – without at any stage telling Pinero how they had come by the idea.

The Squire opened at the St James's on 29 December 1881. It was an immediate success, but the critics could not fail to see its resemblance to *Far From the Madding Crowd*. When Hardy announced that an earlier adaptation had been sent to the Hare and Kendal management the previous year, there was a buzz of comment, although it did not affect the commercial success of *The Squire*, which continued to run at the St James's Theatre.

Hardy travelled up from Wimborne to see the play. He attended a performance in the company of Lewis and Comyns Carr. They sat in a box and tried to determine how nearly the piece resembled *Far From the Madding Crowd*.

The most important difference was the farcical portrayal of a clergyman in *The Squire*: a plum part for a comedian such as John Hare.

Lewis advised Hardy that he might have a case. Both plays presented a similar situation. He gave his opinion without enthusiasm: he knew Hardy's temperament. The long delay of a lawsuit followed by the ordeal of an appearance in the witness box would prove intolerable to the novelist. Lewis was right. Hardy would not proceed against Hare and Kendal.

Meanwhile, the papers had blown the affair up into a public controversy. Plagiarism was good copy: they fanned the flames as hard as they could. The *Illustrated Sporting and Dramatic News* suggested that a management with a sense of fair play should put on the Hardy adaptation and let the public judge between the two.

A management rose to the challenge and the Hardy–Comyns Carr play was produced at the Globe Theatre on 29 April 1882. It got respectful notices, but achieved none of the success of *The Squire*. Like the Lewises' friend, Henry James – whose agonized strivings to succeed as a dramatist were yet to come – Hardy remained fascinated by the theatre and yet strangely maladroit when he tried to write for it.

Hardy remained on friendly terms with the Lewises. He and his wife were to be among the guests at the wedding of their son, George Lewis the Second, in fourteen years time.

Lady Colin Campbell has been described as a glamorous nymphomaniac. Whistler called her his 'lovely leopard'; she posed nude for a 'Harmony in White and Ivory', which, it was rumoured, was destroyed by an outraged Mrs Whistler. But Lady Colin and Trixie Whistler disliked each other anyway. They once quarrelled so violently that Whistler ordered both wife and sitter out of the house to cool off.

Lady Colin Campbell was beautiful. Dark, with an athletic

figure and an audacious, gipsy look, she had been born Gertrude Blood, daughter of an Irish landlord. She met Lord Colin, son of the Duke of Argyll, in 1880. After courting her for the best part of a morning, he asked her to marry him. The duke was furious. A mésalliance! Nothing short of *lèse-majesté*, even for a younger son.

But Lord Colin defied him. He and Miss Blood were married in July 1881. Her family were present; members of the ducal house of Argyll were not.

An unusual feature of the honeymoon was that a nursing sister had to travel with the happy pair to look after Lord Colin. The modern reader will hardly need to be told that the bridegroom was suffering from 'a specific complaint', was in fact so ravaged by syphilis that he was practically an invalid.

By the time Lady Colin visited Lewis at Ely Place, her marriage was dead. Neither she nor her husband expected anything from it. But in the course of its disintegration great bitterness had been engendered.

Lady Colin arrived at Ely Place in a hurry, at half an hour's notice. Lewis's reputation was now such that prospective litigants almost raced each other to his office. When Lady Colin had told him the history of her marriage, Lewis at once filed a petition for divorce, charging Lord Colin with cruelty as well as adultery – a wife, it will be remembered, always had to prove cruelty as an extra; a husband could get a divorce on adultery alone. In this case the writ-servers must have passed each other in their frantic scurry across London. In the event Lewis's man got there a few minutes before his counterpart served a cross-petition on Lady Colin.

As well as alleging cruelty, Lady Colin was accusing her husband of committing adultery with a former housemaid called Mary Watson. On a cross-petition he named four co-respondents. Cynics were to joke that Lady Colin had selected representative lovers from every walk of life. Those named were: the Duke of Marlborough; Captain Shaw (chief of the London Fire Brigade); Dr Thomas Bird (a society physician whose patient Lady Colin was); General Butler (an eminent soldier). Butler had ducked the writ-server by leaving for France as soon as he heard about the case; the jury at the trial solemnly censured him: 'It is our opinion that, in not coming forward in the interests of justice, General Butler is convicted of conduct unworthy of an English officer and gentleman.'

For several weeks (beginning on 26 November 1886), the most expensive talent at the English bar debated the sordid details of the Campbell marriage. Lewis briefed Sir Charles Russell for Lady Colin; Lord Colin had Robert Finlay (a future Lord Chancellor). Sir Frank Lockwood (a future Solicitor General) acted for Captain Shaw; Sir Edward Clarke, who had recently been made Solicitor General and knighted, for Dr Bird. The Attorney General, Sir Richard Webster, represented the Duke of Marlborough.

The medical evidence was reminiscent of the Mordaunt case. The nub of it – and the basis of Lady Colin's charge of cruelty – was that her husband had, on their honeymoon, infected her with venereal disease. Concealing the fact that one had such a disease before entering into a marriage was ground for an annulment even in 1886; infecting one's wife could be construed as 'cruelty' and thus an ancillary reason for a divorce.

Dr Bird had been called in by Lady Colin to treat her. It was easy, her counsel said, to see why Lord Colin had included the doctor among the co-respondents. Lady Colin denied the charges relating to all four men. There was evidence from maids and footmen. One maid deposed that she had observed Lady Colin and Captain Shaw in 'a position from which only guilt could be inferred'. A waiter at a Purfleet Hotel said that Lord Blandford (as he then was, before becoming Duke of Marlborough) and Lady Colin had spent a weekend there as husband and wife. While admitting that he had spent a weekend at that hotel, the duke stoutly maintained that the lady with him was not Lady Colin but a 'woman about town'. (Oscar Wilde, writing to a friend on 15 December 1886, said, 'I had a long talk with George Lewis last night. He is very nervous about Marlborough's cross-examination.') However, the cross-examination passed off without any particular gain to Lord Colin.

But a great gain to him was medical evidence produced to show that Mary Watson, the housemaid cited by Lady Colin, was a virgin. This demolished Lady Colin's cross-petition.

Edward Clarke was in fine sardonic form: 'Mr Finlay [Lord Colin's counsel] seems to believe that if a man is found alone with a woman it implies that adultery has taken place. If a man is accused and does not attend to deny it, he is guilty of the charge imputed. If he does attend and denies it, then he is guilty of perjury as well as of the offence of which he was charged.'

Finlay had made great play with the fact that Dr Bird was alleged to have been discovered asleep in Lady Colin's bedroom. Clarke derided this: 'I do not think there is much in that to prove improper conduct. Had Lord Colin found him *awake* the case might have been stronger.'

Trifling details, gathered together to incriminate his client – that was all Lord Colin could produce, Clarke said. He made light of the fact that Lady Colin had addressed the doctor in her letters as 'my Cockioly Bird'.

Lady Colin went into the witness box to offer an unusual defence. She could not possibly have committed adultery, she said, because she simply would not have had time to do so. What Shakespeare called the 'deed of darkness' would have taken too long to be fitted in at any point of her day. Consider: she had to manage her house in Cadogan Square; act as hostess for Lord Colin, who was a Member of Parliament; deal with an extensive correspondence; teach working girls at night school; and help maintain a soup kitchen at the Stepney Mission. What *time* was there for adultery in such a busy day?

It took the jury over three hours to arrive at their verdict. Their deliberations included trooping off to the house at Cadogan Square to see for themselves exactly how much could be seen through the keyhole of Lady Colin's drawing-room. Their decision, when arrived at, was wholly inconclusive. They could not find Lord Colin guilty of adultery with the virgin Mary Watson; and neither could they find Lady Colin guilty with any of the four co-respondents.

Now Lady Colin had to make her life alone, knowing that she was now 'a notorious woman' because her sexual conduct had been impugned in open court. But she put a stoic face on it and went on to make a career as a journalist. She wrote for the *World* on pictures or on travel; and had a regular column in the *Queen*, advising readers in the manner later made famous by Emily Post on such questions as the use of visiting cards when making calls, the correct way to handle fish knives and finger bowls, and how to address titled personages. In middle age she became crippled with arthritis, and – still tirelessly writing – made an Italian spa, Salso Maggiore, a vogue with her readers in the *World*. Robert Hichens, the novelist, knew her at this time, and wrote of her stoic qualities and how she still, many years later, 'had to turn a brave face to the curious world, which whispered about her wherever she went'.

She became a friend of the Lewises and a regular guest at 88 Portland Place. She must have met Gilbert and Sullivan there; it is not recorded what she said when they lampooned her friend (and alleged lover) Captain Shaw in *Iolanthe*:

O Captain Shaw!
Type of true love kept under!
Could thy brigade
With cold cascade
Quench my great love, I wonder?

20

Beware the Member for Chelsea

ONE HOT DAY in late July 1885 a young woman called at Ely Place. The appointment had been arranged by her sister-in-law, Mrs Ashton Dilke, a widow who lived at Hyde Park Gate.

The young woman who walked into Lewis's office that morning, giving her name as 'Mrs Virginia Crawford', was twenty-three years old. She has been described as 'pretty, but hardly beautiful' and as having a particularly loud voice. Fair in colouring, she had blue eyes and a retroussé nose (some people bluntly called it a snub nose). But what must have been most apparent to Lewis that morning was her self-confidence – a self-confidence born of an iron and calculating self-control. How confident and how self-controlled she was, not only Lewis but the whole world would learn before the year was out.

Lewis did not know Mrs Crawford or her husband personally but he would certainly have heard of the Crawfords and, through mutual acquaintances, have been able to plot fairly accurately their social and financial position.

Virginia Crawford had been born Virginia Smith, daughter of an immensely rich north country shipbuilder called Thomas Eustace Smith, who was Liberal MP for Tynemouth. She was one of six daughters, none of whom got on with their mother, Ellen Smith, a society gossip who was said to have had a number of love affairs since her marriage. Rich in their own right, four of the Smith sisters married rich men considerably older than themselves – and two of them, it was said, did so to get away from their garrulous and overbearing mother.

Certainly Virginia married Donald Crawford to get away from her mother. Crawford came from Edinburgh; he was an academic lawyer who had been a Fellow of Lincoln College, Oxford. Rich, aloof, and pompous, he was what Dickens might have described as 'rather a buttoned-up kind of man'. He was twenty-two years older than Virginia Smith, who married him when she was only eighteen.

The marriage was never happy. It would not be over-simplifying things to say that Virginia discovered she had merely exchanged one prison for another. Five years later, in that summer of 1885, there was considerable tension between the two of them. Crawford was suspicious and watchful. He suspected Virginia of having a lover. Over a long period he had received anonymous letters suggesting this.

He was in a curious state of mind. He, too, was unhappy in this marriage: wanted to end it. But one had to have evidence of adultery to obtain a divorce – and vaguely phrased anonymous letters weren't evidence. He needed certainty. And then, suddenly, his young wife provided it. Or so it seemed.

A few days before Mrs Crawford went to see Lewis at Ely Place, her husband had received another anonymous letter. It had been awaiting him when he arrived home on the night of 17 July 1885. He slit open the envelope and read, 'Fool, looking for the cuckoo when he has flown, having defiled your nest. You have been vilely deceived but you dare not touch the real traitor.'

Nowadays no one could take seriously anything couched in such ludicrously melodramatic terms, but this hit Crawford hard. It came as the culmination of a series of such letters. The first had reached him as long ago as 1882 – more than three years previously – and had warned him that his wife Virginia had, along with her sister Helen (who was married to a stockbroker called Robert Harrison), been 'carrying on' with medical students at St George's Hospital. Robert Harrison had been a patient in St George's at the time and the two sisters were accused of using that as a cover for their bad behaviour. The letter ended mysteriously – and without apparent relevance to the flirtation with the medical students – with the phrase, 'Beware the Member for Chelsea.' (The Member of Parliament for Chelsea was Sir Charles Dilke.)

Presumably Crawford had been puzzled by that letter. Certainly he ignored it. Then, nearly three years later, in March 1885, another letter arrived. It stated bluntly that his wife, Virginia Crawford, was the mistress of Sir Charles Dilke and frequently visited him at his house at 76 Sloane Street. This letter appeared similar in handwriting and general appearance to the first one, and the earlier reference to 'the Member for Chelsea' – Dilke – was of course a link.

A month later a third letter arrived, markedly different in handwriting from the others. This said that Virginia Crawford was associating with an officer called Captain Forster.

It may be asked: Why was Crawford so slow to confront his wife with these accusations? Was it sensitivity, a reluctance to believe there was any truth in the allegations? Or was the delay strategic – granted that he himself was sick of this marriage and was eager to find grounds for divorce?

These questions can never be answered. What is certain is that, immediately he read the fourth letter, Crawford marched into his wife's bedroom. She was waiting for him. (Why? Did she know that the sealed envelope had contained an anonymous letter? If so, how?)

He told her he had received the letter; she asked what was in it.

He read the letter aloud. Then he said, 'Virginia, is it true that you have defiled my bed? I have been a faithful husband to you.'

'Yes,' she replied. 'It is true; it is time that you should know the truth. You have always been on the wrong track, suspecting people who are innocent, and you have never suspected the person who is guilty.'

'I never suspected anybody except Captain Forster,' Crawford said.

'It is not Captain Forster,' his wife said. 'The man who ruined me was Charles Dilke.'

Virginia Crawford was a liar – but a liar of genius. She had the gift of mixing truth and falsehood with the dexterity of a master conjuror. Even now, nearly a century later, it is still impossible to say why she perjured herself to ruin Sir Charles Dilke.

Dilke was the victim of a plot, a conspiracy – there is no doubt of that – and Virginia Crawford stood at the heart of it. It hinged on her, and on the false testimony she gave. But what were her motives?

She had no personal reason to dislike Dilke; indeed, she hardly knew him. So why did she do it? A dozen reasons have been put forward. Each of them involves Mrs Crawford – but each time she is associated with a different figure in the case. And each different involvement predicates a different plot. One has a political rival bribing Mrs Crawford to ruin his unsuspecting colleague, Dilke. Another has a discarded mistress of Dilke's using Virginia Crawford as an instrument of revenge. Yet another theory (the commonest, this) has Mrs Crawford, anxious to end her marriage, using Dilke as a dummy to mask her real, guilty lover. (But why choose Dilke?)

These are some of the alternatives. The case of Charles Dilke and Virginia Crawford is such a delicate equipoise of choices that it could be re-enacted as a game, with cards or counters to stand for its long-dead actors.

No one knows what Mrs Crawford told Lewis when she saw him that July morning. Did he demand to know the truth – whatever that was – or did he accept the version of it that Mrs Crawford wanted him to accept?

That question leads on to another. How far, as a superlatively skilful player of the legal game, was Lewis prepared to go? Did victory for a chosen client justify itself – even if it led to a monstrous injustice being perpetrated on an innocent man?

These are rhetorical questions, and there is no one alive who can answer them. If there were, it is unlikely that their answer could be favourable to Lewis. Mrs Crawford's story, even as first presented – she was to modify it in the course of the case – was not wholly convincing; and Lewis was the last man to be taken in by a liar with a pretty face. Remembering that he was in the habit of rigorously cross-examining clients to make sure that at least they were telling *him* the truth, it seems certain he could have faulted Mrs Crawford's story at half a dozen points. Or did he simply pretend to believe her and proceed to act for her on the basis of testimony which he knew in his heart to be false?

None of this sounds typical of Lewis but the fact remains that he did act for Virginia Crawford – fighting for her over a long period with all his usual vigour – and never referred to the case either publicly, or as far as can be ascertained, to any friend or relative.

When Virginia came to him with her story, Lewis would have already known several of the principals. He would have met Sir Charles Dilke on a number of occasions, and might have had some professional contact with Donald Crawford. And, through their friend Henry James, the Lewises knew a woman called Christine Rogerson who was to play an important part in the case.

Henry James disliked Dilke. He regarded him as essentially a hollow man, with an imposing presence and a plausible eloquence masking an essential mediocrity. Few people would have agreed. Many saw Dilke as a not-so-dark horse running for the highest political office – with every prospect of achieving it.

Sir Charles Wentworth Dilke was forty-three when Mrs Crawford made her 'confession' to her husband. He had been educated in an unconventional way, travelling widely with his grandfather in both England and France; then going to Trinity Hall, Cambridge. He was a Francophile when it was unfashionable to be so; he was also that rare and, some would say, contradictory animal: an intellectual who was also a professional politician. In his younger days he had been a republican, at a time when English republicanism could still be taken seriously – that is, up to the 1870s. But he had long since turned his back on such heresies and was a friend and colleague of Joseph Chamberlain. He had known minor office as President of the Local Government Board. In that summer of 1885, before Mrs Crawford made her revelations, the Liberal government had just fallen. They had, however, an excellent chance of returning to power. If they did, there were exciting possibilities for Dilke: the most exciting of them being that he might succeed Gladstone as leader. Dilke was more popular than the other possible choice – Joseph Chamberlain – and had fewer enemies in his own party. Best of all, Gladstone himself wanted him as heir apparent.

Having known tragedy, he was now happy in his private life. He had been married briefly to a brilliant but erratic woman who had died in childbirth. Now he was unofficially engaged to Mrs Emelia Pattison, widow of Mark Pattison, Rector of Lincoln College Oxford. (George Eliot is believed to have based the characters of Dorothea Brooke and Mr Casaubon in *Middlemarch* on the Pattisons.) Emelia Pattison was a woman of strong character who could be described as a bluestocking of the best kind. She was soon to marry Dilke – in the very eye of the storm – and give him endless comfort and support.

Dilke's private life had not always been so straightforward. In 1868, when he was twenty-five, a young man first entering politics he had had an affair with Mrs Ellen Smith, Mrs Crawford's mother (thus surfaces the first of the several available plots), and the affair had been resumed, briefly, in 1874 after Dilke's first wife had died. There was also some question about his relationship with Mrs Christine Rogerson.

Christine Rogerson, born Christine Stewart, played an equivocal role in London society. She was the daughter of a hostess well known in her day, a Mrs Duncan Stewart, but Christine Stewart never fitted any conventional pattern. She married a man called Rogerson, an amiable alcoholic many years older than herself, and when she tired of him, she hinted to Henry James, she poisoned him, although everyone had attributed the death to cirrhosis of the liver. By the time she got round to telling this story, it was impossible to judge its truth, but Henry James was sufficiently impressed to say of her, 'if she had been beautiful and sane, she would have been one of the world's great wicked women'.

The reference to her sanity has some relevance: in the course of the Dilke case she was certified a lunatic and was therefore not available to give evidence. She soon reappeared, however, and remained on terms of uneasy friendship with both Mrs Crawford and the Dilkes.

On the surface, her role was that of friend of the family. An old friend of Dilke's – perhaps more than a friend – who had overwhelmed his new fiancée, Emelia Pattison, with protestations of affection. But she was also a friend of Virginia Crawford and she had stage-managed assignations between Mrs Crawford and her lovers. Someone with a foot in both camps.

She was a ubiquitous, not-wholly-trusted figure, described as having bright eyes and short curly black hair, who wore always a linen shirt with starched collar and cuffs, a black leather belt, a black tie in a sailor's knot, a dark grey skirt and square-toed Highland shoes with silver buckles. After the death of Rogerson (whatever its cause) she was a frequent visitor at Dilke's house, 76 Sloane Street. She was a great friend of an old uncle of Dilke's; and was thought to have been the uncle's mistress. On his death, gossip said, she had continued in that relationship with Dilke himself and had hoped to marry him. When Emelia Pattison came on the horizon, Mrs Rogerson was infuriated: a woman scorned (thus another alternative scenario begins).

It is hard to know what Dilke thought of Christine Rogerson. Emelia Pattison certainly distrusted her. When Mrs Crawford made her melodramatic 'confession' to her husband, it was Mrs Rogerson who at once ran with the bad news to the Dilkes.

Mrs Crawford's allegations formed the basis of a divorce suit Crawford brought against her. (As the male partner in a marriage, he only had to prove adultery.)

Apart from Dilke's youthful affair with Mrs Ellen Smith, there was already a link between him and the Smiths. His brother, Ashton Dilke, had married another of the Smith girls, Virginia Crawford's older sister Margaret Maye. Ashton Dilke died in 1882. When the Crawford scandal broke, it was his widow, Maye Dilke, who advised her sister Mrs Crawford to consult George Lewis.

Mrs Crawford alleged that Dilke had seduced her soon after her marriage. In 1881, when Virginia was eighteen, the newly wed Donald Crawford and his wife were staying at Bailey's Hotel in Gloucester Road. One day Dilke called to see her while Crawford was out. He made 'amorous proposals' to her and kissed her, but that was as far as it went.

He did not see her till the following February, because she had been staying with her husband in his native Edinburgh. When they returned to London, the Crawfords took a house in Chelsea. One morning – again, when she was alone – Dilke called to see her. This time he was very importunate and she agreed to see him that afternoon at a house 'off Tottenham Court Road'. They spent about an hour there; she committed adultery with Dilke. That was the beginning.

The affair went on, with rather irregular meetings, for some two years. She went to the house near Tottenham Court Road only once more, but early in 1883 she got the opportunity to spend more time with Dilke. Returning from Edinburgh before her husband did, she spent two nights at Dilke's house in Sloane Street. As well as those two nights, there were shorter meetings at Sloane Street and at the house the Crawfords were living in at Young Street, Kensington. At Sloane Street they would go up to Dilke's bedroom; at Young Street they often remained in the drawing-room. Late in 1884, she said, Dilke 'tired of her' and their sexual relationship ended – although they saw each other occasionally socially.

That, in essence, was her story. If you granted that an ambitious forty-two-year-old politician, Under Secretary at the Foreign Office at the time, would attempt the instant seduction of an eighteen-year-old wife a few weeks after her marriage, it sounded plausible enough on the surface. But it all hung on Virginia Crawford's unsupported testimony – and at no time did any part of that testimony get independent corroboration from anyone else. That in itself made her story look less likely – and there was an impressive body of testimony from those in Dilke's employ at his house in Sloane Street to the effect that what Mrs Crawford alleged was impossible. A man of Dilke's standing maintained a considerable staff at his London house – a butler, footmen, housemaids, and other domestic servants – and, as a busy politician, he had a male secretary and a clerk as well. At no time of the day or night would Dilke be alone in the house; therefore, had Mrs Crawford made the number of visits she claimed – at the various times of day she claimed – she must have been seen by *someone*, at least once. She never was, and the staff at 76 Sloane Street all swore to that. If it is argued that these were loyal servants covering up for their master, it can be said that some of Dilke's employees were quite new in his service and owed him no particular loyalty. In any case, such unanimity would be quite impossible to sustain for any length of time if it were not genuine.

But – it must be repeated – Mrs Crawford was a liar of genius. Confronting her husband in her bedroom that July night, she dramatized her story in a way that made it irresistible – not only to him but to a shocked and delighted world that listened open-mouthed when they heard it all repeated in the divorce court early the following year.

First, with a few telling strokes, she painted Dilke as a Svengali figure, possessing absolute power over her. He had taken over her mind and will, she said. Let him command, she must obey. 'Why,' she said, 'if he entered this room at this moment, I believe I should have to do whatever he pleased.'

This was splendid stuff and Crawford was duly impressed. But there was even better to come.

Mrs Crawford told how Dilke had freely discussed his sex life with her. He had a number of mistresses. One of them was the maid who used to dress her, Mrs Crawford, after her sessions with Dilke. A middle-aged woman called Sarah Gray, she had been his mistress for many years. So had Mrs Rogerson; and Mrs Crawford described how anxious Dilke was to bring her and Mrs Rogerson together. 'Together' in the first instance, Mrs Crawford said, in a lesbian sense; when Mrs Crawford set her face against that, Dilke was content with introducing them to each other in a more conventional way. Then they became friends, which they had remained. There was also her, Virginia's, own mother, Mrs Ellen Smith. Dilke told Virginia that he had been her mother's lover; he had first been attracted to her, Virginia, because she resembled her mother at the same age.

But the really electrifying part of Mrs Crawford's story concerned a young maid at Dilke's house called Fanny Gray (younger sister of Sarah Gray). Dilke told Mrs Crawford about Fanny: she was not officially in his employ, but he kept her; she would come and spend the night with him at Sloane Street whenever possible (it should be said at this point that all these statements regarding Fanny Gray were contradicted by the staff at Sloane Street). Above all, he told Mrs Crawford, he wanted to see her and Fanny 'together'. At first she refused; he wore her down with his persistence, however, and eventually she was in the bedroom with Dilke when Fanny also entered the room. Fanny was nude and joined them in bed. After that, she participated in similar threesomes on a number of occasions.

Implying that she enjoyed these encounters, Mrs Crawford went on, 'He [Dilke] taught me every French vice. He used to say I knew more than most women of thirty.'

Not only had Mrs Crawford turned commonplace adultery into a relationship of stunning 'perversity' – ensuring that the Crawford divorce would become a *cause célèbre* of the gamiest sort – but she had also, with amazing cleverness, guaranteed that her story would be believed. Nothing she said was ever to be corroborated and she would be caught out in various lies – but she was never seriously doubted. Her story was accepted without question because no one could believe she could possibly have invented it. Such revelations of vice and depravity would shock hardbitten men of the world – how could a young married lady of good family even imagine such vileness? (Here, of course, we confront again the phoney idealization of the 'lady' that bedevils Victorian sexual mores.) Dilke *had* to have suggested this 'abominable' behaviour to Virginia Crawford – how else could she have known it even existed? As the president of the divorce court was later to express it to a jury, 'This is a most revolting subject, gentlemen, and one which one would be glad to believe untrue; but the question is, do you think Mrs Crawford invented the story? Which is the more probable – that a man should do such things or that a woman should invent them of him?'

Of course the judge and jury both thought that the man in question – Dilke – did do these things. Dilke was after all a man in his forties, who had by his own admission had several mistresses. And – wait! – hadn't Dilke been educated in France? Spent much of his youth in that unfortunate country? That explained a lot. 'Every French vice' – yes, indeed.

The truth was otherwise.

Although the Dilke–Crawford imbroglio was one of the most complex and intriguing of Lewis's famous cases, it is also the one in which his hand was least apparent.

Apart from the intrinsic unlikelihood of Mrs Crawford inventing the details of her affair with Dilke – a supposition that was to be in her favour in the coming divorce suit – there was of course another person involved, a witness whose testimony could sway the court one way or the other: Fanny Gray, Dilke's and Mrs Crawford's alleged playmate.

Unfortunately Fanny Gray had disappeared. She would never give evidence at either of the two trials arising from the Crawford divorce suit. She would, in time, reappear; but her absence during the year or more during which Dilke's fate had to be decided was of course crucial. It also represents another of the fascinating, unsolved choices in which the case abounds: was she bribed or bullied into hiding, and, if so, by whom? By detectives hired by Lewis to get her out of the way so that she could not testify against Mrs Crawford? Or by agents of Dilke, fearful that Fanny would confirm what Mrs Crawford said?

That is one of the unanswered – and unanswerable – questions. Two years later, Fanny, who had by then married a man named Stock, did make a statement denying Mrs Crawford's story, but she always refused to enter the witness box. This was to prove a great disadvantage to Dilke.

Meanwhile, in September 1885, an amazing development occurred. Mrs Helen Harrison, the former Helen Smith, Mrs Crawford's older sister, made a secret approach to Dilke, offering him certain information which could not be other than very damaging to her sister's case.

The approach appears to have been made with great secrecy and, in the Dilke Papers in the British Museum, it is referred to in an enigmatic, even off-hand way. Lewis was Mrs Harrison's solicitor as well as Mrs Crawford's, but it is impossible to say whether he was aware of this secret démarche to the Dilke camp. It seems more probable that Mrs Harrison acted without his knowledge, for Lewis was soon seeking to thwart any advantage Dilke might derive from this information.

It is not known exactly what Helen Harrison did divulge; but it was probably thanks to her that Mrs Crawford had to admit that Captain Forster (the man named in one of the anonymous letters Crawford received) had been her lover for a long time. More importantly, Mrs Harrison gave the Dilke side a lead to the origin of Mrs Crawford's three-in-a-bed story.

Two of the Smith sisters, Helen and Virginia, had married wealthy men nearly twice their age. Presumably they were bored; sexually unfulfilled. Whatever the reason, they both began, very soon after their marriages, to lead a life of considerable promiscuity. This was less remarkable than the fact that they 'hunted' together: worked, indeed, as a team. The troilism that Mrs Crawford had attributed to Dilke had been obsessively practised by her and her sister Helen over a number of years with a number of different men. Their taste was first documented early in 1882 when the two sisters were engaged in a tripartite affair with a handsome medical student at St George's Hospital called Freddie Warner (this was the period referred to in the first of the anonymous letters received by Crawford).

There were many similar involvements with men during the next two or three years. Helen or Virginia would start an affair with a man and meet him *à deux* for a time, but sooner or later he would find himself in bed with both sisters at once.

The man most important to both Helen and Virginia was certainly Captain Henry Forster. He had met Helen in 1881, Virginia in 1882. Then in his early thirties, he was a captain in the Duke of Cornwall's Light Infantry. His photograph – in full dress uniform; heavy moustache with ends carefully twisted and aligned; bold, resolute expression – is a stereotype of the professional soldier of the day: it does not hint at what must have been an insatiable sexuality, for he was catering not only to the Smith sisters in tandem, but to a number of other ladies, including, according to the Dilke Papers, a titled person, believed to be a countess.

A usual place for the sisters to meet men was a house of assignation at 9 Hill Street, Knightsbridge. Such houses were common in London in the second half of the nineteenth century, particularly in West Kensington and Earls Court. They could not be described as brothels – no prostitutes lived there – but they catered to anyone who wished to rent a room for one hour or more. Their main patrons were adulterous couples, and business was brisk from as early as ten in the morning onwards. Pseudonyms were almost de rigueur – Forster, for instance, was 'Captain Green'. He went there often – with Mrs Crawford alone; with Mrs Harrison alone; with both of them at once. They, in turn, went there with at least three other men, both singly and together.

It is clear that, far from being an innocent young bride, seduced by the ogre Dilke, Virginia Crawford had led a life of sexual abandon for at least three years (Dilke's solicitor later described her as 'a common prostitute in 1883').

Of course it has to be asked: Why did Helen Harrison choose to betray her sister to the other side? Betty Askwith, in her *Lady Dilke*, suggests that Helen was appalled at her sister's monstrous attack on an innocent man and was forced by a simple sense of decency into doing something that was sure to rebound on her later.

Not all this information was available to Dilke when Crawford's divorce suit came to court on 12 February 1866; but even a hint of it could have been as devastating for Crawford. But unsupported allegations are worthless. Sworn statements from the housekeeper and other servants at Hill Street were needed. When detectives employed by Ernest Humbert, Dilke's solicitor, went there to get depositions, they found that Lewis had been there before them. According to the detectives' report (and it must be remembered that all these statements come from Dilke's side), Lewis himself had been at Hill Street – acting not only for Mrs Crawford but also for Captain Forster and Mrs Harrison – and had threatened the housekeeper, Mrs Harvey, that if she did not keep her mouth shut he would see that she was 'indicted' (for keeping a house of ill fame). Later, Lewis was said to have remarked of Mrs Harvey and the other staff at Hill Street, 'I have plugged that hole with a hundred pounds.'

The divorce hearing was a curious affair. Even allowing for the fact that Fanny Gray was missing and could not give evidence, Dilke behaved in an oddly euphoric way. He was advised against going into the witness box by his counsel, on the grounds that he would thus be exposed to cross-examination about his past life – and his youthful affair with Mrs Crawford's mother would almost certainly have been brought up. Although it was by no means certain that such a line of cross-examination would be admissible, Dilke appeared to grab at the prospect of not having to go into the box. Clearly he dreaded the dredging-up of past indiscretions; he had been something of a womanizer and, as a politician, was terrified at the damage he might suffer at the hands of an expert cross-examiner like Inderwick, who was leading for Crawford.

It was an easily understood decision but a disastrous one. Had Dilke but realized it, it was his last chance to stand and give battle; he chose to let the case go by default. No doubt some of the blame must be laid on his counsel, Sir Henry James, but perhaps some fatal weakness surfaced momentarily here – thus justifying, in part, the doubt the other Henry James, the novelist, had expressed about his character.

Although Mrs Crawford's confession was the basis of her husband's petition, the case did not attract as much attention as Dilke had feared. The verdict of the court was easily acceptable to lawyers but hard for a layman to understand: Crawford was granted his divorce on the basis of his wife's confession, but, since that confession was not supported by independent evidence, the court did not find that Sir Charles Dilke had committed adultery with Mrs Crawford. Neat, but perfectly inconclusive.

At first, Dilke appears to have thought he was going to ride out the storm. He was wrong. The press took up the case, most notably W. T. Stead's *Pall Mall Gazette*. Stead could be described as the first 'modern' journalist. Bernard Shaw spoke of him as 'an utter Philistine' and this of course was part of Stead's strength. Although he wrote and flourished in the last quarter of the nineteenth century, he had the modern journalist's gift of being able to articulate the dumb paranoia of the masses. He also exploited public prurience by writing stories with a sexual motif in exactly the right excited, denunciatory tone.

Although the 'heavies' like *The Times*, the *Daily Telegraph*, and the *Manchester Guardian* would have been indignant if anyone had accused them of taking their line from a rag like the *Pall Mall Gazette*, this is exactly what happened. At first the comments of such papers on the Dilke case had been friendly, if a little – as with *The Times* – guarded. Now the *Pall Mall* swung into a campaign: why hadn't the member for Chelsea resigned his seat? Why didn't he speak out, vindicate himself? And the serious papers began to echo these demands. Public opinion swelled against Dilke.

Now the *Pall Mall Gazette* gave the campaign a clever twist. It was no secret, Stead wrote, that Dilke's parliamentary colleague Joseph Chamberlain had urged him not to go into the witness box: a disastrous decision indeed. One couldn't help wondering why Mr Chamberlain had chosen to give such bad advice.

The implication was clear: Stead was hinting that Chamberlain had *wanted* Dilke to do the wrong thing and wreck his career – and here we glimpse again one of the alternative conspiracy theories: that of a political rival striving to bring about the fall of a colleague. Chamberlain was upset at these insinuations, and this increased the pressure on Dilke to re-open the case.

At first, knowing little of the law, he thought he could do this easily enough, and his advisers, principally the charming but ultimately ineffectual Sir Henry James, appear to have encouraged him to think so. In fact, there was no way whatever in which he could 're-open' a case already decided in the divorce court. He had had his chance and he had thrown it away.

The divorce, however, had not yet been made absolute. An intervention by the Queen's Proctor *was* a possibility and, probably because of the newspaper agitation, that official did decide to intervene. (The Queen's Proctor is an official of the Crown whose function it is to intervene in any case where a divorce has been granted; and where, subsequently, some question arises of the court having been deceived or of some relevant fact having been concealed.)

At first Dilke was glad, anxious to enter the arena. He had assembled a lot more evidence about Mrs Crawford; about her persistent adulteries with Captain Forster and other men. The staff at Hill Street had now been persuaded to talk. He still feared the witness box, but he was eager to see Mrs Crawford, the arch-liar, being cross-examined by a master like Charles Russell, whom his solicitor hoped to brief.

Nothing like that happened. What Dilke had not grasped was the fact that, technically, he was now excluded from the suit altogether. He could appear as a witness but – and this was the vital deprivation – he could not be represented by counsel. The prospect of seeing Virginia Crawford exposed as a perjurer by Russell had vanished because the parties to the case were Crawford and the Queen's Proctor. And the Queen's Proctor would have no axe to grind for Dilke. In fact, the man who filled the office of Queen's Proctor soon proved himself entirely hostile to Dilke.

When the case was heard, before the president of the Probate, Divorce, and Admiralty Division of the High Court, Sir James Hannen, and a special jury ('special' in that it consisted of wealthy City men, who would dislike Dilke for political reasons), the Queen's Proctor was represented by Sir Walter Phillimore, an ecclesiastical lawyer of note (later to be a judge) but quite without experience in the divorce court. In any case, he was not Dilke's counsel; he only favoured him in so far as he was seeking to test the validity of the decree nisi awarded to Crawford.

In the event Phillimore was faced by Henry Matthews, QC, for Crawford. Matthews was one of the roughest, not to say most brutal, cross-examiners at the bar. Moreover, as a Tory and a Roman Catholic he felt personal animus against Dilke, the Liberal and former republican. Pitted against such an advocate, Phillimore appeared ineffectual – and in any case it was not his duty to defend Dilke against Matthews.

Dilke duly went in the box and did even worse than could have been expected. His inability to give a straight Yes or No, his incorrigible tendency never to use one word when he could use twenty and his general indecision and fuzziness told heavily against him; it contrasted strongly with Mrs Crawford's assurance and self-confidence. The crisp way in which she answered every question soon built an illusion of reliability in the listener's mind. To give a single instance of how far the court was hypnotized by the manner, rather than the matter, of her testimony: when at one point she was asked to draw a plan of Dilke's bedroom, she did so without hesitation and the drawing was handed up to the judge and then to the jury. Only after the trial was it established that the plan was wildly inaccurate and could have been merely imagined. But that did not matter. She had kept up the illusion of being a brisk, truthful, no-nonsense witness.

As if Matthews's relentless cross-examination were not enough, the president soon showed a marked hostility to Dilke, allowing Matthews great latitude and harshly snubbing Dilke when he tried to protest.

Nothing went right for Dilke. Certainly Mrs Crawford was forced to admit her adultery with Captain Forster, but that did not help much.

Lewis must have felt triumphant when the president ended his charge to the jury. Throughout the trial Mrs Crawford had displayed a smiling aplomb; at every turn Dilke had showed himself shambling, indecisive. No one can know what else was in Lewis's mind – some regret that lies were about to triumph over truth? Some feeling of compassion for a man who, whatever his failings in the past, was in the process of being ruined for an act he did not commit? Or was it enough for Lewis that he had won?

The jury only took a quarter of an hour to decide. The decree of divorce awarded to Donald Crawford must stand. The intervention by the Queen's Proctor was dismissed.

This was the end for Dilke.

From being the man who was tipped to succeed Gladstone as Prime Minister, he became that uneasy, very English figure: the public man blighted by scandal. Deprived of a future, he tried to fill the present with restless travel and desultory attempts at writing. He wanted to resign from his clubs but his friends dissuaded him. It would look, they said, like an admission of guilt. The Queen, with her usual gusto for punishing others, wanted Dilke expelled from the Privy Council. (It particularly incensed her that he would still be able to write 'Right Honourable' before his name.) She tried to bully Gladstone or Salisbury into arranging it and they would have been pleased for Dilke to resign but this, again, would have been thought an admission of guilt, so he refused.

In the period following the second trial Dilke obsessively sought evidence to vindicate himself against Mrs Crawford's charges. He spent a great deal of money in having teams of detectives – their efforts co-ordinated through a solicitor called Pridham – root out every detail of Mrs Crawford's life of debauchery. They accumulated a mass of evidence but, tragically, it could never be used. No court, no tribunal, existed at which it could be heard. Even the second trial in which the Queen's proctor intervened had been too late. Dilke's only hope of vindication lay in his being prosecuted for perjury after the second trial. Then he would certainly have cleared his name. In a criminal trial the Crown would have had to prove its case. Mrs Crawford would have entered the witness box under very different circumstances. No longer sheltered, as she had been by Matthews and the grossly partial president of the Divorce Court at the second trial, she would have had to face cross-examination by someone of the stature of Edward Clarke, and her lies would, inevitably, have been exposed.

Needless to say, no government did Dilke the favour of allowing him to be prosecuted. They knew what the result would be. Much better have him quiescent as a backbencher (he got back into Parliament, for the Forest of Dean, in 1892), too old to be considered for office (no Prime Minister would have given him a post in any government, anyway). Let him talk, let him dream, while younger men got on with the business of politics.

It only remains to ask which of the series of alternative plots was the one used to ruin Sir Charles Dilke. Apart from Mrs Crawford and the plotters themselves, Lewis must have known the answer to that question. Dilke himself claimed to know it but, if he did, he never named his enemy.

What is the evidence for each of the alternatives? All of them, of course, have Mrs Crawford as the linchpin of the plot. Granted her co-operation, what fellow conspirators present themselves? There is the jealous political rival theory – which, in effect, points the finger at Joseph Chamberlain. While there is probably no reason to endorse Stead's innuendo that Chamberlain deliberately gave Dilke advice which he, Chamberlain, knew to be wrong about not giving evidence at the first trial – after all, Sir Henry James gave the same bad advice – Dilke's investigators after the second trial did come up with a curious fact. They got hold of a notebook kept by a private detective who had been watching Mrs Crawford on behalf of her husband (no doubt with a view to catching her out with Captain Forster). On Wednesday, 15 July 1885 – only two days before her confession to Crawford – Mrs Crawford called at Joseph Chamberlain's house in Princes Gardens, Kensington. She was seen to enter the house and soon afterwards Chamberlain himself arrived. The watching detective believed she left some hours later in a closed carriage.

This is quite sinister in its implications, because when the storm broke Chamberlain maintained that he did not know Mrs Crawford at all, and never told Dilke that she had called on him only two days before she made her confession to her husband.

The whole incident arouses suspicions that are hard to dismiss, although Dilke himself refused to believe that Chamberlain was capable of such Iago-like treachery. And there is another curious circumstance, involving another case in which Lewis was closely involved: the Parnell–O'Shea divorce suit. Chamberlain was associated with Captain O'Shea; he encouraged him to start the divorce proceedings that wrecked Parnell. There is an echo of Dilke here, to say the least. As Roy Jenkins felicitously puts it, 'there develops a temptation to treat Chamberlain with the suspicion which normally falls upon someone who has been present at the scene of an unsolved murder and is later found committing an almost exactly similar crime'.

Then there is the woman scorned plot: the discarded mistress using Mrs Crawford to wreak vengeance on Dilke. There are two obvious candidates: Mrs Rogerson and Mrs Ellen Smith. This is in essence the same plot, whichever woman is preferred. With Mrs Rogerson, the provocation is Dilke's engagement to Emclia Pattison – when Mrs Rogerson had every reason to think he intended to marry her, if he was going to marry anyone. Mrs Rogerson would have been able to provide the details of Dilke's daily routine and of his establishment at Sloane Street that Mrs Crawford needed. The saucy story of troilism with Fanny Gray came out of Mrs Crawford's own extensive experience and was then grafted on to a backcloth of convincing detail furnished by Mrs Rogerson.

The Ellen Smith scenario would be much the same. There, Dilke's engagement to Mrs Pattison would hardly be a factor. But we know that Mrs Smith cherished a sense of grievance against Dilke. She felt he had used her; then cast her aside. She was particularly angry that he would no longer dine at her house. And of course it would be natural for Mrs Crawford to feel some animus against her mother's ex-lover. Ellen Smith would not know so much about Dilke's house and domestic arrangements, but these could be easily obtained from Mrs Rogerson.

The scapegoat theory – Mrs Crawford substituting Dilke for Captain Forster and hoping thus to get her freedom while protecting Forster – can be combined with any of the scenarios already mentioned. The question, why Dilke? draws the explanation from Roy Jenkins that Virginia Crawford clearly had a streak of exhibitionism in her that made her positively enjoy the storm that her accusations aroused. She chose him because he was a famous man: smearing him would bring her the widest possible publicity.

But all these theories revolve around the character of Virginia Crawford herself. How could she have acted as she did, lied as she did?

Looking at her, photographed in straw boater and wide sailor collar, she seems the personification of youth and innocence, half smiling, looking out towards a life that promises her everything. How can one blame the people she fooled? They could not see the cold, black, dead core that was the real Virginia. Although the word has been debased to mean everything from a mass murderer to a petty delinquent, she can only be described as a psychopath. Hervey Cleckley called a pioneer work on the subject of the psychopath *The Mask of Sanity*, and Virginia Crawford could assume any number of masks. The gentle 'artistic' young wife; the 'common prostitute' she was in the 1880s; the Catholic pietist, abounding in grandiose professions and good works, that she became after 1889. All were equally masks – the saint's as true or as false as the whore's – and all through a long life (she lived to be eighty-five) she assumed the mask of the moment with everyone she met. No one ever called her bluff.

21

Saving the Chief

By the late 1880s Lewis was the one man in London everyone wanted to fight their battles for them. As we have seen, they literally raced each other to Ely Place to secure his services before their enemy did. To have him fighting your corner, it was believed, doubled your chances of winning: his very name was a powerful ju-ju to a prospective litigant. He was known everywhere, as famous and ubiquitous as Fry's Cocoa or Pears Soap. He had been satirized by Gilbert and Sullivan; caricatured by 'Spy' in *Vanity Fair*. And, as usual, the Prince of Wales knew a good thing when he saw one: Lewis was not only his legal adviser but also his friend.

All this, of course, made enemies for Lewis – particularly the royal connection. Success is never wholly pleasing to everyone and then there was the question of his being a Jew. Anti-semitism was an engrained attitude among the English upper class, certainly among the kind of people who made up the original Marlborough House set. So engrained was English anti-semitism that it had a casual, taken-for-granted quality. But attitudes acquired a new edge of bitterness when the Prince began to discover that some of his best friends were Jews. It was not quite sufficient to say that he was friendly with a banker like Sir Ernest Cassel simply because he wanted to borrow money from him. However appalling his traditional circle found the fact, the Prince often enjoyed the company of outsiders. In January 1890 Miss Winifred Sturt (later Lady Hardinge) was staying at Sandringham. She wrote to her fiancé Charles Hardinge that she found 'George Lewis, the solicitor,' an odd fellow-guest, and was amazed to find baccarat being played into the small hours.

Clearly Miss Sturt bracketed Lewis with the baccarat as evidence of a deplorable lowering of royal standards. It is Lewis's profession rather than his race that is being challenged here. What the great mass of humanity would term 'work' would be regarded as a degradation by someone of Miss Sturt's education and background. Presumably someone had to sweep the streets or prepare corpses for burial or practise the law – but Miss Sturt did not expect to encounter such persons as fellow guests at Sandringham!

Such prejudices aside, by virtue of his association with the Prince, Lewis might have been thought at this time to be wholly identified with official attitudes. Such a judgement would have been mistaken. Not only did Lewis remain the friend and champion of the arch-radical Henry Labouchere, but he was soon to clear the name of the man who was anathema to the English Tory establishment: Charles Stewart Parnell.

The story of Parnell and the letters which Richard Pigott forged and *The Times* published has often been told, most notably by Dr F. S. L. Lyons in his *Parnell*. But few if any of Parnell's biographers have given Lewis more than a walk-on part in the drama. It was Lewis's keen observation and bloodhound persistence that enabled Pigott's letters to be unmasked as the forgeries they were. Sir Charles Russell's cross-examination of Pigott is justly famous – but Lewis provided the basis for Russell's attack. To use an appropriate Irishism: Lewis made the cannonballs; Russell only fired them.

Lewis's first dealings with the Irish Parliamentary Party – nationalists elected to represent Irish constituencies with the object of achieving Home Rule – was in 1884, when William O'Brien, an Irish Nationalist MP and editor of *United Ireland*, was sued because of an article in that paper exposing a homosexual scandal at Dublin Castle, the administrative nexus of British rule in Ireland. The allegations concerned such figures of the official hegemony as Gustavus Charles Cornwall, Secretary of the Post Office, and Captain Martin Kirwan of the Royal Dublin Fusiliers, a cousin of Lord Oranmore. The article caused anger in establishment circles, but this was prudently suppressed till O'Brien raised the matter in the Commons (where he was covered by parliamentary privilege). Then Cornwall and Kirwan were forced to sue *United Ireland*.

O'Brien found he could get no evidence to support his allegations. The Irish police would tell him nothing, obviously fearing for their jobs if they said anything against the gentry at the castle. So he went to see Lewis, who advised him to approach ex-Inspector William

Meiklejohn, one of the rogue detectives who had been jailed for corruption after the Turf Frauds. Since his release, Meiklejohn had built up a flourishing private enquiry agency and O'Brien was delighted to hire him.

Meiklejohn had not been in Dublin long before he discovered a widespread circle of homosexual activity that included 'men of all ranks, classes, professions, and outlawries – from aristocrats of the highest fashion to outcasts in the most loathsome dens'.

Thanks to Meiklejohn's probing, and despite the hostility of the judge, *United Ireland* won the libel action. This Dublin Castle scandal foreshadowed the Cleveland Street case with which Lewis was to be concerned a few years later. O'Brien was grateful to Lewis for putting him on to Meiklejohn; thus was forged a link between Lewis and the Irish Parliamentary Party. When in 1888 Parnell found himself in danger through the Pigott forgeries – to which *The Times* was lending authority by publication – it was to Lewis that O'Brien appealed to save 'the Chief' (as Parnell was known to his followers).

Cold, aloof, unsmiling, master of all the parliamentary arts, Parnell found it easier to inspire dog-like devotion than simple liking. His most fanatical followers were quite unable to relax in his company; he aroused mixed emotions in women, who felt protective towards him and yet were repelled by his coldness.

Years later, Lewis said, 'Parnell was an entire stranger to me until the day when he called on me. He asked me if I would represent him and the other Irish MPs. I knew very little of Irish politics, and I told Parnell that I would give him my assistance on one condition – that he would give me his word of honour that he would come to me at all times, when I wanted him. He gave me his word and faithfully kept it.'

Lewis admitted that at first he felt thwarted by the cool, disdainful carapace Parnell presented to the world. Only after many months did he feel he knew the man at all.

Easier to know – but perhaps even harder to like – were Parnell's mistress Katharine O'Shea and her husband Captain O'Shea. Katharine O'Shea – plump, vivacious, over-talkative – struck Lewis as essentially commonplace: strange casting for the tragedy she was to play out with Parnell. Captain O'Shea was almost the stereotype Irish charmer – and yet Lewis could smell the rage inside him. Labouchere had introduced Lewis to the O'Sheas. It was an open secret in journalistic and political circles that Katharine O'Shea was Parnell's mistress. While Parnell was able to ensure that O'Shea kept his seat in the House of Commons, O'Shea maintained an uneasy complaisance. Dr Lyons has aptly compared him to a time bomb; as the years passed, the ticking from the bomb got louder and louder.

Lewis and Katharine never liked each other, although she was to have good reason to be grateful to Lewis, both at the time of the Parnell Commission and many years later. She expressed this gratitude when she wrote her memoirs, although there is a certain falsity about her references to Lewis's 'keen brown eyes reading the hidden secrets of the soul', and to the 'exquisite' way Lewis was dressed.

The foundations of the plot to destroy Parnell went back some years. In 1881 Parnell had felt the need of a newspaper which could serve him as an instrument of propaganda. So, with the help of sympathizers in America, he bought three moribund journals – the *Irishman*, *Shamrock*, and *Flag of Ireland* from a man called Richard Pigott. Pigott was a seedy opportunist who professed extreme Irish Nationalist opinions but was in fact wholly venal. As a sideline, he collected and dealt in pornographic books and drawings.

The sale of the papers involved some correspondence. On his side, Parnell signed one or two business letters. Pigott filed away Parnell's signature for future use.

By 1885 Pigott – always chronically hard up – was in dire need of money. Perhaps the most complex of all the villains Lewis was to encounter, Pigott, smut-hound and political hack, was also a devoted and loving father. A widower, he cared passionately for the welfare of his motherless sons. Having approached a number of politicians with suggestions for journalistic work and been rebuffed, Pigott came in contact with a young man called Edward Houston.

Houston had been on *The Times*. He remains a shadowy figure on the fringe of the case, but he must have been somewhat naive to be as impressed with Pigott as he was. The point was that Pigott suddenly appeared, genie-like, and offered confirmation of what Houston, a Tory who loathed the Irish Nationalists, most wanted to believe: that Parnell had been behind the Phoenix Park murders (when Lord Frederick Cavendish and T. H. Burke were assassinated in the Phoenix Park in Dublin).

Pigott recognized in Houston the perfect dupe. For some months Pigott travelled around Europe on expenses furnished by Houston, meanwhile feeding his paymaster's credulity with 'reports' that were the stalest cloak-and-dagger fantasy. These served for a time but eventually, Pigott realized, he would have to come up with something better.

Meeting Houston in Paris in July 1886, Pigott told him that two agents had provided letters which proved conclusively Parnell's link with the murders. These agents were, he claimed, actually in the hotel where this meeting was taking place but had to remain unseen. Houston was delighted – so delighted that he gave Pigott £500 'for the men downstairs' (who of course did not exist) and £105 for himself.

Now Houston approached the British government with the letters Pigott had sold him, but was everywhere rebuffed. He thought of his former employers at *The Times*. The manager of the paper saw the letters and, without questioning Houston about their origin, referred them to the paper's owner, John Walter. Having consulted his solicitor, Joseph Soames, Walter decided to buy them.

Granted the doubtful origin of the letters – Houston refused to say where he had got them – one can only attribute to Walter's recklessness the same motivation as Houston's: he so wanted to believe Parnell guilty that he grabbed at anything that would sustain that belief.

Euphoric as *The Times* appears to have been about the letters, they made one or two token gestures towards caution. They got an authentic example of Parnell's signature and compared it with the signature on the letters, which were also shown to Sir Henry James (counsel to Florence Bravo and Charles Dilke). James expressed doubts, but his objections were brushed aside. Walter and his editors passionately wanted the letters to be genuine. Parnell secretly condoned violence and murder: everyone knew this was true; the letters confirmed it; therefore the letters were genuine.

The Times started a series of articles entitled 'Parnellism and Crime' in their best Thunderer tradition, alleging that Parnell was associated with 'avowed murderers'. The Home Rule movement was a 'foreign conspiracy'. Then they published the first of the Pigott letters, in which Parnell was made to say that condemnation of the Phoenix Park murders was the only course open to him, but that Burke (one of the victims) only got his just deserts.

The propaganda war against Parnell got off to a good start. *The Times* articles only reflected what everyone had always wanted to believe. Parnell led the Irish in the Commons and he had the typical Irish traits: he was hypocritical, violent, and bloodthirsty.

Naturally Parnell repudiated the letter as a forgery; but this was considered a feeble response; not adequate. Public hostility increased but after some months it seemed he was going to ride out the storm. Then a member of his own Irish Parliamentary Party thought himself libelled by a reference in one of the articles. He sued and lost ignominiously; in the course of the case, *The Times*'s counsel, Sir Richard Webster, introduced further letters which were said to have been written by Parnell (they were, of course, more forgeries by Pigott).

The fact that the accusations embodied in the letters had been made in a court of law forced Parnell to take action, especially when his bitter enemy Joseph Chamberlain had taunted him in the Commons with being unwilling to face an enquiry into the letters. Parnell contemplated a libel action, but eventually the Parnell Commission was set up. In effect, it would be a trial: Parnell against *The Times*.

In the months of preparation before the Commission, Lewis and Parnell got to know each other better; but their mutual exchanges remained untouched by any warmth. Lewis missed the normal pattern of the solicitor–client relationship. Parnell's icy pride would not admit any dependence on anyone – except perhaps on Kitty O'Shea.

Like everyone else who met Parnell, Lewis was baffled and intrigued by the man's opaque and glacial personality and his calculated eccentricities. Thus his appearance was always changing: sometimes his beard was full, sometimes close-cropped. Sometimes he would dress formally; at other times in a fur cap and a knitted woollen vest of bright scarlet.

And yet, in the months before the Commission sat, Parnell did develop a kind of dependence on Lewis. Some fifteen years later, Lewis described how Parnell had followed him one night to Ashley Cottage. Parnell had been at Ely Place earlier in the day and, after leaving Lewis, he had been nagged at by some question he had forgotten to ask during the interview. Lewis answered it as best he could; then, 'after a long conversation I drove him to the railway station [Walton-on-Thames] so that he might catch the last train; and, noting his anxiety and wishing to gain his confidence, I put out my hand and said to him, "I should like you to give me your entire confidence – you may trust me as you might your brother."

'We shook hands earnestly, but somehow I do not think I thoroughly gained from him what I wanted at that moment.'

Lewis believed he did gain Parnell's whole confidence later, but he could never be sure. No one could be sure of anything with Parnell – not his closest henchmen, not even the woman who claimed to know his heart and mind, Kitty O'Shea.

Not only was Lewis's the eye that first detected the key-point of Pigott's forgeries, but he also deserved Parnell's gratitude for briefing the one barrister – with the exception of Edward Clarke – capable of making the most of that discovery.

Charles Russell had been born in Newry, County Down, in 1832, which made him a year older than Lewis. Even so, it could be claimed that he belonged to the stable of brilliant barristers whose abilities were first spotted by Lewis, men like Edward Clarke and, much later, Rufus Isaacs (later Lord Reading). Charles Russell had been a success on the Northern Circuit. Lewis had been interested in a newspaper report of a case Russell had done in Liverpool and had tried him out with a brief in the High Court in London. Russell performed brilliantly: an historic association had begun.

On the surface Russell and Lewis had little in common. Russell was a Catholic and an Ulsterman; Lewis was a Jew and a Londoner. Russell was big in physique and gesture, often described as 'flamboyant'. Lewis was of average height and moved quietly and with deliberation. Russell carried a pack of playing-cards with him wherever he went and would play with anyone at any game; he loved horses and was something of an expert on form. Lewis never sat on a horse in his life – although he was a familiar figure in the Royal Enclosure at Ascot.

And yet these two very different men became friends at once. Both had a histrionic streak. In court Russell had to have his essential stage-properties beside him – a snuff box and a bright-coloured bandanna handkerchief – and they became as well known as Lewis's monocle and fur coat.

By the time Lewis offered Russell the brief to appear before the Parnell Commission, the Ulsterman had made his name. He had cut his teeth in London on several Labouchere libel cases – the most notable of them concerning a swindler named Lambi Pasha whom Labouchere was alleged to have libelled in *Truth*. Lambi Pasha pretended not to know English; Russell's cross-examination was so framed as to trap him into admitting that he did. Lewis never forgot that cross-examination. Now he knew that Russell was the man to unmask Richard Pigott, for both Russell and Lewis were well aware that this was, in Lewis's own words, 'the greatest case I have ever had in my life'.

From the beginning Lewis had accepted Parnell's word that the letters sold by Pigott were forgeries. Whatever else he was, Parnell was not a liar. Granted that the letters were forgeries, how had Pigott obtained a specimen of Parnell's signature? Lewis questioned Parnell closely about what contact there had been between Pigott and the leaders of the Irish Parliamentary Party. After some thought, Parnell mentioned the sale of the *Shamrock* and the other papers.

Lewis spent a whole day staring at the facsimiles of the letters that had been published by *The Times*. When he rose from his desk – his eyes smarting, his head aching – he had reached a certain conclusion about one of the letters.

Meanwhile, the Commission, which had been sitting for some time, was approaching the point where it wished to call its most important witness: Richard Pigott. He was not in London – the Commission was sitting at the law courts in the Strand – and no one was certain where he was.

At this point Labouchere gave a helping hand. One of his leg-men on *Truth* found Pigott in Ireland and persuaded him to come to London, on the excuse that there was a business deal brewing there that could be of advantage to him. When Pigott arrived at Euston, Lewis's clerk was there to meet him – and serve him with a subpoena to appear before the Commission.

Still believing in the business deal, Pigott came to Labouchere's house in Grosvenor Gardens. He was shown into a room on the ground floor, to find himself confronting Labouchere and Parnell. They accused him of forging the letters, but he remained self-possessed: evasive, even flippant.

Then Lewis came into the room. Parnell and Labouchere withdrew, leaving Lewis alone with Pigott.

'I'm in a difficult position,' Pigott said. Lewis had served a subpoena on him and now he might find himself prosecuted for perjury. Speaking as a lawyer, what would Lewis's advice to him be?

Lewis replied carefully that, since Pigott had not forged a negotiable instrument (for example, a cheque), he still had a chance of saving himself. If he confessed to *The Times* and stayed out of the witness box, he could not be prosecuted.

'*The Times* will give me five thousand pounds,' Pigott said. 'I want to know what *you* will give me.'

A few minutes later Lewis left Pigott and rejoined Labouchere and Parnell who were waiting in another room. He told them what had been said, adding that Pigott had promised to make a full statement the next day but wanted a word with Labouchere first.

Pigott then repeated to Labouchere that *The Times* would give him £5000 if he would give evidence for them at the Commission. What would Parnell's side give him to stay away?

'Nothing!' Labouchere said. What they wanted were the originals of the letters that had passed at the sale of the *Shamrock* and the other papers. He, Labouchere, would give Pigott £1000 for them.

Pigott left without giving a definite answer. Next day he called at Ely Place to see Lewis. He was trapped, he said. He had to stay the course: stick to his guns. *The Times*'s solicitor Joseph Soames had also served a subpoena on him.

Russell's cross-examination of Pigott is famous, comparable with Carson's of Wilde. Pigott in the box created an impression more pathetic than sinister. Fifty-four years old, white-bearded and bald-headed, he was described as looking like a 'rather cheapened Father Christmas'.

When Russell stood up to cross-examine him, the atmosphere was taut with expectation. On the table in front of Russell were facsimiles of the letters quoted in *The Times*, including – most importantly – the one that had been put in as evidence in the unsuccessful libel suit brought by Parnell's aide:

> Dear E, [believed to be Patrick Egan, concerned in the sale of the papers] What are these people waiting for? This inaction is inexcuseable [*sic*]. Our best men are in prison and nothing is being done. Let there be an end to this hesitency [*sic*]. Prompt action is called for. You undertook to make it hot for old Forster and Co. Let us have some evidence of your power to do so. My health is good, thanks.
>
> Yours very truly,
> Chas. S. Parnell.

Lewis's examination of the letter had enabled him to spot two misspellings – and he suspected Pigott might be unaware of these. Lewis knew that, once someone gets in the habit of spelling a word wrongly, that habit can persist all his life. So now Russell began his cross-examination with: 'Mr Pigott, would you be good enough, with My Lord's permission, to write some words on that sheet of paper for me?'

Pigott appeared surprised. An usher put a sheet of paper before him and he sat awaiting Russell's dictation. Russell asked him to write down 'livelihood', 'likelihood', his own name, 'proselytism', and then ' Patrick Egan' and 'P. Egan'. Then, casually – as if as an afterthought – 'hesitancy'. 'With a small "h",' Russell added.

When Russell saw what Pigott had written, he knew Pigott was guilty of the forgeries. He had misspelt 'hesitancy' just as it had been misspelt in the facsimile letter.

But Russell did not immediately confront Pigott with this. Slowly, even gently, he kept drawing the noose tighter, ever tighter. There was a gladiatorial excitement in the spectacle but many of those who witnessed it pitied Pigott, even though he was only getting what he deserved. Russell's skilful questioning built up a picture of a petty blackmailer and begging-letter writer, living on his wits, surviving only through humiliating shifts and contrivances.

When the Commission adjourned on the second day after Pigott had gone into the box (it was a Friday afternoon), Parnell remarked, 'Mr Lewis, let that man be watched. If you don't keep an eye on him, he will leave the country.'

The next day Pigott called again at Labouchere's house. Labouchere said afterwards that he looked like a ghost. He signed a full confession, which was witnessed by the well-known journalist George Augustus Sala. This was sent by special messenger to Lewis, who rejected it. What Parnell needed was a confession made in open court.

Later that day, Pigott sent for a Dublin solicitor called Shannon. Changing his tack again, this time he swore an affadavit that he had forged only some of the letters. Lewis thought this was probably a last desperate bid to get money from *The Times* on the basis that, if they held such a statement, they might still be able to claim that a few of the letters were genuine.

Later still on the Monday, Pigott sent a message for Lewis to call on him at Anderton's Hotel in the Strand.

He was a man hunted, distraught. As Lewis said, 'Pigott would not speak to me in the coffee room but took me up to his bedroom. He said he wanted to confess – he had to confess. He told me he had traced Parnell's signature by holding it over a window-pane. He had the loaded pistol with which he later shot himself, so my position there in the bedroom was possibly one of personal risk.'

Pigott promised to write out his confession and send it to Lewis, and the next day he duly posted it from Paris. For the first time leaving nothing out, he confirmed that he was the sole originator of the letters; he had based the forgeries on genuine letters from Parnell, tracing the signatures on a windowpane as explained to Lewis.

Having posted this final confession, Pigott left for Spain. On 28 February 1889 he arrived in Madrid and took a room at the Hotel Embajadores, using a false name. He spent the day wandering about Madrid, but when he got back to the hotel the police were waiting for him.

He went up to his room. The police followed him. At the moment a police inspector entered the room, Pigott muttered something and bent over an open suitcase which was standing on a chair beside the bed. The inspector sprang forward, tried to grab him. But Pigott had a revolver in his hand. He thrust it into his mouth and pulled the trigger.

In his last conscious moments – between the opening of the bedroom door and pulling the trigger – Pigott must have thought of his four boys, now to be orphans. Lewis and Labouchere later opened a fund for them; and in fact Labouchere made himself responsible for their education and welfare till, with new surnames, they were ready to go out into the world.

Lewis was right; this had been his greatest case – at least, no other case of his ever attracted more public attention. The Commission sat for fifteen months and, in Lewis's own words, 'involved the honour of sixty-five members of parliament [the Irish Parliamentary Party] as well as the honour of Parnell himself'.

It certainly made some new enemies for Lewis. Lord Salisbury's government had done all it could to help *The Times*.

The Times's solicitor had been given access to Dublin Castle files in the hope of linking Parnell in some way with the Phoenix Park murders.

The Tory administration was so closely identified with the Pigott letters that it could hardly conceal its dismay at Lewis's and Russell's triumph.

But Joseph Chamberlain and the other Parnell-haters in Parliament swore that they would get him yet. There was always the 'time bomb' – Captain O'Shea, most dangerous of cuckolds – ready to be detonated with devastating effect.

22

Daisy and Mina

1888 – THE YEAR that brought the fame and anxiety of the Parnell Commission – also brought into focus for the last time a question that had always troubled Lewis. His firstborn child, his daughter Alice, was now twenty-two years old. Gracious, attractive, she always seemed happy – smiling, serene, and composed. Indeed, her very serenity distanced her from the other children; made her appear a little aloof. Of course the gulf had always been there – no easier to bridge because neither Alice nor Elizabeth would admit its existence. Lewis was left puzzled, turning the matter over in his mind until a new case blotted it out.

Now, however, the question was going to be resolved – or perhaps left unanswered for ever. Some months ago a young man called Abraham Lionel Hart had told Lewis of his desire to marry Alice. It had been an awkward meeting, cracking with formality: not made easier by the fact that Lewis was the most successful solicitor in London and Hart a mere beginner at the Bar. But Lewis liked young Hart; he had already given him a few briefs. In fact he approved of him. He knew his family: solid London-Jewish merchants, and doubted if Alice could do much better.

But did she love this young man? Or did she want to marry to get away from a family where she felt herself in some way cut off from the mainstream of love and warmth? Could this early marriage be a form of escape?

He questioned Alice. Was she really happy marrying Lionel? Of course. Was he the one man above all others that she wanted to marry? Certainly he was. However Lewis phrased what was essentially the same question, he got the same answer. The master inquisitor who could tease a secret out of the most impenetrable of witnesses found his own daughter smiling, serene, and quite impenetrable.

He shrugged inwardly and gave up, decided it was better to concern oneself with practical matters: the marriage settlement, arrangements for the wedding. Here, Elizabeth would come into her own. She would never be closer to her stepdaughter than on the morning of 21 January 1888 when Lewis gave his daughter away to Lionel Hart.

But for Lewis there would always remain a scar, half cicatrized, on the surface of memory: the belief that he had never really understood his eldest child.

It was in the next year, 1889, that Lewis was caught up in a matter that has caused him to be presented in an unfavourable light by several of Edward VII's many biographers, who quote Lord Charles Beresford's angry gibe about Lewis's 'lickerish servility', but ignore Edward Clarke's view that Lewis behaved in an awkward situation with perfect correctness.

Daisy Brooke, later Countess of Warwick, has already been quoted on the intellectual prejudices of the Marlborough House set. She was the most beautiful and spirited of all Edward's mistresses. When Daisy was eighteen, Queen Victoria had honoured her (or so the Queen thought) by choosing her as a suitable wife for Edward's younger brother, Prince Leopold, Duke of Albany. Daisy politely but firmly refused him. The Queen was most displeased – especially when Daisy accepted a proposal from Lord Brooke, eldest son of the Earl of Warwick, the next morning.

For a few years all went well. If not exactly complaisant, Brooke was certainly tolerant. From the first, Daisy said, he accepted as inevitable her many admirers.

Daisy loved fox-hunting, while her husband had a passion for shooting. It was on the hunting field that she met Lord Charles Beresford (son of the Marquis of Waterford and brother of Marcus, trainer of the Prince's horses). 'Charlie B', as he was called, could have served Ouida as a hero if she had chosen to write about sailors. In 1884 he had been in Egypt, commanding steamers on the Nile that were carrying troops intended to relieve Gordon at Khartoum (they arrived too late). Surrounded by the corpses of his fellow officers, who had all been killed at the wells of Abu Klea, Charlie B remarked that it would have been intolerable to die without knowing who had won the Derby!

Daisy Brooke could hardly be expected to resist such a figure –

especially as he was also an intrepid rider to hounds. An affair began, played to established Marlborough House rules. But Lord Charles's wife, a Junoesque woman ten years older than he was, deeply resented her husband's tireless pursuit of other women. She watched Daisy and her husband with mounting rage.

The affair went on but, at the beginning of 1889 – ten years after the birth of her first child – Lady Charles became pregnant again. Since his wife was a woman of unassailable virtue who had never accepted the conventions of the Marlborough House set, Lord Charles was obviously still enjoying full conjugal relations with her.

Daisy was furious. How dare her lover impregnate his own wife? It was obscene – and she wrote to tell him so. Unfortunately Charles was away at sea. Lady Charles claimed the wifely prerogative of opening her husband's letters. . .

'Mina' Beresford's anger can be imagined. But she did not, indeed could not at once tax her husband with the letter. She went along to Ely Place. Lewis had acted for all the Beresfords – up to this time, at least. Lady Charles showed him the letter and asked him to keep it for her. Lewis at once locked it in the appropriate black deed box, and his clerk saw to it that the box was returned to its right place in the strong-room.

Lewis advised Lady Charles not to take any precipitate action, although he was aware that the rage inside her was only damped down and far from extinguished.

Still not telling her husband about the letter, Lady Charles persuaded him to take her to the south of France. Curiously enough, their villa was only two miles from Daisy's villa and she was staying there at the time. (It is not known what, if any, contact there was between them.)

When Daisy got back to London she learned that Lewis had the letter – which of course represented a considerable threat to her. Somehow she had to get that letter back.

She knew Lewis was a friend of the Prince, so it was to the Prince she went now: a beautiful woman in distress, eyes a-dew with tears, looking – of course – quite irresistible.

So the Prince found her, at least. He looked at her, listened to her, and was deeply moved. Yes, he was a friend of George Lewis. If Lewis had the letter, the obvious thing was to call on him and see how things could best be arranged. Although it was nearly midnight he went straight to Portland Place.

Lewis listened to what Edward had to say. Then they went together to Ely Place. The letter was taken out of Charles Beresford's box in the strong-room and Lewis showed it to the Prince. The Prince read it and then told Lewis that he proposed to keep it. Lewis replied that this was not possible: the letter must remain in his custody. After some further argument, the Prince gave the letter back to Lewis. (There is little doubt that, if he had been allowed to keep it, the Prince would have destroyed it at once.) Lewis told Edward that, in letting him read Daisy Brooke's letter, he had gone as far as he was prepared to go. The Prince then left.

This was undoubtedly the most controversial act of Lewis's whole professional life. It has been described as 'astounding' and 'unprincipled'; when Lord Charles heard of it, he denounced Lewis in sulphuric terms. Lady Charles's anger against Lewis was such that a year later she approached Sir Edward Clarke and asked him whether she could prosecute Lewis for breach of trust: he had, after all, shown the Prince a letter entrusted to him for safekeeping.

Clarke gave the opinion that a solicitor was not subject to a criminal prosecution, but that a civil action could be brought against him. He did not think that would succeed in this case. The nub of Clarke's opinion – very unwelcome to the Beresfords – was that the Prince had acted as any other gentleman might have done towards a lady in distress. And Lewis had not committed any breach of trust in showing the Prince the letter and allowing him to read it. If he had yielded up the letter, letting it go out of his possession, that would have been a different matter.

Of all the counsel then practising at the bar, Clarke was probably the most highly regarded. His vindication of Lewis may have impressed his fellow-lawyers; it did nothing to mollify the Beresfords.

Assuming that Clarke pronounced correctly on the strictly legal aspects, why did Lewis show the Prince the letter? He and Edward were friends but it is a solicitor's duty to maintain inviolable the secrecy of a client's affairs. Nothing the Prince said should have affected Lewis's sense of duty towards Lady Beresford.

It has been suggested that Elizabeth had some part in persuading Lewis to show the Prince the letter. It is argued that she was a woman of strong social ambitions and would therefore have been anxious to do anything the Prince asked, simply because he asked it. But this appears plausible only on a most superficial reading of Elizabeth's character. Ambitious she may have been, but her sense of independence was stronger than her ambition. And while she no doubt felt pleased and honoured that the Prince was her husband's friend as well as his client, Elizabeth was no slavish admirer of royalty. She was German and Jewish, of cosmopolitan background, concerned with the arts to an extent that would have been utterly incomprehensible to the men and women of the Marlborough House set. At the last analysis, Elizabeth's heroes painted pictures, wrote books and poems, played Beethoven magnificently in her drawing-room.

Indeed, it might be more plausible to cast Lewis himself as the courtier doing his Prince's bidding. A lot of the criticism of him was along these lines. But again, it must be remembered that Lewis had not obeyed the Prince without question. He had let him read Daisy's letter; he had stopped short of handing it over.

The most likely interpretation of Lewis's behaviour is that he *was* guided by his loyalty to the Prince, but was still aware of his duty towards Lady Beresford: thus he compromised. He reasoned that the Prince would sooner or later know what was in the letter – as would a great number of other people if the case came to court – and everyone's interest might actually be solved if the Prince saw it, so that he might act as a peacemaker between the blazing Daisy Brooke and the still-smouldering Mina Beresford.

But the Prince soon abandoned the role of peacemaker. He had fallen in love with Daisy and they began a hectic affair. Soon the Prince was displaying a fierce hostility towards Mina Beresford.

Lord Charles, home from sea, confronted an intolerable situation. Not only was his wife being treated in an appalling fashion – and from the moment he knew of the letter, he sided with her – but the Prince had taken Beresford's place in Daisy's bed. To social chagrin was added the torture of jealousy.

On Daisy's behalf, the Prince kept demanding the letter back. The Beresfords kept refusing. The Prince grew more insistent; the Beresfords more defiant. Then Edward presented his ultimatum. If they persisted in their defiance, they would no longer be persona gratia in any circle in which he, the Prince, chose to move.

Enraged at this injustice, tormented by sexual jealousy, Charles Beresford quarrelled violently with the Prince – he is said to have actually struck him – before going back to sea in command of the *Undaunted*. By now the Prince was just as angry as the Beresfords.

He imposed on them the modern equivalent of outlawry: no loyal subject would entertain the Beresfords; they were to be socially ostracized. Although Albert Edward could be good-natured, he rarely forgave anyone and defiance of this kind aroused in him the stubbornness and vindictiveness he inherited from his mother.

Another delicate matter with which Lewis was concerned around this time also hinged on love – a rather different variant of the emotion that Daisy and Mina, Charlie B and the Prince all found so exhausting. In other words what was then sometimes described as 'the love that dare not speak its name'.

Homosexuality became more dangerous after 1885. More dangerous, that is, in that the homosexual was much more likely to find himself punished by the law. The Criminal Law Amendment Act of that year made homosexual behaviour a live issue with the police. For the first time in several centuries the homosexual found himself in effective danger of arrest.

Although the Act is often spoken of as a piece of witch-hunting legislation – Travers Humphreys described it as a 'blackmailer's charter' – it was in fact originally directed only at child prostitution and the kind of juvenile white slave traffic exposed by the journalist W. T. Stead. The bill as drafted was not intended to deal with homosexuality at all, although – almost by accident – it became a powerful instrument against homosexuals. This was entirely due to Lewis's friend Henry Labouchere, who was MP for Northampton at the time. Liberal and radical in most areas, Labouchere cherished a vindictive hatred of homosexuals.

He intervened at the committee stage of the bill which was taken in the House of Commons late on the night of 6 August 1885. Labouchere put down an amendment that would make homosexual acts in private between males of *whatever age* a criminal offence. The age proviso is important because the whole thrust of the bill was to prevent the corruption of youth – and now Labouchere had distorted it to include all homosexuals in all circumstances. Although the Establishment was often hostile to Labouchere and his proposals, this time they were happy to accommodate him.

Lewis, incidentally, never pronounced on the law relating to homosexuality at all. Granted that his views on divorce were far ahead of his time, his attitude might be expected to be liberal, but no word of comment is recorded.

The homosexual underworld soon realized the kind of climate the new legislation had created. Rather as Prohibition in America called into being a world of organized crime, so the Criminal Law Amendment Act vastly enlarged the number of homosexual prostitutes, panders, and blackmailers. Such people had always existed, of course, but the fact that those to whom they catered could now be imprisoned gave the business a new and profitable dimension. That the act greatly increased the risks of homosexual activity was proved by the fact that the few years following its passing saw two major scandals – the Cleveland Street affair and the Oscar Wilde case – whereas a whole century prior to 1885 had yielded only one of comparable fame, that of the Bishop of Clogher in 1822.

There are always those to whom danger is an aphrodisiac and certainly the chance of being 'rented' (blackmailed) was no deterrent to someone who had once been close to George and Elizabeth Lewis: Oscar Wilde.

The question of Wilde's homosexuality has been debated a thousand times; the story of his fall told at least as often. How, at the very peak of fame he succumbed to a *nostalgie de la boue* that dragged him into a world of homosexual pimps and prostitutes, unemployed ostlers, and army deserters whom he chose to entertain at the Café Royal and the Savoy Hotel. Many of the rich, both homosexuals and heterosexuals, had always regarded 'the lower orders' as one vast brothel: a cornucopia of available pleasure ranging from governesses to illiterate slaveys on the one hand; and from office boys to ex-pickpockets on the other. What Wilde was doing was not new: the dangers were.

It is significant that Wilde should have been closest to the Lewises when he was still making his way. Undoubtedly, as Wilde became more successful, there was some cooling-off on one side or the other, and this could hardly have been a case of Wilde 'outgrowing' people who had been kind to him as a young man. ('Outgrowing' in this context usually means that the now successful man finds his old friends socially inferior.) An ambivalence developed on both sides of the relationship. The Lewises did not like the change they saw in Wilde; he resented this, although he was aware he *had* changed and not for the better.

This was the situation when Wilde approached Lewis on behalf of a young man he had met some time before and who was still a student at Oxford, Lord Alfred Douglas. As Wilde was to write in *De*

Profundis, his long, angry, and for many years unpublished letter to Douglas:

> Our friendship really begins with your begging me in a most pathetic and charming letter to assist you in a position appalling to anyone, doubly so to a young man at Oxford: I do so, and ultimately through your using my name as your friend with Sir George Lewis, I begin to loose his esteem and friendship, a friendship of fifteen years standing. When I was deprived of his advice and help and regard I was deprived of the one great safeguard of my life.

The 'position appalling to anyone' was some predicament in which Douglas found himself. In *De Profundis*, however, he was writing in a very different mood from that which held him in 1892. Then, he wanted to impress Douglas with his power and influence – he was at the very top of his success – and what more natural than that he should invoke 'my friend George Lewis', the most subtle and puissant lawyer in London? Lewis would be able to fix it – and fix it Lewis did, at a cost of £100. No doubt this was a pay-off to some homosexual blackmailer who was 'renting' Douglas. No doubt Lewis arranged it so that the blackmailer would not be able to come back for more; and he probably used some tough private operator like ex-Inspector Meiklejohn to work out the details. Douglas was saved and was, one hopes, appropriately grateful to Wilde for invoking Lewis. But from the moment Wilde asked this favour, his friendship with Lewis began to decline. Wilde knew that Lewis's discretion was absolute but he knew, too, that in asking this favour he had made Lewis aware of the nature of his own relationship with Alfred Douglas. The world might accept that Wilde was 'posing' for effect, but Lewis would know better.

Meanwhile, Wilde remained in the grip of an extraordinary euphoria. Physically he had grown flabby: the 'fat white slug' metaphor crops up more and more in descriptions of him around this time. And he grew ever more reckless and obsessive in his pursuit of louche and easily purchasable young men. Later he would say he was 'feasting with panthers' and describe this as the time 'when I was playing with that tiger, Life'.

23

Baccarat

The Baccarat Scandal became one of the greatest of Victorian *causes célèbres* because it illuminated the dilemma of the Prince of Wales: caught as he was between self-indulgent pleasure on the one hand and his desire to win the esteem of the people who would some day be his subjects on the other. The Prince loved every kind of gambling – and not only the Queen but also a large section of the public were fiercely opposed to gambling. A majority rather liked the Prince's sporting image, but even they thought he should exercise discretion.

And yet here he was discovered at the house of people who weren't even aristocrats but nouveaux riches; and the fact that he had been there had only come out because another guest had been accused of cheating at baccarat. So the Prince's friends were not only vulgarians but card-sharps as well! Perhaps worst of all, there had been a determined but inept attempt by several courtiers to suppress the facts of the scandal because they were afraid the Prince would be involved in it.

This is how the papers would have presented the facts to the Man on the Clapham Omnibus; and, in essence, they had them right.

They were certainly right to imply that the Wilsons (the Prince's hosts on this occasion) were nouveaux riches. What they did not explain was why the Prince's circle was being continuously enlarged to include more and more such people. The reason was that it was becoming more and more expensive to entertain the Prince. The days when his entourage included mostly well-born if slightly raffish young aristocrats and their wives – the kind of people who made up the original Marlborough House set – were over. Now his circle took in not only a lawyer like George Lewis or bankers like the Sassoons or Cassel, but also members of the increasingly rich and powerful class of industrialists whose ever-growing fortunes from manufacture were overtaking those of the old landed gentry. It was the Prince's policy to arrange his social life so that members of this last group – whose wealth and power were, generally, on the wane – should meet the new men who were to some extent to replace them.

And, from a harshly practical point of view, the Prince needed the new men. They had the money required to entertain him – and he was an expensive guest. More than one of the earlier Marlborough House set had been brought to bankruptcy through their friendship with him; and – although he was capable of generous acts – HRH had little sympathy for ruined courtiers. He moved on to people like the Wilsons, who had the money to entertain royalty with the kind of lavishness that royalty demanded.

Arthur Wilson was a shipping magnate. In 1889 he and his brother had divided between them more than £1 million profit from their firm's fifty steamships (an astronomical sum in terms of 1980s purchasing power). It would be entirely accurate to describe the Arthur Wilsons as social climbers: he and his wife were lucky to be living in an era when money could almost literally buy social advancement. Arthur Wilson had gone straight for the quickest method through which a rich man could penetrate local county society – the hunting field. Any Master of Fox Hounds had to have a lot of money: thus a parvenu with enough financial resources could buy admission into local society. Arthur Wilson was Master of the Holderness Hunt.

Mrs Wilson appears to have had genuine gifts as a hostess. Her husband bought a house in Grosvenor Square and there his wife and daughter enjoyed the kind of social life they craved.

The Baccarat Scandal occurred at the country home of the Wilsons: Tranby Croft near Hessle in Yorkshire. It was early September 1890 and the Prince was going to the autumn race meeting at Doncaster, a big event in the north of England. Normally he would have stayed with Christopher Sykes at his seat, Brantingham Thorpe, but Sykes was one of those who had beggared themselves entertaining the Prince. So the Prince was glad to accept the invitation from the Wilsons – with whom he had never stayed before.

The composition of the party is important: a nice mix of Marlborough House and moneyed new-arrivals. Heading the second group were the hosts, the Wilsons. Also present were their pretty daughter Ethel and her husband Edward Lycett Green, another arriviste, who had bought into county society through becoming Master of the York and Ainsty Hunt; and the Wilsons' son Stanley (always known as 'Jack').

On the Marlborough House side, the Prince's current favourite Daisy Brooke – bestowed on him by the Beresford letter row – should have been there. She excused herself at the last moment: her step-father had died. Her crying-off can hardly have put the Prince in a good mood; but there were plenty of other friends accompanying him. Reuben Sassoon, the banker; Lady Brougham and Vaux; the Earl and Countess of Coventry; General Owen Williams and his wife; Lord Edward Somerset; a young subaltern called Berkeley Levett (who however was also a friend of the Wilsons); Count Lutzow; and the sadly-exploited Christopher Sykes.

The most important guest of all – a lion among the jackals that thronged Tranby Croft – travelled down with the Prince. Sir William Gordon-Cumming was the antithesis of Arthur Wilson and his son-in-law Lycett Green. Gordon-Cumming despised such men as jumped-up money-grubbers; they, in turn, hated him for his arrogance, his inbred assumption of superiority. It is hard to see where any point of contact could have existed – even under the aegis of the Prince.

Gordon-Cumming claimed descent from Charlemagne and was a lieutenant-colonel in the Scots Guards. He had served with great distinction in the Zulu War; and, like Lord Charles Beresford, had survived the fearful battle of Abu Klea during the Gordon Relief Expedition. He was tall and handsome and – unmarried himself – a tireless and successful seducer of other men's wives. With a huge estate in Scotland and an income of £60,000 a year, he was well qualified to be a friend of the Prince and would often lend him his house in London for an unspecified but fairly obvious purpose.

The Prince had invited Lewis to come to Tranby Croft as a member of his party, but Lewis had a previous engagement and declined. If he had gone with the Prince, that week in September, it seems likely that his counsels might have prevailed and the whole tragedy been averted.

On the evening before the first day of the Doncaster Meeting, the guests at Tranby Croft assembled to play baccarat. A devotee of the game, the Prince brought with him his own unique set of counters inscribed with the Prince of Wales feathers.

Baccarat is usually described as a simple game. The banker sits in the centre. He announces at the start how much there is in the bank. This represents his maximum possible loss. (At Tranby Croft that evening the amount was £100.) The other players are divided into two tableaux (that is: teams); one tableau sitting at each side of the banker. Each tableau has a representative and the banker deals one card to this representative and one to himself. Then this is repeated: six cards having been laid down. The players then look at their cards. The object is to get cards that amount to a total of 8 or 9 points. The player from each tableau declares his cards and, if the dealer cannot equal them, he loses that side of the table. Any player can stake as much as he likes (subject to the banker's limit). Except for the representative of each tableau, the other players can stake without receiving any cards – trusting simply to what happens to the cards dealt to the representative. The result is declared: the bank wins or loses. There is a croupier sitting opposite; he takes care of the counters representing the amount in the bank; pays those who have won and collects from those who have lost.

At Tranby Croft, that night of 8 September 1890, baccarat was played on an improvised table – actually on three whist tables pushed together. There was no line on the cloth covering the tables to indicate where stakes were to be placed.

Play began with the Prince dealing from four packs of cards. Mrs Wilson represented one tableau, which included her son Stanley and the young officer Berkeley Levett. The second tableau comprised, among others, Sir William Gordon-Cumming, Lord Edward Somerset, and General Owen Williams.

Gordon-Cumming was a very experienced player: no one was surprised when he appeared to be doing well.

Then, suddenly, Stanley Wilson thought he noticed something odd about Sir William's play. He saw that Gordon-Cumming had three red counters in front of him: he won £15 on these – three times his original stake. Later, when Lord Edward Somerset received cards as representative of the tableau to which young Wilson and Gordon-Cumming both belonged, Wilson thought he saw Gordon-Cumming looking to see what cards Somerset had (perfectly permissible, of course, in a member of the same tableau). Somerset had a 'natural', a nine and a court card, and, Wilson later alleged, as soon as Gordon-Cumming noticed this, he put down three more £5 counters and was paid for them.

Stanley Wilson whispered to Berkeley Levett, who was sitting next to him, 'My God, Berkeley, this is too hot!'

'What do you mean?' Levett demanded.

'The man next to me is cheating.'

'Impossible!' Levett said. 'You must be mistaken.'

Stanley Wilson told him to look for himself. Levett watched Gordon-Cumming for a time, then turned to Wilson and agreed, 'It is too hot!'

The two young men discussed it after play finished for the night and Wilson told his mother. Early the next morning, he also told his brother-in-law, Lycett Green, who professed great astonishment. Wilson said he was sure Gordon-Cumming had cheated.

That night the butler was told to set out a long kitchen table for the night's play. It was covered with a green cloth and a line drawn on it with chalk.

On this second night, the Prince was banker; General Williams was croupier. Gordon-Cumming was late coming to the table. He sat next to Ethel Lycett Green (her husband had already told her that Gordon-Cumming had cheated). Opposite to Gordon-Cumming was Berkeley Levett.

The kitchen table was narrow, and it cramped the players' movements. Lycett Green was in an aggressive mood. If he caught Sir William cheating, he had said, he would denounce him immediately. In fact at least five people were watching Gordon-Cumming's every movement: Stanley Wilson; Mrs Wilson; Lycett Green and his wife Ethel; Berkeley Levett. They were all waiting for him to cheat – almost willing him to cheat.

Human suggestibility being what it is, he did not disappoint them. In other words, anyone who expects to witness a given phenomenon will rarely fail to witness it. Of the five persons watching, only Levett did not later claim to have seen Gordon-Cumming cheating.

Despite this, the game went on, and Lycett Green did not carry out his threat to denounce Gordon-Cumming then and there. The gathering broke up with at least surface amiability. The Prince, of course, still knew nothing of the alleged cheating.

Next morning they were all off to Doncaster, where the St Leger was being run. At the races Stanley Wilson and Berkeley Levett told Lord Edward Somerset about their suspicions. He advised them to talk to Lord Coventry and General Owen Williams. These were, he said, older men with great experience of the world.

Wilson and Levett took this advice. The reaction of the two courtiers to the story was a curious one. They accepted Wilson's accusation without question – even, it seemed, with relish. Williams was a lifelong friend of Gordon-Cumming and yet both he and Lord Coventry at once assumed that Gordon-Cumming was guilty and adopted an extremely hostile attitude towards him, without – it has to be said – letting him speak a word in his own defence.

The Prince was told. At eight o'clock that evening Lord Coventry and General Williams went to see Gordon-Cumming, who was in his bedroom, dressing for dinner.

Lord Coventry said, 'Some of the people staying in this house object to your manner of playing baccarat.'

'Good God!' Gordon-Cumming said. 'What do you mean? What do they say?'

'They say you are cheating at cards.'

'It is an abominable falsehood,' Gordon-Cumming said. 'Who are my accusers?'

'Stanley Wilson and Berkeley Levett.'

'Surely,' Gordon-Cumming said, 'you are not going to believe a pair of inexperienced boys before me?'

He then asked to see the Prince of Wales. Lord Coventry and Williams said they would let him know about that.

Even allowing for the fact that General Williams and Lord Coventry were sycophants who fawned on the Prince and that from the first both were blinded by fear of a scandal that might touch their royal master, their attitude towards Gordon-Cumming was still remarkable. Clearly Williams's 'friendship' for his old comrade masked deep-seated rancour and jealousy. There is no rivalry more bitter than that among professional soldiers; and now the mediocre Williams saw delivered into his hands a brother-officer whose achievements had always outstripped his own.

After some delay Williams told Gordon-Cumming that the Prince would see him, but that he, Williams, and Lord Coventry would also have to be present.

Confronting the Prince, Gordon-Cumming denied the charge. 'I utterly deny I have done anything of the kind,' he said. 'Your Royal Highness can see what a terrible thing this is for a man like myself who has attempted to lead for twenty-five years the life of an officer and a gentleman.'

'What can you do?' the Prince asked. 'It is five to one.'

'Something must be done, sir,' Gordon-Cumming said.

After a moment's thought he suggested that the whole matter should be referred to the appropriate military authority: his own commanding officer (of the Scots Guards) or the Commander in Chief, the Duke of Cambridge.

But the two courtiers would not have that. At this moment the unfortunate Gordon-Cumming was in their power and they did not want to relinquish their captive – especially as he might well get a fair hearing from the military authorities. They ordered him from the room and consulted with each other. (The Prince had left by this time.)

After some time they summoned Gordon-Cumming. There was, they said, only one way to avoid a horrible scandal – particularly serious as it would involve HRH. That was to sign a document they had prepared.

> In consideration of the promise made by the gentlemen whose names are subscribed to preserve silence with reference to an accusation that has been made with regard to my conduct at baccarat on the nights of Monday the 8th and Tuesday the 9th September 1890 at Tranby Croft, I will on my part solemnly undertake never to play cards again as long as I live.

'Why, that is tantamount to an admission of guilt!' Gordon-Cumming exclaimed. 'What satisfaction would it be to two honourable gentlemen like yourselves for me to sign a document like this?'

Williams and Lord Coventry said he had no option. He *had* to sign. If he didn't, Wilson, Lycett Green, and the others would broadcast the story at Doncaster tomorrow.

Gordon-Cumming looked at the statement again. 'But I am innocent, he protested. 'How can I sign this? It's a confession of guilt.'

Incredibly, it has to be remembered that at this stage Gordon-Cumming still did not know exactly what he was being accused of doing. 'But what do they say I did?' he reiterated but naturally Williams and Lord Coventry preferred to keep him in the dark.

Not only was Gordon-Cumming the victim of the animus of these two courtiers; the Wilsons were also pressing that some action be taken against him. And the Wilsons, in their turn, were being pressured by Lycett Green, who had an obsessive and inexplicable hatred of Gordon-Cumming. (Why? Did Lycett Green fear the colonel's expertise with young wives?)

It was not unnatural that Gordon-Cumming should hesitate to sign a document that admitted guilt to a crime he did not commit. What is strange is that he did, after hesitating a little longer, agree to sign – strange, that is, in view of the defiant, combative nature of the man. But Gordon-Cumming may have thought there was, after all, little alternative. If Lycett Green and his friends did make these allegations against him at the Doncaster meeting, his name would be befouled for ever. No denial he might make could ever reverse the impact the story would have the first day it was told. It would be seized on, sniggered at, trumpeted across England.

He signed, still protesting his innocence. General Williams, tireless in his lust to humiliate, insisted that he leave first thing in the morning. He protested that this would cause talk – and the only reason, surely, he had just admitted to doing something he had not done, was precisely to avoid that: to suppress scandal. Williams brushed that aside.

Later that evening the Prince called everyone together and read out the document. Those present had to sign it and promise secrecy.

They all did so – the Prince, Lord Coventry, General Williams, Arthur Wilson, Stanley Wilson, Lord Edward Somerset, Captain Arthur Somerset (cousin of Lord Edward), Lycett Green, Berkeley Levett, and Reuben Sassoon.

This done, the Prince must have indicated some degree of relief. But Captain Arthur Somerset was a realist. 'This will be no secret, sir,' he said.

'Not when gentlemen have given their word?' the Prince asked.

'Nothing in the world that was known to ten people was ever kept secret,' was the sombre reply.

Captain Somerset was right. The secret was not kept. And in the weeks that followed the party at Tranby Croft, Gordon-Cumming realized he had been cheated. He had been persuaded to sign the confession on the grounds that this would end the matter, scotch this ugliness at its source. He saw now that this had not been the true intention of Williams and Lord Coventry. Now he realized that he had been invited to put his head in a noose; he had foolishly accepted that invitation and it was only a matter of time before someone began to pull on the rope.

Gordon-Cumming wrote to the Prince saying that he hoped the Prince would give him the benefit of the doubt, pleading that nothing need change in their relationship. The Prince did not bother to acknowledge the letter. Although he had championed Valentine Baker after his debacle, the two cases were very different. Baker had somehow managed to frighten a young woman out of her wits in a railway carriage; Gordon-Cumming had contrived to cause the Prince personal embarrassment. The Prince could turn on a former favourite in a second, changing from affectionate good-fellowship to tigerish hatred – and this happened now.

The unfortunate man tried to keep at least the externals of life going as before. It was not easy. The pledge he had given not to play cards aroused suspicion everywhere. As he put it himself, 'This will even debar me from playing sixpence and a shilling rubbers of whist in the barracks.'

Then he got an anonymous letter. It was in French and had been posted in France. It said that people were beginning to talk about what had happened at Newmarket (a mistake, of course) that autumn, and warned Gordon-Cumming, if he came to Paris or Monte Carlo, not to touch a card. 'They have talked too much about it.'

That the blow had been expected did not make it less crushing for Gordon-Cumming. He sent the letter to General Williams, who tried to brush him off by stating the obvious: that the mention of Newmarket showed that its writer did not know much about the house-party at Tranby Croft.

What was important to Gordon-Cumming, of course, was that the secret was out. Rumours were spreading. A week or two later, Gordon-Cumming wrote to Williams again, saying that 'a lady' had told him that the affair was being talked of all over London. Again, he got no satisfaction from Williams, who was clearly quite indifferent to the promise given to Gordon-Cumming in return for the signed confession – that no one would talk about the affair. The Prince may have believed the promise would be kept; for Williams, it was simply a useful device to get Gordon-Cumming to convict himself out of his own mouth.

Gordon-Cumming telegraphed the Prince with a request to see him. The Prince refused. Now Gordon-Cumming had no choice but to take legal action, for the story of his cheating was being told everywhere and he was encountering widespread hostility. He went to his solicitors, Wontners, and instructed them to demand an apology for the statements made by Lycett Green, Stanley Wilson, Berkeley Levett, Mrs Arthur Wilson, and Mrs Lycett Green. If he did not get this, he would start a slander action against them.

There was, of course, no hope of an apology, so the battle was joined.

The Prince arranged for Lewis to represent all the defendants – the Wilsons, the Lycett Greens, and Berkeley Levett.

Knowing Lewis's reputation for settling difficult society cases before they ever came to trial, the Prince may have hoped that he would manage to effect some face-saving compromise. If so, he was deceiving himself. Feelings ran deep and bitter on both sides.

Lewis's first act was to answer Wontner's letter in identical terms on behalf of all the defendants. The gist of the reply was that anything any one of them had said he or she was prepared to substantiate in a court of law. Then he had to formulate a general accusation against Gordon-Cumming that would serve each of the defendants individually and jointly. Lewis sought this unity of testimony largely because there were discrepancies between the statements of the defendants and he wanted to smooth these out in a single blanket statement. The formula ultimately arrived at was: 'I saw the plaintiff cheat at baccarat by placing a larger stake on the table after the cards had been declared in his favour than he had originally laid down.'

Since what was alleged was a criminal act – even though this was to be a civil action – the burden of proof lay on the defence.

Later, Lewis proceeded to interview people other than the defendants who had sat in on the game, but he could not find anyone else who was prepared to say they had seen any cheating.

Up to this point the facts of the case have been recounted on the basis that Gordon-Cumming was innocent. Was Lewis once again on the 'wrong' side?

Most of those with knowledge of the case – including Sir Edward Clarke – consider that he was, although the Baccarat Scandal did not raise the kind of questions posed by, say, Mrs Crawford's accusations against Sir Charles Dilke. It seems unlikely that the Wilsons and the Lycett Greens were deliberately perjuring themselves – they believed that they had seen Gordon-Cumming cheating – but the quality of their testimony was dubious in the extreme. If two people, both with perfect eyesight and standing together, both observe the same event, their attempts to describe it will invariably show some points of difference. The testimony of eyewitnesses, in fact, is highly idiosyncratic – which is why personal identification tends to be a nightmare that has produced many miscarriages of justice.

It was so in this case. The whole unsteady pyramid of evidence against Gordon-Cumming was based on the testimony of a single young man: Stanley Wilson. Wilson knew little of the game of baccarat; nor did Berkeley Levett, whom Wilson invoked when he thought he saw Gordon-Cumming cheating ('My God, this is too hot!'). And the first reactions of both young men were not wholly serious. They were full of glee at having caught a formidable and not over-popular figure out in something discreditable. That night Berkeley Levett is said to have thrown himself across his bed and exclaimed to Stanley Wilson, 'Think of it – Sir William Gordon-Cumming caught cheating at cards! What on earth are we to do?'

'What they did, of course, was to tell the Wilsons and the Lycett Greens – who reacted instantly, displaying an already-existing hostility towards Gordon-Cumming. It would be fair to say that, once Lycett Green in particular heard the young men's allegations, the unfortunate baronet had no chance. However slight their acquaintanceship and for whatever reason, Lycett Green hated Gordon-Cumming and it was only too easy for him to carry his wife and her parents, the Wilsons, along with him. By the second night, when they settled down to catch Gordon-Cumming cheating, they were conditioned, programmed, to see what they afterwards claimed they saw. A single seed of suspicion, sown by Stanley Wilson, soon burgeoned into an apparently impressive body of testimony from five people.

So much for what might be called the negative aspect of the case against Gordon-Cumming. More positively, there is the question of motive. What had he to gain by cheating? Money? – the stakes were not large, and in any case he was as rich as the Wilsons themselves. Moreover, unlike the Wilsons, he was a figure of great social and professional prestige – why risk it all for a game of baccarat? And, lastly, he was a skilled and experienced player, more than a match for the others around the table. No one, in fact, has ever been able to suggest a reason for Sir William to have cheated. He had nothing to gain and everything to lose.

Lewis decided to brief Sir Charles Russell, who was a man with a passion for every game of chance: one only had to watch him dealing a hand to see that: the cards seemed to leap from his fingertips. Who better to discuss the intricacies of play at Tranby Croft?

Writing a brief for Russell, Lewis stressed that it was highly desirable that the Prince's name should be kept out of the case. It seems certain, indeed, that, when he was writing the brief, Lewis may have still hoped that a military enquiry (instigated by the Prince) would have dismissed Gordon-Cumming from the army and thus silenced him for ever. In fact the Prince had hinted that, if the officers on the enquiry recognized their 'duty', they would give Gordon-Cumming short shrift, thus taking everyone off the hook.

HRH was disappointed. To his intense annoyance, the Adjutant General, Sir Redvers Buller VC, suspended the enquiry pending the result of Gordon-Cumming's action for slander. This must have disappointed Lewis too.

It was clear that the Prince wanted to deny Gordon-Cumming any chance to clear his name in open court. The military enquiry having been suspended, the Prince now suggested a similar investigation to be conducted at the Guards Club – again hoping that the club's committee would take the royal hint and kick Gordon-Cumming out without further ado. (If the Guards Club expelled him, all his other clubs would follow their lead.)

But the Guards Club declined. The Prince was infuriated. He resigned himself to the fact that the case was going to come to court. He must rely on Lewis and Charles Russell to protect him as best they could.

The Prince soon learned of another annoying circumstance: the then Solicitor General, Sir Edward Clarke, had been briefed for Sir William Gordon-Cumming. One of Her Majesty's law officers representing a man who had incurred the Prince's displeasure! At that time the law officers of the Crown were allowed to accept private briefs but the offence rankled and the Prince never forgave Clarke. The more as the Prince had to ask Lewis to approach Clarke on the delicate matter of the baccarat counters with the Prince of Wales feathers on them. Mention of these might excite hostile comment. Could copies be produced in court that lacked the Prince's emblem?

Lewis went round to Clarke's chambers and made the request.

Clarke looked at the copies. He told Lewis he would use them – adding that he could, however, promise nothing.

With Clarke appearing for Gordon-Cumming and Russell leading for the five defendants, the public – including the usual 'fashionably-dressed women' – were promised a battle of giants.

Standing in the wings behind Russell, Lewis must have been glad that John Duke Coleridge, Lord Chief Justice of England, was on the bench. Lewis would have remembered Coleridge's jury-swaying speech in the Overend Gurney trial, over twenty years before. Coleridge was deeply committed to the status quo and Lewis knew that in this case the judge, at least, would do all he could to protect the Prince.

Coleridge was seventy that year of 1891 and he was tired of the game of the law, which he had played so long, so brilliantly – and, many thought, so unfairly. Today he introduced a touch of *opéra bouffe* by having his young and fashionable wife sit beside him on the bench wearing, as the *Star* said, 'the smartest of arrangements in black velvet, open jacket, and white satin waistcoat with gold buttons'.

The *Star* also noted that, throughout the trial, Lewis entered the court in the company of the Prince.

Clarke opened the case for Gordon-Cumming by saying that this case involved the honour of a gallant soldier and he went on to describe Gordon-Cumming's achievements in various campaigns – the Zulu War, Tel-el-Kebir, and the Nile Campaign.

Clarke then dealt with the technicalities of the alleged cheating, arguing that Gordon-Cumming's highly individual method of play had caused his accusers to mistakenly – but quite sincerely – think he was cheating. His client was a very experienced player and he kept a sheet of paper before him on which he recorded the result of each coup and he would put his stake on this paper. If he won, he let the winning stake remain there, adding a counter to it from his personal reserve and letting the winning counter given him by the croupier also remain on the paper so that his second stake would be three times the size of the first.

With all his skill and eloquence, Clarke now approached the one decisive, suicidal act of folly which Gordon-Cumming had committed: the signed confession.

Clarke reiterated the fact that although his client had signed this document, he had – even as he did so – asserted his total innocence. If Gordon-Cumming had really been cheating, he would never have signed. What would he have had to gain by doing so? It would have served him much better simply to brazen the matter out. No, Clarke said, he had signed only because of the pressure brought to bear on him by men he admired and respected – the Prince of Wales, General Williams, and Lord Coventry. Why did these men, all of them old friends of Gordon-Cumming, believe it essential that he sign this document. Because – and now Clarke spoke with the hypnotic intensity that gave his advocacy its power – they were terrified of scandal. They were fearful that the mere mention of the fact that the Prince had acted as banker at a baccarat table would be considered disgraceful by a large section of society. They were, Clarke continued, quite mistaken in that: 'There is nothing in the whole course of this case which carries any imputation upon the Prince of Wales.'

But – Clarke hammered it home – Williams and Lord Coventry quite clearly believed there was: that the Prince's presence at such a gathering would cause a scandal. Anything that could be done to avoid public knowledge of the fact would have to be done. That was why Gordon-Cumming had been coerced into signing the document.

Gordon-Cumming proved a good witness, intelligently supporting his counsel's line of argument. On the whole, he stood up well to cross-examination by Charles Russell.

Lewis and Russell had decided that the signing of the confession was the hinge of their case. Clarke's arguments were plausible – but a little subtle for an English jury at that time. So Russell laboured the common-sense aspect: 'Why should anyone sign a paper admitting he had cheated if he hadn't cheated?'

Although Russell got Gordon-Cumming to admit he had 'lost his head', at this point the case could still have gone either way. Now Clarke put the Prince of Wales into the box. Not surprisingly, he was treated with some delicacy by both Clarke and Russell. Clarke established that HRH had known Gordon-Cumming for many years and that nothing had ever occurred to cause the slightest suspicion as to his methods of play.

Russell was equally cautious. He was content to elicit the fact that the Prince had not met Gordon-Cumming since the time of Tranby Croft.

Then Clarke called General Williams. At this point Gordon-

Cumming's chances looked so good that Lewis and Russell discussed the possibility of withdrawing from the case and apologizing to Gordon-Cumming: making some face-saving statement to the effect that their clients had made a genuine mistake.

The fact that Lewis and Russell contemplated such a course is probably the most eloquent argument for Gordon-Cumming's being innocent of the accusations against him. But the habit of winning was engrained in both men. An apology, however cleverly phrased, smelt of defeat – and that was repulsive to Lewis and Russell alike. They decided to go on.

That decision was justified, although this was not immediately apparent. In fact, right up to the moment that the Lord Chief Justice began to sum up, it looked as if Clarke would win.

His speech for Gordon-Cumming has been considered one of the most eloquent and closely-reasoned that he ever made. He stressed the paucity of the original 'evidence' against Gordon-Cumming – how it was based on the observation of a young man who hardly understood the game of baccarat, blown up into a scandal by the eager Lycett Green, and then taken up by the whole Wilson family. He discussed the behaviour of the two courtiers, General Williams and Lord Coventry, and said of them: 'If they are to have the credit that they doomed their old friend to a life of misery and suspicion out of loyalty to their Prince, at least let Sir William Gordon-Cumming have credit, too, that while protesting his innocence he signed that paper to serve the Prince.'

At that moment the sympathy of the court – and of the public outside the court – lay with Gordon-Cumming. Clarke had won them over, as he had so often won the sympathy of judges and juries in the past. But John Duke Coleridge was no ordinary judge. As soon as Clarke sat down, he adjourned the court till the following morning. No doubt Lewis – and Clarke too – knew why. Coleridge meant to let a night elapse before he began his summing-up. The immediate effect of Clarke's arguments would, Coleridge presumably hoped, have faded a little from the jurors' minds. It is known that the Lord Chief Justice spent that night preparing a summing-up that was in every respect a speech for the five defendants, rebutting every argument advanced by Clarke with a skill and eloquence equal to Clarke's own. As Clarke himself was to put it many years later, it was a matter of discussion among lawyers as to who was the greater advocate: Charles Russell or John Duke Coleridge. On his showing in the baccarat trial, Clarke wryly concluded, Coleridge was the better man.

By any criterion, Coleridge's summing-up was extraordinary – extraordinary both in the dialectical skill he displayed and in the fact that he was a judge addressing a jury and thus owed at least lip-service to the ideal of impartiality. No advocate could have been more partisan than Coleridge in his charge to the jury in this case. Point by point, he answered Clarke's speech. Suave, mellifluous, he lulled the jury into accepting the arguments for the defence while at the same time quietly demolishing those advanced by Clarke. He read aloud those portions of Stanley Wilson's testimony most inimical to Gordon-Cumming. He even suggested that Clarke, as a law officer of the Crown, should not have accepted a brief in a case involving the Prince.

Although Coleridge's behaviour was going to save Lewis's clients, Lewis must have felt as Clarke did about the cynical manner in which Coleridge degraded his high office. If Edward Clarke was universally regarded as a hero of the law, then John Duke Coleridge must be remembered as one of its villains – for who can excuse an unjust judge making a mockery of his function, not out of stupidity or ignorance, but out of calculated arrogance and perversity?

Lewis had won again. After a withdrawal of only thirteen minutes, the jury found against Gordon-Cumming.

There was a loud hissing all over the court, which the Lord Chief Justice chose to ignore, although all the junior barristers joined in. Later the Wilsons and the Lycett Greens, accompanied by Lewis, were confronted by an angry crowd who booed and shouted insults. Lewis led his clients back into an empty court-room and they remained there until attendants were able to smuggle them all out by a back door.

The press were equally hostile to the verdict. The *Daily Chronicle* spoke of 'the amazement of all cool critics of the evidence' and remarked of Coleridge, '[the defendants] had the inestimable advantage of the impassioned advocacy of the Lord Chief Justice of England'.

Labouchere was scathing in *Truth*. He expressed a particular contempt for the courtiers who had forced Gordon-Cumming to sign the confession: 'The scene reminds me of what must often have occurred in the dungeons of the Inquisition. "Recant, or –" And often the victim did recant.'

The *Manchester Guardian* summed up public feeling by saying that decent people all over the country had followed the case each day with growing shame and indignation.

Once again, Lewis had advised the Prince to go into the witness box and give evidence, thus showing that he had as much respect for the institutions and process of the law as the humblest of his mother's subjects. And once again, however reluctantly, the Prince had followed that advice. But considerable hostility had been aroused against him – not only among the considerable section of the middle class who disapproved of gambling and were aghast at the thought of their future monarch acting as a banker at baccarat, but also among those who were naive enough to believe that popular fantasies about 'fair play' and 'sportsmanship' cut any ice with the Prince and his friends. An American paper summed up the general feeling about the Prince's facile concept of friendship by saying that, if five of his friends agreed to turn on a sixth, then the Prince would unquestioningly turn his back on the odd man out while the other five threw him to the wolves.

None of this comment helped Gordon-Cumming. He was ruined – more starkly even than Dilke – and he had to face a longer, colder banishment than did Valentine Baker. (Banishment in Gordon-Cumming's case in the social, not the geographical, sense.) He married a charming American girl soon after the case and had several children; but the marriage does not appear to have been happy. His wife was described as a 'very old woman' when she died at the age of fifty-two. William Gordon-Cumming himself lived on to be eighty-one, having endured forty years of social ostracism, cut off from the only kind of life that, for him, had any meaning.

As usual, the Prince was grateful to Lewis for his support; and it seems likely that it was the Baccarat Scandal – rather than the Parnell Commission, as is often claimed – that won Lewis his knighthood two years later.

The Queen was angry with everyone: with her son; with Edward Clarke; most of all – it is gratifying to know – with the man who contrived to be both bully and toady: General Williams.

24

The Cuckold's Revenge

LEWIS ALWAYS DESCRIBED the vindication of Parnell before the government Commission as his greatest achievement, but there was a sequel to the case which meant that the triumph wrought by Lewis and Russell would ultimately be worthless.

Captain O'Shea was never the urbane kind of *mari complaisant* commonly found in the Marlborough House set. His defenders maintain that he was not, at the beginning, aware of the true relationship between his wife and Parnell. That is hard to believe. Even if he gave Parnell the benefit of the doubt during the early days, the truth must have been forced on him sooner or later. The knowledge bred an anger that grew into an obsessive hatred. O'Shea only tolerated Kitty O'Shea's liaison with Parnell because he got something out of it: Parnell was responsible for his having a seat in Parliament.

By the 1880s, however, the affair was so blatant that few men could have been expected to tolerate it, whatever the advantages. Parnell had given Kitty O'Shea two daughters – legally, they were O'Shea's children, but the name of their true father was widely known in political and journalistic circles. It was a fairly open secret that did not find its way into print. Neither Parnell nor O'Shea were popular men. 'The Chief' was detested for his coldness and aloofness and for the nuisance-value of his phalanx of Irish members. O'Shea was outwardly agreeable but was distrusted; with his oiled curls and super-confident manner, he seemed the essence of the Irish 'chancer', a stock figure from a novel by Charles Lever.

But, whatever the extent of hatred between the two men – patron and patronized, triumphant seducer and cuckolded husband – mutual interest maintained an uneasy truce for many years. Then in 1885 O'Shea lost his seat as member for Clare.

Although he had lost it through his own feeble performance as an

MP, he blamed Parnell and expected him to find another constituency where he, O'Shea, could be elected without difficulty. Parnell tried – he had little option – but by now too much was known about O'Shea, and about his curious situation vis-à-vis Parnell. Parnell could not foist him on the Irish Nationalist Party any longer and when O'Shea was certain of this, he turned to an enemy of Parnell's, Joseph Chamberlain, and sought his help.

A question mark hangs over Chamberlain's behaviour in the Dilke case, and that must cause us to view with suspicion the part he played in the O'Shea–Parnell affair. It seems doubtful, however, that O'Shea needed much incitement against Parnell. In turning to Chamberlain, he was probably influenced by a number of factors. Even at this late hour, he was full of chagrin that Parnell could no longer help him, and he might have cherished the forlorn hope that Chamberlain might revive his moribund political career – especially if he, O'Shea, were instrumental in bringing down Parnell. Even so, it is easy to over-estimate Chamberlain's part in the imbroglio. Sexual jealousy was no doubt the strongest element in O'Shea's hatred for Parnell.

Money came into it too – a great deal of money. Kitty O'Shea had an immensely rich aunt, a Mrs Wood. Kitty was her favourite niece and had received a large allowance from her aunt over the years. (Captain O'Shea had siphoned off enough of that allowance to maintain a bachelor establishment in London.) Mrs Wood had no knowledge of the strange triangular relationship between the O'Sheas and Parnell. She was very old and it was clearly in everyone's interest to contain any hint of scandal until Mrs Wood was safely dead.

But she lived on. Even after O'Shea lost his seat in the Commons she survived, well on into her nineties, hanging on to life as if to thwart his revenge.

At last she died: in May 1889. As expected, she left the bulk of her fortune (some £250,000: several million in terms of 1980s purchasing power), to Kitty O'Shea. Because of the way the will was drafted, Kitty's husband could have no claim on the estate; and her brothers and sisters, equally aggrieved, immediately began proceedings to have the will set aside.

O'Shea naturally set about exploiting the situation. If, in the course of the action challenging Mrs Wood's will, it could be shown that Kitty had been deceiving her aunt over her adulterous relationship with Parnell, then the case for overturning the will would be strengthened. There was no need for O'Shea to postpone his revenge any longer – indeed, revenge might now prove financially profitable. He filed suit for divorce, citing Parnell as co-respondent. The time bomb had exploded at last.

As we have seen, there was never much warmth between Lewis and Kitty O'Shea. What was more – and this was unusual for him – Lewis admitted it. He told W. T. Stead that she was 'a very charming lady but an impossible one'; and his distrust of her went further than that. For Kitty's part, a certain impatience with Lewis comes through, even in her rather gushing memoirs. Some antipathetic chemistry worked between them, and they fell out during the course of the divorce action. Kitty put great emphasis on the fact that O'Shea had also committed adultery – as he certainly had on numerous occasions – and on the fact that he had turned a blind eye to her affair with Parnell. But Lewis pointed out that no amount of blackening O'Shea could save Parnell. Any involvement in a divorce case must ruin a politician.

Kitty O'Shea herself always believed that her husband would have been amenable to a bribe – either straight cash or a share in Mrs Wood's estate. Kitty later told Henry Harrison, one of Parnell's biographers, that for a payment of £20,000 O'Shea would have allowed her to divorce him, instead of his divorcing her. (No doubt some allegation of cruelty could have been dredged up to add to his adulteries.) Because the Wood estate had not yet been admitted to probate – and the challenge by Kitty's brothers and sisters meant greater delay and made her expectations doubtful security to borrow against – it was found impossible to raise this sum. Kitty O'Shea is thought to have fallen out with Lewis because he did not try hard enough to find this money – and it is clear that he *could* have raised a sum like £20,000 easily enough, given the enormous prestige he enjoyed in the City of London.

The fact that Lewis did not get on with Kitty would not explain his passive attitude in such a critical situation. He probably demanded a more positive stance from Parnell himself – it was *his* career that was threatened, after all – and Parnell did not respond. He displayed, indeed, a strange air of resignation. And, although Lewis and Parnell had achieved a satisfactory working relationship during the time of the Pigott letters and the fight with *The Times*, now Lewis confronted again something opaque in Parnell's nature – and for once simply shrugged his shoulders and admitted defeat. He had briefed Frank Lockwood (afterwards to prosecute Oscar Wilde) for Kitty O'Shea, but in the event the case was allowed to go by default.

The divorce proceedings were mercifully short. Although Kitty had cross-petitioned with an allegation of adultery between O'Shea and her own sister, Mrs Steele, the judge dismissed that at once for lack of evidence. The sole issue was the question of adultery between Parnell and Mrs O'Shea and that was abundantly proved.

The Times described the case as 'a story of dull and ignoble infidelity untouched so far as can be seen by a single ray of sentiment or a single flash of passion and comparable only to the dreary monotony of French middle-class vice, over which M. Zola's scalpel so lovingly lingers.'

The story of Parnell's political collapse and subsequent death is well known. Lewis did not see him again. A year or two later he spoke of him as 'a man of immense power, possessing the mind of a statesman . . . a very great Irishman'.

Lewis and the volatile Kitty O'Shea (she married Parnell shortly before his death but no one ever thought of her as anything but 'Kitty O'Shea') were to meet again, despite their disagreements. Indeed, she had to turn to Lewis for help many years later. Although she eventually did get most of her aunt's money, she had little capacity for handling it. She found herself comparatively poor, thanks to embezzlement by a dishonest solicitor. It was then she thought of Lewis. They had not been in contact for years, but she approached him and, by putting pressure on the defaulting lawyer, he was able to recover a proportion of the money lost.

25

Sir George

On 3 June 1893 George Henry Lewis was knighted. Both Mr Gladstone and the Prince of Wales had strongly urged that he should receive the accolade. Officially, this was in recognition of his work in establishing the truth about the Pigott forgeries before the Parnell Commission. No doubt Gladstone and his colleagues did feel Lewis should be honoured for the part he played, but the Prince could not be expected to show much concern for the vindication of the troublesome Irish leader. The recent Baccarat Scandal must have bulked much larger in the royal mind.

It would be easy to see Lewis as either a slavish courtier – which was how the jeering crowd saw him, as he shepherded the Wilsons out after the baccarat trial – or as the conscience of the Prince. The truth lay somewhere between the two. Lewis was always concerned with what today would be called the Prince's 'image'. He realized – as for that matter did the Queen's advisers, who were constantly asking her to modify her stance of grim, unrelenting widowhood for similar reasons – that, however great the instinctive respect for the Monarchy, royal personages have to maintain a living relationship with their subjects or that respect will evaporate. That was why Lewis warned Edward against acting as if he were above the law; advising him always to enter a court and give evidence if required to do so. This often went against the grain with the Prince. As we have seen, there was a very real conflict in his mind as to how he should behave. When confronted with, say, the aggressive Charles Beresford, all Edward's instincts led him to act royally: to demand obedience.

And similarly, in the baccarat case, he had an 'Off with his head!' reaction to Gordon-Cumming for the trouble he was causing. Always Lewis had to stand at his elbow and remind him that, great as his powers were, they were strictly limited in a parliamentary democracy. However reluctant the Prince might be to hear this, when it came to the point he would swallow his toad and do as Lewis advised.

The knighthood got a good press. The English love to institutionalize their public figures and 'George Lewis' was an institution even before he became 'Sir George'. Now thirty-seven years in practice, he was the most famous solicitor that ever wrote a brief. A firm like Freshfields, solicitors to the Bank of England, enjoyed a more impersonal renown. Famous advocates like Charles Russell and Edward Clarke might loom theatrically in the public mind – titans whose jousting you read about in the papers – but they remained essentially remote, whereas everyone felt he knew George Lewis.

In 1893 he was sixty years old, but, according to a contemporary description, 'despite the hair, the sweeping moustache, the whiskers all being grey, he somehow looks a young man. There is not a hint of age in the glance or in the slight upright figure or in the soft clear deliberate voice. . .'

Thus the rather gushing George Smalley, but the portrait is confirmed by others. The fur coat was still an essential adjunct, but the single eyeglass had now given way to gold-rimmed spectacles. He was still something of a dandy in 'a brown frock-coat, brown waistcoat, and a scarf fastened with a scarf-pin of sapphire set in diamonds, a gift from the Prince of Wales. . .'

The public persona had been created a long time ago but now the knighthood confirmed it – impressive, authoritative, solid as the throne Lewis served so well. It changed little over the eighteen years he still had to live. All the people who wrote about him speak of his 'deliberation' – in speech, in walk, in gesture – and of his 'penetrating' eyes. All enlarge on the secrets Lewis knew and would never reveal. Soon after being knighted, he was interviewed by Harry How. Asked about 'the secrets of London', Lewis said, 'I have not kept a diary for over twenty years. When I found that my business was becoming so confidential, I determined that I would never chronicle another thing – so when I die the confidences of London society die with me. At one time I thought the fact of my not keeping a diary – for reference sake – might lead to some severe observations in court, as all lawyers are expected to keep such a book. But a Lord Justice told me he was perfectly certain that no judge would ever blame me.'

For a number of years previous to this, Lewis – who had fought and won so many battles in the searchlight glare of open court – had been well known for his skill in settling and 'arranging' cases that never came there. How many such cases he handled will never be known, but their number is believed far to exceed that of those that did come to judgement.

Elizabeth Lewis was now a famous hostess – everyone who was anyone had come to her house, and for an unknown, particularly in the arts, the drawing-room at 88 Portland Place could prove the ante-room to success and future fame.

The guests at the Lewises fell into several tiers. Establishment figures that Lewis – professionally eminent as he now was – knew as a matter of course. Sir Charles Russell (in a few years to be Lord Russell of Killowen, Lord Chief Justice); Sir Edward Clarke (who had been Solicitor General and had then rather marred his chances by appearing for Sir William Gordon-Cumming; he was to bury them finally by being 'pro-Boer'); Sir Richard Webster (Attorney General; later, as Lord Alverstone, to succeed Russell as Lord Chief Justice); and many other eminent lawyers. A lawyer who is remembered only as a politician was a constant visitor: Herbert Asquith, whom Lewis had often briefed at the bar, was Home Secretary in 1892 and was to be Prime Minister when war broke out in 1914. The beautiful Margot Tennant – famous for saying the first thing that came into her head: at once penetrating and *faux naif*; soon to become Asquith's second wife – had been coming to Portland Place for some time.

But for Elizabeth the artists would always come first. Hardy had returned to Dorchester and was rarely seen in her drawing-room. Neither was Meredith, who left his home at Box Hill less and less frequently, disabled as he was by ill health and increasing deafness. But Henry James was more faithful than ever. He was going through a difficult time, artistically, in the early 1890s. He felt that with his long novel *The Tragic Muse* he had reached a dead end; and he had embarked on his disastrous campaign to succeed as a playwright. (At Elizabeth's, of course, he would meet theatre people who would at least agree to read his plays: Ellen Terry, the Wyndhams, Mary Anderson, Beerbohm Tree.) Wilde came less often. There had been no disagreement, not even a 'coldness' – but things had changed, and both the Lewises and Wilde himself were aware of the fact.

One of the clever young men who thronged Elizabeth's drawing-room had written a *roman à clef* – really a kind of burlesque – based on Wilde and his entourage. The book was *The Green Carnation* and the young man was Robert Hichens. The publisher William Heinemann liked the book and asked Lewis to read it for libel. Lewis told Heinemann to go ahead and publish. *The Green Carnation* had a great success, but was unfortunately overtaken by Wilde's own downfall, which appeared to give Hichens' light-hearted burlesque a cutting edge he had never intended.

Hichens remained a great friend of the Lewises. Described as having 'the voice of a curate and the eyes of a satyr', he appears in fact to have been an agreeable young man, who wrote a string of now-forgotten bestsellers, many of them with North African themes – *Call of the Blood*, *Bella Donna*, and *The Garden of Allah* among them.

His great friend E. F. Benson was also a regular visitor at Portland Place. Benson was the son of a former Archbishop of Canterbury and the brother of Robert Hugh Benson, who became a charismatic Roman Catholic priest and a facile novelist. E. F. Benson had himself become a bestselling writer through the 'Dodo' series of light novels, based on the devastating chatter of Margot Tennant, whom Benson may well have first met at Portland Place.

Both Benson and Hichens were charming lightweights, poised and amusing, the kind of young men any hostess invites because they keep the party running on well-oiled wheels. Altogether more remarkable was another young man, Max Beerbohm, brother of the actor Beerbohm Tree, whom Lewis had known for a long time. Still at Oxford, Max could already draw with precision and an antic wit: he would soon blaze his way into fame through his contributions to the *Yellow Book*. Meanwhile, 'Katie' Lewis, the Lewises' youngest daughter, regarded Max with extraordinary interest. She was only fifteen and Max Beerbohm, it was often said, appeared to have been born old, but there was some strange chemistry between them, which would assert itself fully in a few years' time.

Of all the friends of the family, the closest remained the Burne-Joneses. Edward Burne-Jones had long been accepted by the establishment. Hundreds of reproductions of his works had been made by a German photographic company; he had been awarded countless foreign medals and honours; Exeter College, Oxford had made him an honorary fellow; the University itself awarded him a doctorate. In a year's time, in 1894, Gladstone would ask Queen Victoria to make him a baronet. And yet, through all this piling-on of honours, Burne-Jones remained unpompous and unspoilt, direct and even childlike in character.

Not all childlike adults like real children, but Burne-Jones did. He was particularly fond of Katie Lewis. He had painted her a number of times when she was a child and wrote her a charming series of letters, illustrated with his drawings. These would be published with great success many years later under the title *Letters to Katie*.

As Katie grew up, it was apparent that she could startle and dazzle just as effectively as her mother, but perhaps with greater charm. Like her mother, she wanted her own way and, like her, usually got it; but, while Elizabeth occasionally went too far and irritated people, Katie charmed them. More than any of the Lewis children, she was the darling of the famous men and women who were her parents' friends. When she was in her cradle, Oscar Wilde wrote of her, 'Katie has now ceased to be the modern Hero and now gives up to Gertie.' During Katie's teens, Henry Irving and Ellen Terry bombarded her with letters and presents. But, through all this attention, she liked Burne-Jones the best.

Her sister Gertrude was twenty-two in 1893. If Lewis could see Elizabeth's likeness in Katie, he saw his mother's in Gertrude – although there were those who descried in her a flicker of her father's dry wit. Whether or not she did resemble Lewis, Gertrude certainly adored him. She would be waiting for him when his brougham arrived from Ely Place in the late afternoon: to offer him a glass of port, a newspaper, his cigar. (Elizabeth, who in the Victorian age would be expected to perform in this wifely role, would usually be out or busy arranging some social event.) When Gertrude knew that her father was particularly hard-pressed – immersed in a heavy case perhaps – she would arrange a quiet game of cards for him with an old friend like Charles Russell or Labouchere.

'George the Second' was waiting in the wings, soon to be a partner in an enlarged Lewis and Lewis. He was nearly twenty-five; on leaving Oxford, he had gone straight to Ely Place to spend several years as an articled clerk.

Physically, he resembled his father. He was slight, with delicate features, and in him some of his father's traits were intensified. Like his father, he always dressed immaculately. If Lewis was diplomatic, George James Lewis was a diplomat. He was to become a most able lawyer, heading a fashionable practice that was very different from that conducted by his grandfather in the 1840s and 1850s.

Socially, he had nothing to learn, and at his mother's parties he was every bit as poised as the charming Benson or the indispensable Hichens.

And at the centre of all this stood Elizabeth, initiating and orchestrating everything from the lunch-time 'open house' the Lewises maintained during the London season to dinner-parties so elaborate and brilliant that they could be called banquets. At her elbow stood Parkes, her butler and adjutant, quietly marshalling the forces below stairs, while in the bowels of the house the erratic and alcoholic Gramecy functioned brilliantly amid a mounting frenzy of pots and pans.

The New Year's Eve dinner party the Lewises gave every year was acknowledged to be the high point of the season. The numbers that attended varied between sixty and a hundred: an extraordinary sampling of lawyers, politicians, writers, actors, painters, sculptors, and musicians – an elitist gathering indeed, but representing an elite of talent rather than of money or power. As the artist Graham Robertson was to put it, 'It would be easier to list the notabilities absent than those present.'

Elizabeth loved charades – she transmitted her passion to her children – and charades had therefore been a feature of the Lewises' parties ever since the early days at Taviton Street. No one – not Paderewski nor Henry Irving – ever had to sing for their supper at Portland Place, but, with guests such as Charles Wyndham, the Bancrofts, George Alexander, and Ellen Terry playing it was inevitable that these performances would become more elaborate and sophisticated with each New Year. In fact, they ceased to be charades at all and became theatrical productions in their own right, brilliantly staged and directed: sometimes original pieces of a fantastic and fairy-tale nature; sometimes parodies of West End successes – often with actors from the actual production mocking their own current performances for the enjoyment of their fellow guests. A young actress called Mary Ansell acted in one of these skits (although she was not appearing in the play that was parodied) and this brought her and her fiancé to Elizabeth's attention. Mary's fiancé started coming to Portland Place too. He was a tiny Scot, forever sucking on a pipe that seemed to dwarf him. His name was James Matthew

Barrie and he married Mary Ansell in 1894. The Lewises and the dinner parties they gave were to bear on his life in several ways he could never have foreseen.

26

Outlawed Noblemen and Perverted Telegraph Boys

AT THE AGE of sixty-one Lewis appeared as active as ever. The physical persona, the identifiable outer shell that had served him for so long, would serve him for a long time yet. At sixty-five he would look very much as he had at forty-five.

And yet in his sixties a man's powers are failing. However vast his experience, however shrewd his judgement, he cannot work as hard as he could when he was forty – even though he may seek to persuade himself that he can. For fifteen years – since the death of his Uncle George in 1879 – Lewis had been alone in his business. Lewis the man and Lewis and Lewis the firm had been one.

Now that was to be altered. In 1894, three new partners joined the firm: three young men who for several years past had been working in the long downstairs office in Ely Place as assistants to Lewis.

The first of them was Lewis's son, 'George the Second' who was admitted a solicitor and made a partner in Lewis and Lewis on the same day in August. Next came a young man called Reginald Ward Edward Lane Poole. He was already a solicitor, having been admitted in January 1891 while working as an articled clerk. The third was George James Lewis's cousin – Lewis's nephew, son of his Uncle George – Henry Reginald Lewis (always known as 'Harry'). He had been admitted as long ago as 1888, but was now being made a partner, together with his cousin and Reginald Poole.

There was no question of Lewis abdicating. For fifteen years, Hercules-like, he had upheld the vast administrative and consultative burdens of the busiest legal firm in London, and he had no intention of letting go now. He would distribute more of the routine work among these three young men; they could lift some of the burden of correspondence; they could see minor litigants – although Lewis would continue to interview (some might think 'interrogate' a better word) anyone who wanted to be taken on as a client. But he would retain to himself all major decisions; he would continue to hold the lines of command for a long time yet – by the time he relinquished them, 'the heir apparent', young George, should be ready to take over.

However, Lewis the protagonist, the ruthless fighter for 'my client, right or wrong' – the champion of the abominable Mrs Crawford and the despicable Wilsons – was much less in evidence after 1894. During the last part of his life the law reformer re-emerged. Not only did he battle ceaselessly for several victims of judicial injustice (only one of whom he represented initially), but he spoke and lobbied to bring about the changes he believed in.

Some of the causes he espoused at the beginning of his career had been achieved before 1894. The two Married Women's Property Acts – of 1870 and 1882 – had extended the equitable doctrine that a woman should be in the same position in respect of property as her husband. The 1882 Act, particularly, established by statute what highly paid lawyers had previously won for women able to pay their fees; and Lewis derived great satisfaction from that.

In contrast, the situation with regard to divorce remained unchanged. The odds still stood monstrously loaded against the woman. A wife still had to prove cruelty (or perhaps bestiality or incest!) in addition to adultery against her husband; he could still divorce her for a single act of infidelity. Little progress had been made. A bill seeking to bring in divorce for desertion had been defeated in 1892. Lewis said to Harry How in 1893, 'Fancy a young girl just married; her husband commits a crime for which the sentence is life-imprisonment. Don't you think it monstrous that the woman should not be allowed to marry again? I would go farther. If a man deserts his wife for three years and upwards, she too should be free!'

Lewis would agitate for the reform of the divorce laws for the rest of his life; but he would not live to see reform achieved.

Another *bête noire* of Lewis's, the bar on a prisoner giving evidence on his or her own behalf, would be abrogated with the Prisoners Evidence Act of 1898, although this created what many lawyers still regard as a two-edged sword that can as easily hurt as help a defence. Lewis's other main concern was the lack of a court of criminal appeal.

The Serafino Pelizzioni case, nearly thirty years earlier, had first convinced him of the necessity for such a court; and one of the cases in which he would shortly be involved would offer an irresistible argument for its establishment.

Several years previously, a High Tory journalist called Charles Whibley had written in the *Scots Observer* (reviewing Oscar Wilde's *The Picture of Dorian Gray*):

> Mr Wilde has brains, and art, and style; but if he can write for none but outlawed noblemen and perverted telegraph boys, the sooner he takes to tailoring (or some other decent trade) the better for his own reputation and the public morals.

This was, of course, less a review than a personal jeer at Wilde. The 'outlawed noblemen' was a reference to Lord Alfred Douglas; 'perverted telegraph boys' to the male brothel in Cleveland Street, off the Tottenham Court Road, where youths, including telegraph boys, had been available to the patrons. But, however scurrilous, these few lines manage to embrace, in a grimly prophetic way, the attitude that precipitated Wilde's downfall – in which Lewis, despite his old friendship with Wilde, was to play a merely peripheral role.

Even without the embarrassment of Lewis's having had to extricate Alfred Douglas from the clutches of a blackmailer, Wilde and the Lewises would probably have drifted apart. The extraordinary success of plays like *Lady Windermere's Fan* and *The Importance of Being Earnest* and the money they brought only helped to fuel Wilde along his chosen course of self-destruction. Leaving the rumours aside – and Lewis, with contacts ranging from the Cabinet to private investigators like Meiklejohn, heard them all – Wilde had clearly suffered some deterioration of character. He had lost the faculty for self-criticism essential to the artist. As Hesketh Pearson said, 'As he became more prosperous, he became more preposterous.' Meeting Conan Doyle in the street, he asked him if he had seen his, Wilde's, latest play. Doyle said he had not. 'Ah, you must go,' Wilde said. 'It is wonderful. It is genius.'

But it was the rumours that counted. The message on the visiting card that the Marquis of Queensberry left for Wilde at the Albemarle Club – 'For Oscar Wilde posing as somdomite [sic]' – contained one key word: 'posing'. Right up to the debacle of the Wilde-Queensberry libel case, Wilde benefited from the assumption that he was 'posing' as something he could not possibly be. He was protected by the Victorian *pudeur* he despised: just as no one believed that a sweet young thing like Virginia Crawford had done the things she undoubtedly had done, it was hard to believe that a witty wealthy dramatist like Oscar Wilde enjoyed going to bed with stable boys.

There is no point in retelling the story of Wilde's feud with the 'Scarlet Marquis' (Lord Queensberry). We are concerned here with how Lewis touches the story.

When Queensberry threw down the gauntlet in the shape of the ugly, misspelt message on the visiting card, Alfred Douglas wanted Wilde to consult his old friend Lewis. But Wilde had earlier consulted another solicitor, C. O. Humphreys of Humphreys, Son and Kershaw, about Queensberry's threats.

Why did Wilde not go to Lewis? Quite apart from old friendship, Lewis was quite simply *the* solicitor to go to in 1895.

The answer can only lie in the passage from *De Profundis* already quoted (on page 241), in which Wilde talks of having forfeited Lewis's affection. No doubt Wilde did feel sad at the crumbling of his relationship with George and Elizabeth, but – it has to be said – a more compelling motive was probably vanity. With Wilde, vanity transcended self-preservation. He preferred to deal with Humphreys, a stranger who could be fooled, rather than with Lewis, who knew him too well. Humphreys asked Wilde whether he would give him his word that there was no truth in the allegations made against him. Wilde assured him that there was no truth in them. Humphreys was satisfied. 'If you are innocent,' he said, 'you should succeed.'

A warrant was applied for, seeking Lord Queensberry's arrest on a charge of criminal libel against Wilde, and Queensberry was duly arrested. He immediately consulted Lewis, who agreed to act for him.

If Wilde's motive in not going to Lewis is fairly clear, how do we explain Lewis's agreeing to represent his old friend's arch-enemy, Queensberry? He may well have felt hurt – even allowing for the cooling of the friendship – that Wilde had not consulted him. But that is some way short of giving support and counsel to Wilde's opponent.

Presumably – and this is uncharacteristic of Lewis – he *was* sufficiently hurt to take up what might be called the cab-on-the-rank attitude: I am a solicitor sitting in my office awaiting clients; my services are available to anyone who chooses to seek them. That might be plausible if Lewis's choosiness in accepting new clients was not already legendary. Neither in reputation nor personality can John Sholto Douglas, eighth Marquis of Queensberry, have appealed. Lewis must simply have shrugged and hardened his heart when he heard that Wilde had initiated proceedings through Humphreys.

Queensberry came before the Great Marlborough Street magistrate, Robert Milner Newton, on a Saturday morning, 2 March 1895. After the evidence for the prosecution had been outlined – the delivery of the card at Wilde's club and other, earlier, insults – Lewis jumped up and addressed the court: 'I venture to say that when the circumstances of this case are more fully understood – that Lord Queensberry, acting as he did under feelings of great indignation –'

Milner Newton interrupted him, 'I cannot go into that now.'

Lewis persisted. 'I do not wish this case to be adjourned without it being known that there is nothing against the honour of Lord Queensberry.'

That sounds like committed advocacy. And yet, immediately the court rose, Lewis told Lord Queensberry that he could not go on acting for him.

In the whole of Lewis's career there is no incident even remotely resembling this one. If his decision to act for Queensberry was not in character, his sudden withdrawal from the case is even less so. Why did he do it?

Mr H. Montgomery Hyde, the definitive biographer of Oscar Wilde, says that Lewis presumably found it repugnant to act against a man with whom he had been on terms of friendship. No doubt this is true, but why had not this objection applied when the marquis first approached Lewis?

Did Elizabeth play any part in Lewis's abrupt withdrawal? Did she urge Lewis to bow out for old times' sake? Could it be that Lewis, listening to the proceedings at Great Marlborough Street – and perhaps knowing more than anyone else in court what Wilde's private life was really like – had a sudden vision of the gulf yawning in front of Wilde: of the utter ruin that awaited him?

Stunned by Lewis's rejection, Lord Queensberry found himself walking the Strand in the hope that he could find a solicitor who was open on a Saturday afternoon. By chance he found Charles Russell Junior (son of Lord Russell of Killowen), a partner in the recently established firm of Day and Russell. They acted with great vigour on Queensberry's behalf in the subsequent trial.

Wilde knew in his heart that he should have consulted Lewis. Immediately after he had seen his case against Queensberry collapse, he and Lord Alfred Douglas took a cab to Ely Place. (This was during the few hours between the end of the Queensberry trial and Wilde's own arrest that evening at the Cadogan Hotel – the magistrate at Bow Street, Sir John Bridge, is said to have delayed issuing a warrant to give Wilde a chance to get out of the country.) Lewis saw Wilde and Douglas at once, but had to tell them that there was nothing he could do.

'If you had come to see me in the first place,' he said, 'I would have torn up Queensberry's card and thrown it on the fire and told you not to make a fool of yourself.'

27

Cyanide

On 26 March 1896 George James Graham Lewis married a young and beautiful woman called Marie Hirsch. Like his mother Elizabeth, Marie Hirsch came from Mannheim, that splendid seat of the Palatine. Like Elizabeth, again, Marie came from a solid Jewish-mercantile background. The Hirsch and Eberstadt families were acquainted but were not close friends.

Like his father before him – and indeed, the parallels come thick and fast – young George met his future wife while on holiday in Germany. (Incidentally, the marriage was an example of the social and cultural links that still held between English and German Jews at the end of the nineteenth century.) His son's courtship and marriage must have struck Lewis as having an almost predestined quality. More than thirty years ago he had gone to Frankfurt and brought home the tragic Alice Victorine Kann, his young bride who was to live so short a time; then, a few years later, he had gone to Mannheim and returned with George's mother, the brilliant and indestructible Elizabeth Eberstadt.

Elizabeth and her new daughter-in-law got on well together – although Marie not unnaturally found her mother-in-law rather formidable. Not that Elizabeth was ever unkind to her. Ordinary unkindness was not in her nature, it was rather that she appeared to address the world from a kind of Olympian plateau of vigour and self-confidence and Marie felt that she would never be on the same level as her. Though she was never sharp with Marie, Elizabeth's sharp tongue was certainly intimidating. An eminent composer had just been widowed. A gushing lady remarked of the event, 'Poor fellow, now he has only his muse.' 'Bad company!' Elizabeth retorted.

Both Elizabeth and Marie were fond of music; and Marie was soon going to concerts with Elizabeth and helping her to organize the musical side of entertainments at Portland Place. Music, in fact, was to prove an ever-strengthening bond between them as time went on. Although neither of them could know it, their destinies were linked in a strange way, for they both died on the same day, 4 September 1931, Elizabeth at the age of eighty-six and Marie at the age of fifty-eight.

The Lewises knew Lord Randolph Churchill and his wife, the lovely Jennie Jerome. George and Elizabeth had watched from a distance the Aylesford–Blandford imbroglio, and Lewis had congratulated himself that he was not likely to be caught in the backlash – as he had been between Daisy Brooke and Mina Beresford.

Lord Blandford (Randolph Churchill's brother) had eloped with the Countess of Aylesford. Randolph Churchill begged the Prince to use his influence to stop the Earl of Aylesford from divorcing his wife – which would mean, of course, his citing Blandford. When the Prince expressed his reluctance – really, his refusal – Randolph Churchill attempted the crudest kind of blackmail. There were some letters, he intimated, written by the Prince to Lady Aylesford. Perhaps if those letters were produced –?

Of course the Prince was furious. No course of action on Randolph Churchill's part could have been more disastrous. HRH banished the Churchills to a pit of Acheron comparable with that to which he had consigned Charlie B and Mina. Lewis must have felt relieved that Lady Aylesford had not decided to give him her letters from the Prince for safe keeping.

In 1896, when Jennie Churchill had been a widow for scarcely a year, the beautiful Jerome sisters fell into the hands of a swindler. Through the agency of Arthur Cadogan, the second son of the fourth Earl Cadogan, Jennie and her sister Clara (Mrs Morton Frewen) got to know an American called James Henry Cruickshank. He professed to be head of a market syndicate specializing in American stocks. The two society beauties became obsessed with the possibility of making millions: this they called 'the Spec'.

The young Winston Churchill was on his way out to India when he received a cable from a friend in the City informing him that his mother and aunt had not merely been speculating unwisely, they had actually been defrauded. The money was gone. Winston was appalled and he wrote at once urging her to put the matter in Lewis's hands.

When Lady Jennie Churchill saw Lewis she told him that she was not anxious to prosecute Cruickshank and endure all the embarrassing publicity, when they knew they could never recover their money. But Winston insisted it was her duty to do so. Lewis agreed. Swindlers like Cruickshank relied on their victims' shrinking from the publicity of a court case and letting them off by default.

A year later, in November 1897, Cruickshank pleaded guilty at the Old Bailey to obtaining large sums by fraud. There was a subsidiary charge of obtaining credit while an undischarged bankrupt. The Common Sergeant sentenced Cruickshank to four years' penal servitude on each of the two counts, making the terms consecutive so that he received in all eight years' penal servitude. The judge said he had to award a heavy sentence because he could not lose sight of the fact that the prisoner represented 'a large, growing, and dangerous class of men who live and thrive on the follies of mankind. In this crowded metropolis we call London we are surrounded by thousands of the industrious poor struggling – often in vain – to live in decency and comfort, while men like you clothe yourselves in purple and fine linen and fare sumptuously every day.'

Although Winston Churchill thought the sentence severe – he would have given Cruickshank three years, he said – he wrote to his mother congratulating her on her public spirit. Lewis had already expressed his approval.

The three new young partners in the firm enabled Lewis to delegate more of his work, although he could at all times hold in his mind a sort of linear vision of all the important cases with which the firm was concerned – each at its appropriate stage: pleadings, for trial, for appeal (this last could not apply to criminal cases, of course). Lewis once told a young barrister that this power to *visualize* complex and essentially abstract matters of law and fact was a large element in his success; he might have added to it his extraordinary memory. There was nothing affected about his refusal to keep a diary. His memory, throughout his life, functioned as a perfect system for storage and retrieval. To the discomfiture of counsel and, sometimes, his own clerks, he was inclined to attribute this faculty to everyone else. Thus in court he would say impatiently, 'Never mind taking notes; watch the case!' By this he meant that the facial expressions of judge, counsel, and witnesses functioned as valuable weathervanes which must be kept under constant observation.

Most of the dramas of Lewis's professional life were played out in airless courtrooms where bewigged functionaries and archaic phrases tend to distance the observer from the human passions involved. Twice, however, Lewis stood at an arm's length from violent death. Once with Richard Pigott in Anderton's Hotel; once with Whitaker Wright.

Wright was born in the north of England in 1845. He came from a solid middle-class, chapel-going, bible-reading background; and all his life retained a soft northern burr in his speech – which, he believed, people found reassuring. When he was twenty-one he went to the United States. He had little money, but some knowledge of geology and inorganic chemistry. This was just after the Civil War: an era of predatory capitalism, the time of the Robber Barons, and Wright naturally thought of using his talents in mining. With savings of $500 he bought a half-share of a mine in Montana. It turned out to be a success; Wright then sold his share. He had made a start.

He soon became a big operator in the jungle-world of speculative mining, making – and then losing again – two fortunes in the great boom at Leadville, Colorado. After ten years in America he had, he said, achieved the ambition that fired him to leave England: he was a millionaire. More speculation in mining companies followed and he had lost most of his million by the time he decided to return to England in 1889. But he still had enough money to open a small office in Copthall Avenue, not far from the London Stock Exchange.

Wright could not have chosen a better time to return to England. Optimism to the point of euphoria fired the air like oxygen. This was the high-point of an era: Queen Victoria's Diamond Jubilee. The streets blazed with lights. Visitors from all over the world thronged the pavements. This was high noon for an empire. God was smiling – and on England most of all.

Naturally this euphoric, expansive mood affected the financial climate. Everything was going for the best in this best of all possible worlds, so the price of shares – if you held shares – was going to keep rising. How could anyone fail to make a fortune? It was a quintessential bull-market and it made the City of London a Tom Tiddler's ground for company promoters. The great gold-mining boom was at its height and these men, if their promises were to be believed, were offering mines rich enough to pave every London street with gold. In 1897 the *Financial Times* issued a pictorial supplement entitled 'Men of Millions'. It included such creatures of the moment as Barney Barnato, Ernest Teriah Hooley, Colonel North, Woolf Joel, Horatio Bottomley – and Whitaker Wright. The subsequent fates of these men indicate the hubris inherent in the boom they helped to create. Colonel North dropped dead of a heart attack just before the collapse of his companies was announced. Ernest Teriah Hooley and Bottomley went to prison. Barney Barnato committed suicide. Woolf Joel was murdered in his office in Johannesburg.

Wright was mainly concerned with Australian gold mines. In 1894 he floated the West Australian Exploration and Finance Corporation, one of a host of similar companies the price of whose shares on the market was boosted to unnatural heights on a barrage of rhetorical promises and wildly optimistic engineers' reports.

At the centre of Wright's fast-growing financial empire stood the London and Globe Financial Corporation. As Wright said, the purpose of this company was to 'contribute much to the pioneer and profitable task of opening up Western Australia'. Its more immediate purpose, for Wright, was to serve as a launching pad for numerous subsidiary companies – none of which were actually producing gold. Wright's profit from these promotions was £238,436. The most successful of them was Lake View Consols ('Consols' was a touch of genius, suggesting as it did gilt-edged government security.) The price of Lake View Consols rose at one time to £29 a share.

In 1897 Wright was in a position to acquire the assets of London and Globe out of his own resources. He then set about combining London and Globe with another company, Western Australian Finance. The amalgam had a capital of £2 million in £1 shares, of which Whitaker Wright received £605,000. Having appointed himself managing director, he looked around for a titled chairman whose name would inspire confidence with the investing public. (A 'guinea pig', in the City jargon of the day.)

He found a suitable deadhead in Lord Loch, a former Governor of Victoria (the Australian connection was important), but after a few months he resigned on the plea of having other commitments, although he remained a director. Lord Loch recommended another retired proconsul to succeed him: the Marquis of Dufferin and Ava, an ex-Viceroy of India and Governor General of Canada. Lord Dufferin accepted Wright's offer and when it was announced that he was becoming chairman the shares of London and Globe rose £2.

At first everything went well. London and Globe acquired the Ivanhoe mine at Kalgoorie from a small local company and floated a share issue on the London Stock Exchange for £1.5 million – it was proposed, the prospectus said, to also acquire mining concessions in British Columbia and the Yukon.

All these ventures were directly controlled by Whitaker Wright, working with a large staff of clerks in a marble palace in Lothbury, just across the road from the Bank of England. Wright was dealing in millions at this time: everyone said he had the Midas touch. Rumours sometimes fluttered the City that London and Globe were unsound, but the company was known to have made large profits from its holdings of Lake View Consols and it continued to pay modest dividends.

Wright's private life matched his public success. His big town house next to Londonderry House in Park Lane was full of paintings, sculptures, valuable artifacts of all kinds. His country estate, at Lea Park near Godalming in Surrey, was princely in size and boasted a well-equipped observatory and a private theatre. Wright had imported armies of workmen to level hills which obstructed his view and dig artificial lakes. Under one of these lakes he had a billiard-room built with a glass ceiling, through which he and his guests could observe the fish above them. In a nearby grotto, illuminated by coloured lights, genuine Italian gondoliers would ferry visitors through an ingeniously constructed fairyland. Wright had a penchant for things Italian: the estate was dotted with fountains made from Italian marble. His guests at Lea Park included members of Parliament, bankers, peers, and, on at least one occasion the Prince himself. Everyone was impressed with Wright. How could they fail to be when his stable housed fifty thoroughbred horses and his yacht *Sybarita* lay in the Solent, outranking the Kaiser's *Meteor*?

In fairness, it has to be said that men no more honest than Wright died as peers, full of wealth and honours, the object of public admiration. Wright might have ended as just such a figure, if he had not so heroically overreached himself – and if he had been luckier. None of his companies was actually bogus – as were some of those promoted by several of his fellow 'Men of Millions'. Some of his mines eventually produced gold and even paid dividends.

There was a certain irony in the fact that Wright's decline began when he became interested in an enterprise that, like mining, involved excavating below the surface of the earth, but concerning which he had no technical knowledge. The London and Globe took over the financing and construction of the Baker Street and Waterloo underground railway – later known as the Bakerloo Line. Most of the company's liquid capital was tied up in the project. Then, by an unfortunate chance, the shares of Lake View Consols dropped sharply after the rich lode of ore which had caused the shares to be bought was exhausted. Wright foolishly thought he must support Lake View by buying shares in the open market. The result was disastrous. The London and Globe lost £782,000 in a single transaction in Lake View – and yet on 15 December 1900 a balance sheet showed the company to be in a flourishing condition. Only thirteen days after that balance sheet was issued, the London and Globe announced its insolvency.

The collapse of such an important company caused a number of Stock Exchange firms to fail – there had been heavy speculative buying of both London and Globe and Lake Views – and several of Wright's other companies went into liquidation. The Official Receiver, who examined Whitaker Wright, decided that the finances of the whole group had been conducted on a fraudulent basis. The usual system of robbing Peter to pay Paul, popular with dishonest financiers who control a group of companies, had been employed here: accounts had been manipulated in such a way as to conceal deficits, and the dividend paid by London and Globe had not been earned but had been provided by means of loans provided by the subsidiary companies. The balance sheet for the year 1899 showed a fictitious profit of £463,372, whereas there was actually a deficit of £1,600,000.

Although there was a general uproar after the examination by the Official Receiver, and questions were asked in Parliament, the authorities refused to prosecute Whitaker Wright. The reason for the official attitude was that there was a loophole in the Companies Acts: anyone who issued a false prospectus could be prosecuted, but it was not a crime to publish a false balance sheet.

Finally a creditor, a well-known stockbroker called John Flower, applied to a judge in the Chancery division and asked him to sanction a private prosecution. Mr Justice Buckley decided that there was a case under the Larceny Act. He made the necessary order but Wright immediately fled to America.

After a long fight – Wright tried to use his long residence in America to block extradition – he was brought back to England to stand his trial.

Lewis had already met Wright on a number of occasions and it was almost inevitable that Wright should ask him to undertake his defence. Lewis knew this would not be an easy task. The investing public, mulcted of literally millions of pounds by plausible company promoters like Bottomley, Hooley, and Whitaker Wright himself, were looking for someone to punish, and now Wright was delivered into their hands. Times had changed since Lewis faced the directors of Overend Gurney across the Guildhall court. They had been, if anything, more culpable than Wright, but the day was past when John Duke Coleridge had been able to bully and bamboozle a jury into letting the Overend directors go scot free.

Lewis knew that Wright would stand little chance at the Old Bailey with a common jury. He sought and obtained a transfer to the Law Courts in the Strand, where a special jury (that is, jurors with superior property qualifications i.e. richer) would hear the case.

The Crown was represented by Rufus Isaacs and Horace Avory, both senior counsel and both to attain high office – Isaacs as Lord Chief Justice and later Viceroy of India; Avory as a judge. Lewis briefed Lawson Walton (later Attorney General) and Richard Muir (later a senior Treasury counsel; he prosecuted Dr Crippen) for the defence.

The case against Wright was one of labyrinthine complexity. Stripped of a thousand subtleties and convolutions, the nub of it was: had Wright issued a balance sheet knowing its contents to be false? So complicated were the issues of fact and law involved that, when it was suggested that the jurors should be given a copy of the indictment, Mr Justice Bigham said, 'I might as well give the jury Archbold's *Criminal Pleading* or the *Encyclopaedia Britannica*.'

Rufus Isaacs's opening speech for the Crown took five hours. It was masterly – but it was hard even for him to keep a single coherent thread running through the financial maze. Describing the nature of Wright's transactions – all in millions – Isaacs raised a laugh when he said, 'That was an item for £10,000 – not worth talking about!'

As Isaacs went on, the extent of Wright's manipulation became apparent. To give one instance: his statement at the shareholders' meeting that £1 million had been written off during the past year from the value of the assets was a lie. The amount written off was a straightforward trading loss.

On the seventh day of the trial Whitaker Wright left his seat at Lewis's side at the solicitors' table and walked up to the witness box. (The fact that the case was being tried at the law courts spared him the humiliation of standing in the dock, since the law courts normally hear no criminal cases.) With his small goatee beard, gold pince-nez, and black frock-coat he looked a figure of almost exaggerated respectability.

His confidence matched his appearance. He answered his counsel's questions blithely and without hesitation, telling how he had lent the London and Globe £400,000 of his own money which he had previously intended settling on his children. 'There is nothing criminal,' he asserted, 'in one company lending money to another. It is, on the contrary, normal business practice.'

Rufus Isaacs began his cross-examination on a quiet note. Why had Wright gone to America when he knew this prosecution was impending?

'A coincidence!' Wright replied. He had already booked passages for himself and his wife. Lewis, sitting in the middle of the court and watching the faces of the jury, realized that they were not impressed.

The cross-examination went on. Soon Isaacs was deep into the maze of loans and reciprocal loans, payments and cross-payments.

'You received all this money as chairman of one company from yourself as chairman of another?' Isaacs asked.

'I do not like your way of putting it,' Wright said. Then he added, 'The money was paid by one *company* to another.'

Isaacs forced Wright to admit that he had made 'slips' on two occasions when asked about the true state of affairs. In a letter to Lord Dufferin he had said that the amount of profit shown reflected a deduction of £500,000 from the market value of the shares, whereas he ought to have said 'cost' or 'par value'.

On the whole Wright kept his temper under Isaacs' probing, but once he burst out that the court would like him to be chairman, secretary, and everything else to the company.

'No!' Isaacs said. 'I think *you* were quite enough.'

Towards the end of the cross-examination, Isaacs was pressing Wright hard: relentlessly quoting him against himself.

'You said over one million pounds sterling had been written off for depreciation?' Isaacs demanded. 'That was untrue?'

Wright began to look worried and mopped his forehead.

'I do not admit that at all,' he said. 'You must take the whole report together.'

'You said over a million sterling,' Isaacs repeated. 'Have you any doubt that this statement is absolutely untrue?'

Wright floundered: 'In its connection it is true. But I ought to have said "loss and depreciation". It was an extempore utterance.'

For several hours Rufus Isaacs kept at it, tearing away what remained of Wright's credibility. When Isaacs at last sat down, Richard Muir tried to reverse the balance a little by his re-examination of Wright. Even the Crown did not deny that some of Wright's flotations had made fortunes. Lake View Consols had paid over a million in dividends; Ivanhoe a million; and another of his companies, Victoria Gold Estates, almost £600,000.

Wright gave an apparently sincere explanation of his troubles. In the autumn of 1899 all London and Globe's money was tied up in the construction of the Bakerloo Line. Then occurred the debacle with Lake View and the drop of almost £13 in the market value of the shares.

'Things look very different years after they have happened,' Wright cried. 'I'll guarantee to go to the Bank of England and twist and distort anything years afterwards!'

At last he was allowed to step down and resume his seat beside Lewis. During the judge's summing-up – very hostile to Wright – Lewis noticed that Wright was drawing the Roman figure VII on a piece of blotting paper in front of him. Seven years was the maximum sentence under statute for the crime of which he was accused – and seven years was what he got after the jury had returned with a verdict of guilty. Wright stood up with dignity to receive it.

'My Lord,' he said, bowing to the bench, 'all I have to say is that I am as innocent as any person in this court of any intention to deceive or defraud the shareholders.'

After the judge and jury had left the court, Wright turned to Lewis: 'Never mind, Sir George. *I* don't mind a bit.'

Wright and Lewis left the court by a private door, accompanied by the assistant superintendent of the Law Courts and a tipstaff. The four went to one of the consultation rooms near the court in which the case had been tried. The assistant superintendent and the tipstaff withdrew to leave Lewis and Wright to talk privately. At that point, however, there entered the room a Mr Worters, chief accountant of London and Globe, and a Mr Eyre who had gone bail for Wright.

'So this is British justice,' Wright said indignantly to Eyre. 'What have I done? I am amazed. I have done nothing to deserve this.' But then he seemed to recollect himself and said to Lewis and the others, 'Nevertheless you have all been very good. I am most grateful for all you have done for me.'

Lewis poured out some whisky from a bottle Wright had been allowed to have sent in. He handed the glass to Wright, and offered him a cigar from his own case. Wright took out his gold watch and chain and gave them to Eyre. 'I shan't have any use for these where I'm going,' he said. 'Keep them for me till we meet again.'

He talked on for about a quarter of an hour, mainly to Lewis about the possibility of an appeal. He was also concerned with the disposal of his personal property. Then he excused himself and went to the door. The assistant superintendent and the tipstaff were waiting outside. Wright told them he wished to go to the lavatory.

He was only out of the room for a moment; when he returned he asked for a glass of water. This was given to him and then Lewis offered him another cigar. He took it and tried to light it: his hand was shaking violently. A moment later he collapsed and fell back in his chair. He was struggling to speak but could not. A doctor was called immediately from Charing Cross Hospital. When he arrived Wright was still alive, writhing in anguish on the floor. The doctor at first thought Wright had had some kind of seizure. 'He has only a few minutes to live,' he said.

A moment later the writhing ceased. Wright had swallowed cyanide. When his body was searched, he was found to be carrying not only another phial of cyanide but a loaded revolver. The post mortem revealed that the lower side of Wright's tongue was corroded: this meant that he had kept the cyanide in his mouth for some time before he swallowed it fully. Clearly he had been determined to commit suicide if he were found guilty.

Lewis was not alone in thinking Wright deserved some sympathy. He had not set out to be a criminal but, fighting to save the financial empire he had created, he became one. Recalling Wright, Lewis would always compare his fate with that of the directors of Overend Gurney – something of a King Charles Head with Lewis, which he could never forget.

28

A Game of Forfeits

THE YEARS UP TO the turn of the century brought Lewis both joy – the birth of his grandchildren, Elizabeth and Margaret Ellen (daughters of George James Graham Lewis) – and grief in the deaths of Burne-Jones and Charles Russell. Lewis was sixty-seven in 1900. He neither looked nor felt his years; in de Montherlant's phrase, he *dominated* his age – and yet each death of an old friend brought a diminishment, a narrowing of his world of a kind that the survivor at last comes to recognize can only be repaired by his own death.

Burne-Jones died on 17 June 1898. He had seen Lewis only the day before. The Burne-Joneses had dined with the Lewises at Portland Place; there had been no other guests, and after they left Lewis remarked that he had never seen Edward looking better. The following evening, Burne-Jones appeared well and in good spirits, but, as his wife Georgiana was going up to bed, he suddenly remarked, with what she said afterwards was a strangeness in his manner, a yearning quality she had never noticed before: 'I should like to paint and paint for seventeen thousand years.' Georgiana looked puzzled, and then he added, 'Seventeen? Why not seventy thousand years?' He was silent, as if overwhelmed with sadness that it all had to stop.

He died in the early hours of the following morning.

He was buried at Rottingdean, near Brighton, and Lewis enjoyed the melancholy honour of being a pall-bearer. Later there was a memorial service in Westminster Abbey.

This death hit Lewis the hardest. But he was scarcely less grieved when Charles Russell, now Lord Russell of Killowen, died with equal suddenness. Lewis had always liked Russell. He had been closer to him than to any other member of the bar. No doubt he felt a certain pride that he had been the man who helped the tough Ulsterman from Newry conquer the British establishment and end up as Lord

Chief Justice of England. Russell knew what he owed to Lewis; on his appointment, he had written:

> Thank you for your kind words of congratulation. To you, more than to any man in either branch of the profession do I owe the position at the Bar which has led to the present appointment. I hope in it I may not disappoint my friends.

And Lewis said of Russell, 'He had no equal as a cross-examiner. He had no equal as an advocate; there never was a greater man at the English Bar than Charles Russell.'

Not that Lewis was the sort of man to allow himself to be plunged into melancholy, even by the deaths of those he loved. He was too controlled for that – and anyway he had Elizabeth beside him. Elizabeth, with her vitality, her almost-gamine wit, her electric response to every kind of person, would have held him back from old age – if he had ever shown any inclination to embrace it.

She kept inviting new people to Portland Place. The house was as famous now as the Lewises themselves: a palimpsest of friendship crammed with the work of artists George and Elizabeth had known; and with the gifts of grateful clients, the sheer bulk of which had defeated their recipients' capacity to house them. According to the *Strand* magazine there was 'a cellar packed with objects of the greatest value and of the most exquisite workmanship – grand vases, snuff-boxes, Oriental daggers, cigarette-cases, silver-gilt cabinets, and many other things.'

As she got older, Elizabeth enjoyed entertaining more and more. And her son, 'George the Second', loved it as much as she did and was indefatigable at her side (Marie sometimes pleaded the two babies, Elizabeth and Margaret Ellen, as a reason for not being there). Katie was usually there too – Katie was her mother's daughter. She had all her mother's social gifts – and more.

We know about the attraction between Katie and the young Max Beerbohm only from Beerbohm's side. She liked him; she responded to him; keen-eyed observers believed that she would have been willing to marry him. He, for his part, was already interested in Florence Kahn – whom he subsequently married. But the attraction Katie Lewis had for him was real enough; and he felt admiration for George and Elizabeth. (He drew no less than seven caricatures of Lewis, and three of his son, George James Graham.) Max was, however – he admitted – overpowered by the wealth and social success of the Lewises. If he had married Katie, he would have been dependent on her money, at least for a long time to come; he feared being plunged into the social maelstrom which Katie herself enjoyed.

But whatever the keen-eyed observers said, one wonders if Katie, however charmed and attracted, would have married Max. Her niece, Lewis's grandchild Elizabeth (now Mrs Wansbrough) believes that, fascinating and beautiful as she was, she could never find a man who would really stand up to her – and she would not consider marrying a man who would not. Would Max have passed the test?

The Lewises were by now great friends with J. M. Barrie and his wife, Mary Ansell. Whatever Elizabeth thought of Barrie's early, sentimental Kailyard writings, his brooding little-boy-lost quality behind the enormous pipe did not fail to arouse her maternal instincts. Whether she liked Mary Barrie quite so much is not clear. Elizabeth was too shrewd not to sense the malaise already apparent in the Barries' marriage. Mary was clearly frustrated, even lost. She had 'retired' from the stage for no very good reason, but had taken part in the copyright performance of Barrie's *The Little Minister*. (A copyright performance was given to safeguard the author's rights and usually took place as a social entertainment at a private house.) Gertrude and Katie Lewis had also taken part and were described as prancing around as Scottish lassies, 'in beautiful Paquin dresses'.

It was at the Lewises' New Year's Eve party for 1897 that Barrie met Sylvia Llewelyn Davies, and was enchanted when he saw her secreting sweets in her reticule for 'Peter'. (How that meeting led to the creation of Peter Pan has been told in detail by Andrew Birkin in *J. M. Barrie and the Lost Boys*.) She was the wife of a young barrister called Arthur Llewelyn Davies, whose abilities had attracted Lewis's attention. Thanks to Lewis, Llewelyn Davies was not exactly briefless, but he was going through the classic testing-time when so many young barristers are forced to drop out of the race. His wife's meeting with Barrie would profoundly affect the lives of all the Davieses – and Barrie's own life even more.

There is a slight irony in the fact that in neither of the two cases with which Lewis was most deeply concerned over the next ten years – which were the last ten years of his life – was he himself professionally involved. At no time did he represent either Adolf Beck or George Edjali. Both men were victims of injustice – of injustice so gross that it raises questions about the administration and practice of the law in England that have hardly yet been answered. Good did come out of evil in that Adolf Beck's case brought about the establishment of the Court of Criminal Appeal; but the behaviour of certain Home Office officials and of Horace Avory, the prosecuting counsel, was subjected to a whitewashing process unique in British legal history.

Adolf Beck's story began in 1895. He was then forty-four years old. A Norwegian, he had enjoyed a strange and varied career – a fact which did him no good at all when he came into the hands of the law. He had been in turn a seaman, a research chemist, a shipbroker's clerk, and – an extraordinary episode – a singer, starring in Paris at concerts and in grand opera. What was still more extraordinary was that, having discovered this gift, he abandoned it and went off to Peru, where he made a lot of money supplying food to the soldiers fighting in the so-called 'War of the Pacific'. (Peru was helping Bolivia to defend the silver and nitrate resources of Antofagasta against Chile.) In 1885 he returned to England and began to dabble in company promoting, although he was hardly in the 'Men of Millions' class. He was in fact so unsuccessful that, by 1890, he was living on hand-outs from acquaintances and dodging from one cheap hotel to another.

Leaving one of these hotels one evening in December 1895, he was accosted by a woman who was a total stranger to him. When she spoke to him, he denied knowing her.

'I know you!' she said. 'I'd know *you* anywhere.'

'What do you want from me?' he demanded.

'I want my two watches and my rings,' she said.

Foolishly – for it was afterwards cited as an indication of guilt – Beck ran away. But the woman caught up with him and gave him in charge to a constable who had come up, wondering what the fuss was about.

At the police station she said she was a music teacher named Ottilie Meissonier. A German, she lived in Putney. Three weeks ago this man – she was certain it was he – had stopped her in the street and asked if she was Lady Everton. She clearly did not resent such a ploy – was 'music teacher' a euphemism for her real profession? – and got talking. Soon he was telling her that he had £180,000 a year and was a relative of Lord Salisbury. Would she come on a yachting trip to the Riviera? Of course she would. Then, he said, she would need some new clothes. He made out a list of what precisely she would need. He gave her a £40 cheque to cover these. 'Oh – and that jewellery is hardly the thing, is it?' he said, but with such charm that she didn't mind the implied criticism. So he took away a bracelet (he was going to get two black pearls put in it) and a diamond ring (he was going to buy her another, better one and he wanted to have this to get the size of her finger).

And then, of course, he disappeared. The cheque turned out to be on a non-existent account at the Union Bank, Trafalgar Square. And then, three weeks later, she saw the same man, she believed, leaving a seedy hotel in Victoria Street.

Beck was not only so unlucky as to be the victim of mistaken identity: there were a host of other, ancillary misfortunes that began the moment he was held by the police.

At that time there was an epidemic of frauds on women exactly like that described by Ottilie Meissonier. The police were able to produce no less than twenty-three women who all told similar stories. Ten picked out Beck at the identification parades; the others were not certain it was he. The ten positive witnesses were prepared to identify him again at the magistrate's court and duly did so. Beck was committed for trial.

Then Beck suffered another misfortune. An anonymous letter-writer appeared, writing with hate-sharpened pen to call the attention of the police to the fact that the alleged frauds of Beck were very like those of a man calling himself John Smith who had been sent to jail for a five-year term in 1877. (Adolf Beck was in Peru then.) Clearly, the letter-writer went on, John Smith and Adolf Beck were one and the same man.

Fingerprints were not then accepted as a means of identification in Britain, though they were in France. If they had been, Beck would have been released at once.

As it was, a familiar psychological mechanism had been set in motion. Just as the guests at Tranby Croft had expected Sir William Gordon-Cumming to cheat when they watched him on the second night's play, so the police were conditioned to believe Beck to be Smith. The two officers who had arrested Smith actually came forward and swore to this. A handwriting expert, Thomas Gurrin, said that Smith's handwriting and Beck's proved them to be the same man. Beck was committed for trial on an indictment that charged him with theft and obtaining property by deception. Mentioned in the indictment was the fact that he had a previous conviction (the 1877 case) for felony.

The mention of the previous conviction was important because it provided an opportunity for Beck to prove his innocence. If, as the original indictment laid down, Beck was accused of being the man who had been convicted in 1877 under the name of John Smith, he could prove he was *not* – for he could produce witnesses to testify that he was in Peru in 1877.

But Horace Avory, for the Crown, decided to omit all mention of the felony in 1877. Later, in the course of a whitewashing committee of enquiry, Avory was to proclaim in tones of injured innocence that he had done this *to be fair to Beck*! (In the sense that the jury would not be prejudiced by knowledge that Beck had been convicted before.) This would have been plausible if Avory had not known perfectly well that Beck had a cast-iron alibi for 1877: he had been in Peru and there were dozens of witnesses to swear to the fact. It comes to this: Avory knew all the time he was prosecuting an innocent man, and yet he let the case go forward. He did make a half-hearted attempt to put in the 1877 conviction but the judge overruled it. The obvious course then would be for Avory to withdraw the case from the jury. He did not. He let Beck be sentenced to seven years' penal servitude, knowing that he was an innocent man.

This was a deed of extraordinary ruthlessness – and brings Avory right out of the frame of lawyers playing to win at all costs. Russell, Edward Clarke, and Lewis himself all at different times achieved verdicts in the very teeth of the law and the evidence – and no one can blame them, for they fought fairly, even if they elicited a 'wrong' verdict from judge or jury. John Duke Coleridge was, in Clarke's view, an unfair cross-examiner; he was certainly a master of doublethink and doubletalk but he would never have acted as Avory did.

The solicitor who had represented Beck, T. Duerdin Dutton, never slackened his efforts to get Beck released. And, after Beck had served three years, something came to light which must have promised to clear him entirely – even leaving the question of the 1877 alibi aside.

Dutton discovered that the 'John Smith' who had been convicted in 1877 was a man called Wilhelm Meyer. The importance of this lay in the fact that Meyer was a Jew and therefore circumcised. Beck was not circumcised; therefore Beck could not possibly be Meyer-Smith.

All the people concerned with Beck's innocence – and there were now a number of them, including the well-known journalist George R. Sims, and Lewis himself (who knew Sims), regarded this as a heaven-sent deliverance for the unfortunate Beck. Now he *must* be released.

Nothing of the kind happened. The Home Office stonewalled, said that the evidence at Beck's trial was 'overwhelming' – although it was based on personal identification, which was notoriously unreliable. And that was that. The authorities refused to budge. Beck repeatedly petitioned the prison governor; his petitions were as consistently rejected.

In 1901 Beck was released on licence – then called 'ticket-of-leave' – and the campaign to clear his name gathered pace. Beck and the faithful Dutton consulted with Lewis, who agreed with Dutton that in the absence of a court of criminal appeal there was no legal remedy. The Beck case, in fact, only emphasized once more the enormous need for such a court – as had been recommended by Sir James Fitzjames Stephen and a Royal Commission years before, and which Lewis himself had never ceased to advocate. (The Court for Crown Cases Reserved, created in 1848, dealt only with misdemeanours, not with felonies, and was in any event quite ineffectual.)

All that could be done, then, short of some sensational piece of evidence which would automatically vindicate Beck – and, recalling the official response to the facts about Meyer's circumcision, Lewis and Dutton cannot be blamed for wondering what would be needed to move the authorities – was to intensify public agitation about the case. George R. Sims would continue to write articles; Lewis would write letters to *The Times* and the *Daily Telegraph* (which took the establishment side in the Beck agitation) and to the law journals. The Salvation Army – which Lewis admired greatly and often praised – would give Beck financial help while they fought for his name.

And now the unthinkable happened. A new series of frauds started – again directed against prostitutes like Ottilie Meissonier. They acted out the same ritual: the chance meeting, the invitation to become the swindler's mistress, the new outfit that would be needed, the jewels, the cheque.

Again, Beck was arrested. All the evidence that had been adduced in his favour, all the public agitation by Sims, Lewis, and others, seemed to have been for nothing. The police took Beck to a café and conducted a kind of identification parade there. Again, several women swore that he was the man who had swindled them. Again, he was tried at the Old Bailey. But – and this was a first weakening of the entrenched official attitude – the propaganda war waged on Beck's behalf had sown sufficient doubt in the judge's mind for him to postpone sentence on Beck until the next session at the Old Bailey.

Beck remained in jail – but this time the frauds on women went on (they had, during Beck's earlier periods in prison, curiously but no doubt coincidentally, ceased). And on 7 July 1904, two days before Beck had to appear again before Mr Justice Grantham, the real criminal, Wilhelm Meyer, alias 'John Smith', was arrested while pawning the rings he had tricked out of a woman he had asked to be his mistress. (The all-too-familiar routine had again been followed, even to the point of his saying, with tentative charm, 'Oh – that jewellery is hardly the thing!' and taking a ring away so that a new and much larger ring could be made the right size for the lady's finger.)

So far as officialdom is concerned, there is no doubt that Beck might well have been sentenced to another seven years, while Meyer could have also been convicted – both for the same crimes! But this time Beck was luckier. An Inspector Kane of Scotland Yard was interested in Beck's case – he thought he was probably innocent – and was immediately struck by the similar nature of the crime committed while Beck was actually in prison. Kane soon established that the man under arrest was undoubtedly Meyer, and he gave this fact to the newspapers, who naturally made the most of it. Now the authorities had to bend before the storm. Beck was released and received a King's pardon – which, as Lewis pointed out, by its very name perpetuated the injustice, for you cannot be 'pardoned' for a crime you did not commit. Beck also received compensation of £4000.

But Lewis, Sims, and all the other people who had concerned themselves with the case were not prepared to let the matter go at that. 'All's well that ends well' would not apply here. Sims, in his popular journalistic style, and Lewis, with the weight his name now carried in legal and court circles, both pressed for an official enquiry. Eventually the government gave in and announced that one would take place. Its members were: Sir Richard Henn-Collins, Master of the Rolls; Sir John Edge, ex-Chief Justice of India; and Sir Spencer Walpole.

Lewis represented Beck at the hearings. It soon became apparent that the thrust – if such a word can be applied to such essentially circumlocutory proceedings – of the enquiry was directed against the officials of the Home Office rather than against the conduct of judge and counsel at the trial at which Beck had been convicted. Lewis had expected this just as he had expected the defensive attitude of the chairman of the enquiry, who firmly snubbed any question that got too near the knuckle.

Lewis wanted Avory's role investigated, but he was well aware that Avory's own excuse, that he had suppressed mention of the 1877 convictions to safeguard Beck, rather than to simply secure a verdict against him, would be found wholly acceptable by this tribunal.

The outcome was as Lewis had expected. He was able to ask some questions of the handwriting expert Gurrin – exposed as a dangerous charlatan in other cases beside this one – but the real culprits remained immune.

While no one was really pleased with the outcome of the enquiry – which stopped short of censuring anyone in anything but the mildest terms – it was largely instrumental in bringing about the establishment of the Court of Criminal Appeal.

The bill setting up the court was introduced by Herbert Gladstone (son of 'the Grand Old Man'), then Home Secretary. The Home Office, he said, had no power to crush a conviction (as in the case of Adolf Beck). On the other hand, the court of Criminal Appeal would have that power. And the quashing of a conviction by a properly constituted court was infinitely more desirable than any decision by a government department:

> The decision of a court of law is final. There is no legal formality in the position of the Home Secretary. The consequence of that is although he might come to a clear decision, he is always exposed to pressures to reconsider that decision.

And thus, after at least fifty years of protest and lobbying, what Lewis and many other lawyers had demanded was finally achieved. The Court of Criminal Appeal was set up; the writ of error and the Court for Crown Cases Reserved were abolished. In exceptional cases, a further appeal from the Court of Criminal Appeal to the House of Lords was allowed.

Beck died within five years of his release, his £4000 all spent. Clearing his name had become his obsession. Perhaps the fact that he had finally done so destroyed his raison d'être.

Horace Avory, by contrast, lived to be a very old man. He became a judge, famous for his severity and his acerbic presence on the bench. Living far on into his eighties, he became a much-photographed symbol of authority – the stretched parchment mask inhuman and menacing beneath the short wig – as well known to the 1930s as the Hunger Marchers or the Rector of Stiffkey.

Lewis played a similar role in another case – not as famous as Beck's perhaps but notable in that it displayed an element of racialism rarely found in nineteenth-century England; and because not only Lewis but also the creator of Sherlock Holmes were among those who sought justice for the unfortunate George Edalji.

Edalji's father was a Parsee, Shapurgi Edalji, who had married an Englishwoman and had then taken orders in the Church of England. He had later been given the living of Great Wyrley, near Walsall in Staffordshire. This was the so-called Black Country – the industrial conurbation that grew up between Birmingham and Wolverhampton at the time of the Industrial Revolution – and Great Wyrley was a scattered village, neither urban nor truly rural, surrounded by dismal fields, stunted trees, and smoke-blackened hedgerows. The land was scarred with pit workings, active and defunct, and crossed with sluggishly moving canals.

An inhospitable milieu, it would seem, for anyone from the East; but the Edaljis were confronted with worse than a hostile climate. The degree of shock and social chagrin in even a working-class parish in the 1880s (the time when the Reverend Edalji first came to Great Wyrley) at finding their new vicar was a 'nigger' or a 'darkie' is hard to imagine now.

Hostility first broke out in a series of anonymous letters, all directed against the family in the vicarage. In view of what happened later, these letters appear to be highly significant.

On 17 March 1893 the vicar received a letter which said, 'Before the end of this year your kid will either be in the graveyard or disgraced for life . . . Do you think that when we want we cannot copy your kid's writing?'

The most disconcerting aspect of these happenings for the Edaljis was the fact that the police – presumably also fuelled by racial prejudice – were totally unsympathetic. In a mysterious and pointless episode, a key was stolen from Walsall Grammar School. Young Edalji did not attend the school – and yet, when it was discovered on the doorstep of the vicarage, the Chief Constable wrote to Mr Edalji, 'I shall not pretend to believe any protestations of ignorance which your son may make about the key. My information on the subject does not come from the police.'

Thus it is obvious that, as early as 1893, the Staffordshire police had focused their suspicions on George Edalji. But these events were merely a foretaste of the disaster that was to overwhelm the Edaljis ten years later.

In February 1903 a horrible act was committed in the village of Great Wyrley. A horse was killed and disembowelled with great savagery. Then, at intervals of only a few days, other animals were attacked and killed in the same way.

The method of maiming the animal was always the same, but the police could not find any clue to the perpetrator. Every night policemen were posted at various concealed vantage posts – and every night the maiming went on. It seemed that the unknown slayer had the ability to creep up under the very noses of the police, disembowel a horse or some other animal, and then – inevitably covered with blood – escape.

Frustrated at their failure to stop the maimimgs, the local police were out in force on the night of 17 August 1903, combing the fields and hedgerows; keeping watch.

Imagine their anger and horror, then, when the following morning a young coalminer going to work came upon a pony with its belly ripped apart: the grass beneath it a sodden mess of blood. He called the police; they arrived soon after seven; and immediately went to the vicarage to interview George Edalji. By the time they arrived, young Edalji had already left for his work in Birmingham (he was a solicitor).

The police interrogated his parents in his absence. They took from them the clothes he had worn the previous night. His trousers and boots had mud on them – which meant nothing – but the jacket was the garment the police were to claim was incriminating. There were reddish stains on the cuffs, which they alleged were bloodstains. They also claimed that the coat was damp and that there were brown horse-hairs clinging to it. Failing to find a knife or dagger that could have been used for the maiming, they took away four razor-blades.

The police now confronted George Edalji with these clothes. He denied any involvement in the cattle-maimings. Moreover, he was able to provide a totally watertight alibi for the previous night – not only did his father swear that his son had not left the vicarage after 9.20 p.m., but it transpired that two policemen had actually been set to watch the Edalji house. They had kept it under surveillance throughout the night of 17–18 August and they could testify that George Edalji had not left the vicarage between 9.20 p.m. on the night of the 17th and around 7.30 a.m. the morning of the 18th.

This took some explaining away, even for the Staffordshire police – indeed, were it not for the tragic injury Edalji suffered at their hands, one might be tempted to quote:

> Staffordshire born,
> Staffordshire bred,
> Long in t'arm
> And thick in t'head.

Even the testimony of two of their own men did not shake the police's belief in Edalji's guilt – which was presumably based mainly on the colour of his skin; and no doubt on some further resentment that 'darkies' like he and his father should be allowed to enter professions like the law and the church.

Eventually they decided that Edalji was a member of a gang formed for the purpose of horse and cattle maiming. This took care of the difficulty posed by the two policemen's testimony. (There was never the slightest evidence that the maimings were the work of more than one person.)

Steamrollering all objections, the police had Edalji committed for trial at the Stafford Quarter Sessions, blithely ignoring the fact that while he was in custody the maimings continued. Suspecting that this would happen, Edalji had actually refused bail, but it did him no good, for the 'gang' theory enabled the police to rationalize away any flaw in their case. In frantic pursuit of support for the gang hypothesis, they arrested a boy of nineteen who made a confession – although he was actually the owner of the horse which had been killed – which included the sentence 'The horse was killed to keep the game rolling.' Later, after the boy (whose name was Harry Green) had left Great Wyrley and gone to South Africa, he claimed that the police had forced this confession out of him and that he knew nothing of the maimings at all.

Conan Doyle, then at the peak of his fame as a writer, took the role in the Edalji case played by George R. Sims in the Beck case, the only difference being that he wrote more eloquently and in greater bulk of Edalji than Sims did of Beck. Lewis supported Edalji by a campaign of letter-writing and private agitation – for there were establishment figures who would listen to Lewis while they would have dismissed Conan Doyle as a sensational novelist seeking publicity.

Again, as in Beck's case, public indignation at last secured Edalji's release. And Lewis was able to complete the unfortunate young man's rehabilitation by getting his name restored to the register of practising solicitors.

29

A Jewish Voltaire

THE EDWARDIAN AGE had its own special character, but in essence it took up certain themes of the great age that had ended when Queen Victoria died – and then exaggerated, even parodied, them before everything was swallowed up in the consuming fire of the First World War.

For the great mass of the people, the accession of Edward VII – he cocked a snook at his mother, gone to the grave as she was, by not calling himself 'Albert Edward' – did not bring much change. Piccadilly was still a thoroughfare of dignified mansions; there were very few motor cars; top-hats and frock-coats were still worn by gentlemen of leisure, of whom there were still considerable numbers, and long skirts and tightly laced corsets were still *de rigueur* for ladies. But for the Man on the Clapham Omnibus – still drawn by a horse – life remained a difficult business. Money was as hard to come by as it always had been. Wives and children behaved as awkwardly as they always had.

And yet Edward did manage to impose himself on those nine years and one hundred days that he ruled the English people. His reign is often described as vulgar, materialistic, full of outward sham and show – but to what age can these epithets not be applied? Certainly for the rich, and for a large part of the middle class, a high point of comfort and prosperity was achieved in the reign of Edward VII. A hedonistic age? For some certainly. Many writers have instinctively seen the Edwardian atmosphere as that of a long sunny afternoon:

> Rich Jews at Court, in London and at Baden;
> Italian slang and golden chamberware;
> Adultery and racing; for the garden
> Muslin and picture-hats and a blank stare.

Lewis can hardly be one of the 'rich Jews' referred to, although he was rich, a Jew, and often at court. The enclave of financiers around the King is meant – men like Sir Ernest Cassel, Lord Burnham, and the Rothschilds. There is a cartoon by Max Beerbohm showing Cassel, Lord Burnham, and Arthur Sassoon all standing outside the door of Edward's successor. The caption reads, 'Are we as welcome as ever?'

A large number of Edward VII's circle would have reason to ask that question after the King died – this did not apply only to the Jews. As an aristocratic lady remarked on Edward's death, 'There will be a regular sweep of the people who used to be about the court – the Jews, and all the second-rate people that the King preferred to his aristocracy because they amused him.' A cry from the heart, and eloquent of the bitterness the King's friendship with people like Lewis caused among the establishment. The King's mind moved fast beneath that monolithic exterior and this disconcerted his duller advisers. This, too, was why he got on so well with the Jews and the French: they had quicker wits than some of the red-faced riders to hounds.

Lewis would never have to ask if he were still welcome. The last ten years of his life roughly coincided with Edward's reign; by the time his old friend died, Lewis had only a year to live.

Meanwhile, the King honoured him with a baronetcy at his Coronation. The Prime Minister, Lord Salisbury, and his successor, A. J. Balfour, both objected, but the King overruled them. Their opposition hardly sprang from simple anti-semitism, but most likely from the kind of resentment mentioned above. How typical of HRH to spend so much of his time with that lawyer fellow, George Lewis! Not that this would have stopped them consulting Lewis themselves if their sons got into trouble or they wanted to divorce their wives.

Lewis often went with the King to take the waters at Homburg, Baden, or Marienbad – a practice Edward made fashionable. Ostensibly he went to these spas to counter the enormous amount he ate the rest of the time, but the general opinion is that he did not take the medical side of the 'cure' very seriously. As regards diet, it was said, he acted as 'his own doctor' and 'his prescriptions were not severe'. What the King liked about Homburg and the other spas was the opportunity he had to relax there, where the pressures of etiquette and protocol were lifted. He lived in a rented villa, like everyone else. He wore lounge suits in the daytime – sometimes they were of a somewhat flamboyant colour and cut – and a soft grey hat. In the evening he wore a black dinner jacket and black trousers and a soft black hat (a 'Homburg' hat, in fact).

Lewis, too, lived in a rented villa; and in later years, when Marienbad had replaced Homburg as the King's preference, Elizabeth would often prefer staying at home, at Portland Place or Ivy Cottage, to 'following His Majesty to these small German or Bohemian towns', as she put it. Lewis himself would always go if he could. He enjoyed the social life of the foreign spas – brilliant in its way, yet detached from the formality of society at home. Most of the members of the King's set were there at one time or another, among them many of Lewis's clients – people like Lord Burnham; D'Arcy, the gold-mine tycoon; the Marquis of Soveral, the Portuguese Ambassador in London and a great friend of the King, known popularly as 'the Blue Monkey'; Mrs Hall Walker; and many more. At Homburg Lewis introduced Rufus Isaacs, later Lord Reading, to the King. The meeting took place in the Kurhaus: Isaacs had to display some dexterity in dropping on one knee and kissing the royal hand while carrying a large glass of spa water. On another occasion Lewis brought about a reconciliation between Labouchere and the Prince, as he then was. But the two men never liked each other and the reconciliation was short-lived.

The social life at Marienbad and the other continental spas had a deeper political significance too. King Edward met monarchs and statesmen from all over Europe in these small towns. Views were exchanged and differences discussed in a calm, lotus-eating atmosphere. These meetings were the furthest remove from today's widely trumpeted 'Summits'. Thanks to a total lack of publicity, no false expectations were aroused; and thus some of the 'chance' meetings at Baden or Marienbad possibly achieved a great deal.

This aspect of life at the spas was particularly attractive to Lewis. After almost a half-century of stultifying idleness, the King had shown himself to have a real flair for diplomacy. A Belgian diplomat in London wrote:

> The English are getting more and more into the habit of regarding international problems as being almost exclusively within the province of King Edward, for whose profound political instinct and fertile diplomacy they very rightly feel great respect.

Lewis was delighted that his old friend should have marched on to the stage of international affairs with such dignity and assurance.

Lewis was with the King when he paid his first visit to Marienbad since his accession. He went 'incognito' as the Duke of Lancaster – of course everyone knew who he was – but on Emperor Franz-Josef's birthday put on Austro-Hungarian Hussar uniform and, standing on the balcony of his hotel, took the salute as the King of England.

It is pleasant to think of Lewis and the King enjoying this last long Edwardian afternoon together before the sunshine faded and the shadows passed into night.

During the last decade of his life Lewis was far from inactive in the law, although he concentrated on manifest injustices like the Beck and Edalji cases and on general law reform. His son George and Reginald Poole ran Lewis and Lewis very effectively between them (Harry Lewis had left the firm in 1898 to found his own, Lewis and Yglesias), and Lewis noticed – with no particular regret – that the firm was now quite simply the smartest and most influential in London: the ghost of Mr Jaggers would have looked in vain for his admiring clientele of macers and whores and shofulmen in the palatial offices at Ely Place.

One of Lewis's cases of this period is best known to us in a transmuted but not greatly altered form in Terence Rattigan's play, *The Winslow Boy*. This tells the story of a parent fighting for the rights of his son against a blind and self-justifying bureaucracy. George Archer-Shee was a cadet at the Royal Naval College at Osborne; he was accused of forging the endorsement on a postal order – on far from convincing evidence – and was dismissed from the service. George's half-brother (who was a good deal older than he and a Member of Parliament) advised his father, Martin Archer-Shee, to go straight to the great Sir Edward Carson. 'There's only one man who can take on the Admiralty, and that's Edward Carson.'

After investigating the background, Carson did indeed take on the case. But as a barrister he had to be instructed by a solicitor, and Carson advised Mr Archer-Shee to go to George Lewis. Thus the normal procedure was reversed.

But Lewis found that the Admiralty put every possible obstacle in the way of the case being aired. For some time it was not clear how any remedy could be sought by the Archer-Shees. Carson and Lewis at last decided that there was only one way for a private citizen to challenge the Crown. This was by the ancient practice, a Petition of Rights, which claimed hearing by virtue of the words 'Let Right be Done'.

This was the beginning of a hard-fought battle between Carson and the Attorney General, Rufus Isaacs. Isaacs at first tried to silence the Archer-Shees' case entirely on a legal technicality. Carson eventually overcame this, after a bitter court-room wrangle with Isaacs. When the facts came to be considered, it was clear that the case against Archer-Shee was every bit as tenuous as that against the unfortunate George Edalji. Eventually it was heard again before a grossly prejudiced judge, but Carson triumphed and Isaacs, for the Admiralty, conceded that young Archer-Shee had not forged the endorsement on the postal order. He was vindicated on the charge of dishonesty, but was not taken back to the Naval College – this was something the authorities, smarting at their defeat, could not be forced to do. But George Archer-Shee's name had been cleared, and he died four years later in the Great War.

Lewis's last incursion into public life took place in March 1910, when he gave his views to the Royal Commission on the Law of Divorce, sitting at Winchester House, St James's Square. Lewis was asked for his views given his lifelong interest in divorce and expressed himself as very willing to come forward and give them.

He began by saying that he had been admitted a solicitor in 1856 and had practised all branches of law. He had handled thousands of divorce cases, mostly among the wealthy. He had been agitating for over thirty years to change the law in the direction of equality of treatment between husband and wife on the five grounds of adultery, desertion, cruelty, lunacy, and imprisonment for a criminal act for five years and over. In fact, Lewis said, adultery itself should be a ground for divorce for either party. He had known cases where wives had suffered greatly through their husband's conduct. And cruel or lewd behaviour was not the prerogative of any one social class. He had known one case where the husband was a member of Parliament and the wife twice broke down trying to reform him before she petitioned for divorce. Ladies had told him again and again that it was torture for them to remain with the men they had married – yet, with the law as it stood, they could not seek the remedy of divorce.

He agreed with Scots law in this, although he thought their period for divorce for desertion was too long at four years; he would suggest two years after desertion by either party as the ideal.

There was great social injustice inflicted by the law as it stood, for there was no divorce for the poor. They did not have the money to go to the divorce court in London.

The chairman asked on what grounds Lewis thought divorce should be granted. Lewis replied that he thought that, in addition to adultery, desertion, and cruelty, lunacy which lasted two years should be a ground, as should imprisonment for five years or longer. Sir Charles Dibden asked if it would not add enormously to the gravity of a five-year sentence if it carried with it the probability that the convict's wife would secure a divorce.

Lewis said it would, but that his sympathy was entirely with the wife who wanted her freedom. There was laughter when he added, 'even in the case of a company promoter'.

Lewis next dealt with the limitations he thought should be imposed on the lewd details of divorce cases that took up so much space in the papers: 'It is painful for children growing up – say a girl of sixteen – to read such things of their parents.'

Later, he said that he thought the divorce court was 'the greatest court for blackmail in London'. Asked by Lord Gorell if he thought that menaces were uttered under the threat of publication, Lewis cited the case of a man who had relations with a woman and was visited on the following day by a man who declared he was the woman's husband and demanded £500. 'I have dealt with hundreds of such cases in my time,' Lewis added.

Finally, he agreed that it would be correct to describe Lewis and Lewis as 'pioneers' of modern divorce. Other firms like Charles Russell and Co and Withers and Co were prominent in the field, but Lewis and Lewis were pre-eminent.

To the end of his life Lewis wrote letters and gave interviews on divorce and expressed in private his conviction that the English laws on divorce were cruel, socially divisive, and discriminated savagely against women. The fact that he spoke as one of the partners of a long and happy marriage should have made his words the more effective – but in fact there was no serious move to change the law until long after his death.

30

The Last Enchantments

THE LEWISES held their New Year's Eve party as usual on the last day of December 1909. George and Elizabeth welcomed the guests one by one as they arrived. Lewis looked his usual self – dapper, spry, and more than one friend remarked how ageless he was. 'Each New Year and George looks exactly the same. How reassuring!' If he was running a silent roll-call in his mind he gave no hint of it. Yet the list of old friends now absent would be a long one. Echo would have to answer 'Dead!' to many names. Edward Burne-Jones; Charles Russell; Henry Irving; Dion Boucicault; Arthur Sullivan; his brother, Frederick Lewis; Montagu Williams, who had fought so many cases with him in those far-off, early days; George du Maurier and James McNeill Whistler, enemies to the last – Whistler had sued du Maurier for libel over a character in *Trilby* and Lewis had refused to act against du Maurier, thus losing Whistler as a client; the beautiful brawling Mrs Rousby: all of them dead. Labouchere was alive certainly, living near Florence. Wilde was dead – perhaps the most tragic of all the absent friends – and so was Constance, his sad and uncomplaining wife, whom Lewis had acted for after the debacle.

If Lewis looked the same, Elizabeth looked if anything younger, more radiant than ever. Not just dazzling, but incandescent, as Graham Robertson told her. He was a painter who also designed for the theatre and wrote children's plays. He was in his forties but hardly looked it. Like E. F. Benson and Robert Hichens (who remained a faithful visitor at Portland Place but was in Sicily this year), Robertson was one of those young men – bright, witty, yet full of tact – who serve as indispensable aides to every great hostess.

Here too was Elizabeth's reigning lion of the moment: the American painter, John Singer Sargent, who had already painted Elizabeth's portrait. An American expatriate (like Henry James, whose friend he was), he was the quintessential artist for the Edwardians and his suave technical facility has been likened to Fabergé jewellery, but that is unkind: he paid for his success and his facility in loss of critical esteem after his death.

J. M. Barrie was here too: looking unhappy, as he so often did, but tonight it was because Sylvia Llewelyn Davies, whom he had met at an earlier New Year's party here, was dying of cancer. But he came tonight because he did not want to disappoint Elizabeth: more and more she had taken him under her wing in practical matters (emotionally, he remained dependent on Sylvia and her sons), having found him a flat in Adelphi after his divorce and recruited him an inimitable Jeeves figure called Harry Brown, who would remain with him for many years.

Tonight Graham Robertson was taking an important part in the festivities, for the play to be presented on the specially built stage in the back drawing-room at Portland Place – 'a tiny stage with a great tradition,' as Robertson called it – was a burlesque of Robertson's own West End success *Pinkie and the Fairies.*

Robertson wrote the libretto; Paul Rubens the music. There is no doubt that the performance was of the highest professional quality: the performers *were* professionals, the most successful extant. What strikes an odd note today is the essential innocence of such an entertainment for such a sophisticated audience – innocence, not naiveté – but that is typical of the Edwardians.

In this play a 'Fairy Visitant' (Graham Robertson's description) arrives among a family of modern children. They are all complete sceptics and give her a chilly reception. The poor fairy is broken-hearted at the attitude of the children, but then the parents arrive, weighed down with presents and full of Yuletide spirit, talking excitedly of Cinderella and Bo-Peep. Naturally they are enchanted to see the fairy – who responds and waltzes away with the parents, much to the relief of the children, who return to their normal routine: the baby, for example, settles down in his cradle to enjoy a cigar! Nigel Playfair (later a famous actor-manager) played the baby. He is described as convulsing the audience when he sat up in his cradle and uttered 'a withering cynicism'. Playfair said this was his great moment as an actor; Robertson adds, 'it was certainly my great moment as an author'. Their laughter may sound oddly in modern ears, but Robertson adds, 'The sight of that audience, comprising most of the finest intellects in London helplessly rocking with laughter, is an abiding memory.'

It is perhaps best to leave Lewis there, puffing at his cigar, no doubt laughing heartily, gazing at a scene of happiness which one hopes he shared. For there were to be no more New Year's parties. Lewis had the best part of a year of active life left; thereafter, for nearly another year, he was the diminished, suffering prisoner of his room in Portland Place.

Julian Symons has said that the most interesting characters for a biographer are those whose inner lives present some kind of ethical conflict, as do the lives of many artists. Most statesmen and politicians, he goes on, offer instead a mask to the world.

A lawyer – a great lawyer, as Lewis was – falls into neither category. His work is essentially cerebral – interpreting a complex mixture of statute and precedent – and yet he must concern himself with emotions too, and penetrate the innermost thoughts of his clients and their opponents.

Lewis would have liked what Charles Russell said of him: 'What is remarkable in George Lewis is not his knowledge of the law, which is very great, nor his skill in the conduct of different causes, which is unrivalled, nor his tact, nor his genius for compromise. What is most remarkable is his courage.'

No one would have disagreed with that. But perhaps Lewis would have liked best Oscar Wilde's 'he forgives us all'.

Bibliography

Newspapers and Periodicals

The Daily Telegraph
The Hawk
The Illustrated London News
Lloyd's Weekly Newspaper
Merry England
The Morning Post
Nineteenth Century
North London Press
The Pall Mall Gazette
Paul Pry
Punch
The Queen
Reynold's News
St James's Gazette
The Sketch
The Star
The Times
Tittle Tattle
Tomahawk
The Town
Town Topics
Vanity Fair
Weekly Times

Books

Anson, Clodagh, *In Victorian Days*. London, 1957.
Askwith, Betty, *Lady Dilke*. London, 1969.
Askwith, Betty, *The Tangled Web*. London, 1960.

Bennett, A. R., *London and Londoners in the Eighteen-fifties and Sixties*. London, 1924.
Benson, E. F., *As We Were*. London, 1930.
Bent, James, *Criminal Life: Reminiscences of forty-two years as a Police Officer*. London, 1891.
Birkin, Andrew, *J. M. Barrie and the Lost Boys*. London, 1979.
Biron, Sir Chartres, *Without Prejudice: Impressions of Life and Law*. London, 1936.
Boon, John, *Victorians, Edwardians and Georgians*. London, 1928.

Bowen-Reynolds, Ernest, *Seventy-two Years at the Bar*. London, 1924.
Bridges, Yseult, *How Charles Bravo Died*. London, 1956.
Bridges, Yseult, *Poison and Adelaide Bartlett*. London, 1962.
Brome, Vincent, *Reverse Your Verdict*. London, 1971.
Burne-Jones, Lady Georgiana, *Memorials of Sir Edward Burne-Jones*. London, 1904.

Cecil, Lord David, *Max: a biography*. London, 1964.
Chesney, Kellow, *The Victorian Underworld*. London, 1970.
Clarke, Sir Edward, *The Story of My Life*. London, 1918.
Coleridge, E. H., *The Life and Correspondence of John Duke Coleridge, Lord Chief Justice of England*. London, 1904.
Croft-Cooke, Rupert, *Bosie*. London, 1963.

Dicey, A. V., *Law and Public Opinion in England during the Nineteenth Century*. London, 1914.
Dilnot, George, *The Trial of the Detectives*. London, 1928.

Fordham, E. W., *Notable Cross-examinations*. London, 1951.

Gaunt, William, *The Aesthetic Adventure*. London, 1945.
Gaunt, William, *The Pre-Raphaelite Tragedy*. London, 1942.
Gaute, J. H. H., and Odell, Robin, *The Murderers' Who's Who*. London, 1979.
Gittings, Robert, *The Older Hardy*. London, 1978.
Graveson, R. H., and Crane, F., *A Century of Family Law*. London, 1957.

Harrison, Henry, *Parnell, Joseph Chamberlain and Mr Garvin*. London, 1938.
Havers, Sir Michael, Grayson, Edward, and Shankland, Peter, *The Royal Baccarat Scandal*. London, 1977.
Hichens, Robert, *Yesterday: the Autobiography of Robert Hichens*. London, 1947.
Holdsworth, W. S., *History of English Law*. London, 1926.
How, Harry, 'Illustrated Interviews XXIX – Sir George Lewis', *The Strand Magazine*, 1893.
Humphreys, Sir Travers, *Criminal Days*. London, 1946.
Hyde, H. Montgomery, *Carson. The Life of Sir Edward Carson, Lord Carson of Duncairn*. London, 1953.
Hyde H. Montgomery, *Oscar Wilde: a Biography*. London, 1976.
Hyde H. Montgomery, *The Trials of Oscar Wilde*. With an introduction by Sir Travers Humphreys. London, 1948. New and enlarged edition. London, 1962.
Hyde H. Montgomery, *The Other Love*. London, 1970.

Jenkins, Roy, *Sir Charles Dilke: a Victorian Tragedy*. London, 1958.

Langtry, Lillie, *The Days I Knew*. London, 1925.
Leslie, Anita, *Edwardians in Love*. London 1972.
Lyons, F. S. L., *Charles Stewart Parnell: a Biography*. London, 1977.

Magnus, Philip, *King Edward the Seventh*. London, 1964.
Nordon, Pierre, *Conan Doyle*, London, 1966.

O'Brien, R. Barry, *Lord Russell of Killowen*. London, 1904.

Pearsall, Ronald, *The Worm in the Bud: the World of Victorian Sexuality*. London, 1969.
Pearson, Hesketh, *Gilbert and Sullivan*. London, 1935.
Pearson Hesketh, *Labby: the Life and Character of Henry Labouchere*. London, 1936.
Pearson, Hesketh, *The Man Whistler*. London, 1952.
Pennell, E. R. and J., *The Life of James McNeill Whistler*. London, 1908.
Petrie, Sir Charles, *Scenes of Edwardian Life*. London, 1965.
Plucknett, Theodore A., *A Concise History of the Common Law*. London, 1948.

Robertson, Graham, *Time Was*. London, 1931.
Roughead, William, *The Bad Companions*. London, 1930.

St Aubyn, Giles, *Edward the Seventh*. London, 1979.
Smalley, George W., *Anglo-American Memories*. London, 1911.
Smalley, George W., *Some Letters from a Man of No Importance*. London, 1928.
Symons, Julian, *Horatio Bottomley: a Biography*. London, 1955.

Thorold, A. L., *The Life of Henry Labouchere*. London, 1913.
Twyman, H. W., *The Best Laid Schemes*. London, 1931.

Walford, L. B., *Memories of Victorian London*. London, 1912.
Walker-Smith, Derek, and Clarke, Edward, *The Life of Sir Edward Clarke*. London, 1939.
Watson, Eric R., *The Trial of Adolf Beck*. London, 1924.
Weintraub, Stanley, *Whistler: a biography*. London, 1974.
Wilde, Oscar, *The Letters of Oscar Wilde*, edited by Sir Rupert Hart-Davis. London, 1962.
Williams, Montagu, *Leaves of a Life*. London, 1889.

Young, G. M., *Victorian England: Portrait of an Age*. London, 1936.

Index